DARK AGORAS

Dark Agoras

Insurgent Black Social Life and the Politics of Place

J. T. Roane

NEW YORK UNIVERSITY PRESS

New York

NEW YORK UNIVERSITY PRESS
New York
www.nyupress.org

References to Internet websites (URLs) were accurate at the time of writing. Neither the author nor New York University Press is responsible for URLs that may have expired or changed since the manuscript was prepared.

Library of Congress Cataloging-in-Publication Data
Names: Roane, J. T., author.
Title: Dark agoras : insurgent Black social life and the politics of place
/ J. T. Roane.
Description: New York : New York University Press, [2022] | Includes
bibliographical references and index.
Identifiers: LCCN 2022015622 | ISBN 9781479847679 (hardback) | ISBN
9781479831029 (paperback) | ISBN 9781479876129 (ebook) | ISBN 9781479845385 (ebook
other)
Subjects: LCSH: Urban African Americans--Pennsylvania--Philadelphia--Social
conditions--20th century | Working class African
Americans--Pennsylvania--Philadelphia--Social conditions--20th century |
African American sexual minorities--Pennsylvania--Philadelphia--Social
conditions--20th century | Great Migration, ca. 1914-ca. 1970 | City and
town life--Pennsylvania--Philadelphia |
Urbanization--Pennsylvania--Philadelphia | Philadelphia (Pa.)--Social
conditions
Classification: LCC F158.9.B53 R63 2022 | DDC
305.896/073074811--dc23/eng/20221003
LC record available at https://lccn.loc.gov/2022015622

To the memory of my daddy, Earl Roane.

He was an organic historian and I gain my writing power from

carrying his voice with me always.

CONTENTS

Introduction

In his pathbreaking turn-of-the-twentieth-century sociological work *The Philadelphia Negro*, W. E. B. Du Bois describes two distinctive social-geographic phenomena associated with Black migrant cultures in the urban north.[1] First of the two were the institutions of the "vicious and criminal," "congregated" in the "slums of Seventh and Lombard Streets, Seventeenth and Lombard, and Eighteenth and Naudain," that included ordinary sites like street corners and more concerted spaces for drinking, gambling, and prostitution. In addition to examining the effects of social and economic conditions of late-nineteenth century Philadelphia shaping Black participation in crime, Du Bois describes these sites as materializations of a rogue Black migrant wandering, a rural and multicity post–Civil War passage between rural communities, towns, and cities.[2] According to Du Bois, "A large migratory criminal class" that received "training" through its "wanderings" from the countryside to "larger towns" and "eventually" to Norfolk or Richmond, Virginia, before moving on to Washington, DC, finally settled as a group in Baltimore and Philadelphia "sharpened and prepared for crime by the slums of many cities through which they have passed." For Du Bois, migrant wandering co-conspired with the slum conditions of Philadelphia to create the intractable Black criminal class that constituted the underground. The underground, the site of this class's inculcation and the infrastructures grounding its activities, shadowed the formal relations of governance and economy.

Directly adjoining the sites of the city's underground were the worlds of a second social-geographic phenomena, according to Du Bois. These were the *set-apart*—the individual homes that sited prayer meetings and worship services, the temporary street revivals and semipermanent storefronts and rented spaces near commercial districts or within residential blocks—that constituted the primary infrastructures of Black urban spiritual geographies. Relying on the description of an early

Holiness storefront in Philadelphia's Fifth Ward written by Reverend Charles Daniels for a religious publication called the *Nazarene*, Du Bois describes these forms as "little noisy missions," "dozens" of which emerged "in various parts of Philadelphia, led by wandering preachers." According to Du Bois, these congregations' demonstrative worship style and physical interactions with the spirit represented "survivals of the methods of worship in Africa and the West Indies," part of a subset of "customs [that] are dying away." Composed of approximately fifteen people and led by "a very illiterate preacher," the small congregations drew primarily on migrants from the South and sang songs that Daniels considered "repetitions of senseless sentiment in exiting cadences" rather than true hymns. Du Bois went further in a footnote, writing that Daniels's description of the music of the storefronts "hardly does justice to the weird witchery of those hymns sung thus rudely."[3]

Despite the anachronistic, meaninglessness, impenetrability, and discordance attributed to the storefront congregation's singing by Du Bois, the collective production of the church's music led to a "remarkable scene" in which "the whole congregation pressed forward to an open space before the pulpit, and formed a ring" that the "most excitable of their number entered," clapping their hands and in "contortions led the devotions." Excited, feverous, and frenetic, they shouted, sang, prayed, danced, and worshiped ecstatically for several hours "until all were completely exhausted, and some had fainted and been stowed away on benches or the pulpit platform."[4] For Du Bois, this form of congregation was out of line with the vision of social and moral uplift and political action that he attributed to the city's mainstream Black churches. While some of the city's institutional churches functioned in a similar way as political organizations, the "noisy mission" storefront was defined by simplistic cathartic appeal rather than collective mobilization and action, a wandering and repetitious—but charismatic—preacher, and a noisy flock of ecstatic worshippers.

Writing that "the vicious and criminal portion do not usually go to church" but continue to live as "next-door neighbors" in a commingling of "pronounced criminals and prostitutes" with those spiritually and otherwise set-apart, Du Bois identifies a primary social-geographic boundary shaping the trajectory of twentieth-century Philadelphia. Although there was a visible criminal element, this group also had its own socially elevated group, what Du Bois describes as a hidden, well-dressed faction integrated among members of the Black respectable poor and middle classes who nevertheless profited from vice and criminal activity. While for Du Bois, these sites constituted differentiated worlds, this distinction was defined by proximity and significant boundary transgression, helping to give shape to the ways that those in the Great Migration and the post–Great Migration experienced, made sense of, and sought the transformation of the city. As part of these outlooks and worlds, Black migrant communities affected sometimes impermanent edits on their homes and communities, appropriating the infrastructures of the row house, the storefront, the corner, and the tap room or bar to create new and often fleeting possibilities for social existence among the displaced and the condemned.

For outsiders like Du Bois, the relations underwriting these geographies were defined by their transitory nature. According to him, "Away from home and oppressed by the peculiar lonesomeness of a great city, [migrants from the South] form chance acquaintances here and there."[5] What Du Bois dismissed as a rather queer form of Black migrant sociality—defined by rapid passage into and back out of connection— facilitated the annealing of social worlds among the condemned, forming the elementary possibility for working-class Black migrant worldmaking. Black working-class modalities of social existence, born of the dissolution and reality of death and the social alienation stalking familial and social bonds intergenerationally out from slavery, generated dissonant modes of living and expressions of vitality—discordant and disruptive—within the temporal and spatial logics of urbanized industrial modernity. What Du Bois could describe only as sexual and moral impertinence or frenetic and irrational connection, and what later social scientists and reformers codified as Black pathology born of slavery and plantations, indexed small-scale rebellions in the realm of intimacies, the reappropriation of care and other forms of labor to cultivate dynamic worlds, a renegotiation and sometimes rejection of the restrictive visions of affiliation through blood, sex, and property, idealized in late-Victorian, Progressive, and post-Progressive thought as insurers of normal, white, (eugenic) growth, and stabilization for the chaotic industrial city.[6] House and storefront congregations, temples, and mosques, along with other unsanctioned social spaces like those of the street and the tap room, constituted a unique Black vernacular landscape that challenged the predominant vision of orderly urban life channeled through the normative home, the patriarchal family, the institutional church, and the institutions of (legal) secular civil society.

These modalities of social-spatial life come together in this work through my conceptualization of *dark agoras*, which describe insurgent Black working-class migrant formulations of social and geographic connection often at the edges of, or explicitly demoted and excluded from, state-sanctioned majoritarian publics. While *agora* most commonly refers to classical Greek public spaces, and especially markets, associated with citizenship, dark agoras represent a shapeshifting social-geographic formation associated with forms of Black collectivity shadowing public life and haunting the market as the residue of the rich excess of vitality and sociality.[7] In using the language of shapeshifting, I draw on the work of Aimee Meredith Cox, who uses this conceptualization to describe the ways that "young Black women mobilize history, whether officially documented or bricolaged through recall and desire, to give new meaning to social contexts that engender cartographic capacities beyond particular physical or ideological sites."[8] In a different context, Pekka Hämäläinen describes shapeshifting as "recurring metamorphosis, fragmenting and coalescing into smaller and larger units" and, specifically in relation to Lakota history, as "a palpable capacity to adapt to changing conditions around them and yet remain" themselves.[9] Building out from Cox and Hämäläinen, dark agoras are shapeshifting forms in the ways that they embody the complex cartographic and social renegotiation of physical and ideological repression through the skillful and strategic reformulation of presence, absence, form, and aesthetic, as well as by the broader derivation of the excess capacities of the geography of domination, to render other possibilities for configuring living, being, and collectivity. The description of dark agoras as shapeshifting elasticizes the concept to account for its various meanings and significations in different periods, cohering through opacity, through the form of assembly itself, shaped in the originary plantation context and in the insurgent social-spatial formations of the city and by dialectics of enclosure and porosity, confinement and spatial autonomy. Dark agoras name modes of Black assembling constitutive of Black life elided and often purposefully made opaque in a dynamic blurring distinction between resistance to transparency as a cooperative expression of interiority and worldmaking, and the discursive demarcation enacted by majoritarian publics inscribing autonomous forms of Black presence with wretchedness and danger and marking them for confinement, containment, and violent dislocation.

Dark agoras emerged under slavery through the active reinvention of African socialities and consciousnesses about place, identity, kinship, and belonging as the negation of the spatial and temporal features associated with domination and slave mastery, atomizing and rendering their connections dissolvable as a condition of the geographic and economic expansion of what Tiffany Lethabo King underscores as the settler-conquistador order.[10] They name formulations of belonging across the boundaries of plantations, across insurgent infrastructures of care and reciprocity defined by the strategic refutation of the public and the visible, the embrace of the possibilities for alternative social and spatial reproduction in the marginal, hidden, and subterranean.[11] In the context of farms and plantations, they describe unaccounted-for space and time, marking the coordinates of local, regional, and transregional geography associated with what Kathryn Benjamin Golden terms "insurgent ecologies," created primarily to generate the possibility of belonging outside servitude and often in connection to land and waterscapes considered untamed.[12] These forms rendered sites for the unknowable through the spatially unaccounted for, the excess spatial features unmarked on maps and promulgated through everyday acts of spatial refusal, truancy, unsanctioned gathering, meeting stealing, marronage, and insurrectionary rebellion. These forms terrorized the cartographic imaginaries central to dominion, or what Wende Marshall underscores as the theological imperative foundational to Western power and governance that legitimate domination and exploitation through control of the earth and people as property.[13]

Although the radical negation of the planter state that emerged from the rudiments of the quotidian practices of unsanctioned placemaking and sabotage that constituted resistance to slavery and were crystalized during the US Civil War's dislocations, dark agoras were not dislodged in total from the coordinates of the region and the nation. Between the collapse of Radical Reconstruction after 1877 and the consolidation of Jim Crow between the 1890s and the 1920s, the dynamic of opacity, co-

constituted by the internally derived desire for social integrity in the absence of discursive and physical violence and the racial state's renewed demarcation of the Black gathering as an insurgent form of disruption requiring preemptive violence, was given renewed vigor in the enclosures and displacements constituting the dominant spatial features of what Sarah Haley terms Jim Crow modernity.[14] Within a matrix defined by the reinvigorated plantation and a carceral continuum that extended legally and extralegally across rural towns, that enclosed urban neighborhoods, that proliferated prisons and work camps, opaqueness provided modes of urbanized Black sociality with cover, insulating rich if sometimes unintelligible interiorities and collective visioning within a fleeting relationality that registered as the underground, as dodgy and peripatetic, and as the shrouded inchoate congregations of the set-apart, especially those cohering in the territory of the "cultish."

Although dismissed, derided, and policed as outside the terrain of vitality and living, as constituted solely of the corrosiveness of segregation and bound by instability, meaninglessness, and death, these formations and the energy generated between them represents critical loci of Black migrant worldmaking and spatial politics. Here I use the term worldmaking in a similar vein as Adom Getachew, who employs it to think about the anticolonial and postcolonial political formations around the Diaspora that aspired to retool and remake "self-determination." Worldmaking in this sense encompasses modes of horizon generation that scholars can investigate without overdetermining these dynamic efforts collective transformation by their subsequent "failures" to produce a specific set of outcomes.[15] This use of worldmaking is also engaged with what Nijah Cunningham describes through the rubric of Black freedom's non-arrival as a "glimpse [at] the making of worlds within the historical archive that fall outside of the normative horizons and expectations of political emancipation."[16]

Under the umbrella of dark agoras, sites within the often ephemeral geographies of the furtive and fugitive Black underground and the often conspicuous but illegible spaces of heterodox migrant religiosity incubated dissident visions for urban futurity—doing so over and against the dictates of dominant urban reform efforts and their modes of (re)producing race, gender, space, and ultimately, the city itself. Ranging from underground spaces to sacred sites created and inhabited by "cults" and other groups that embraced nonnormative belief systems, the cultivators of dark agoras engaged in a continuum of efforts to express a different horizon for the urban future beyond the emplacement of Black communities in austerity, death, or dissolution. Taken together, dark agoras and the passages, connections, and disavowals across them constituted Black vernacular landscapes, understood as competing territorialities cultivated through the creation of small-scale edits to matters of place that, while not always disrupting dominant social-geographic relations, incubated within its inhabitants visions of urban futures askew, that queried the trajectory of racial capitalist stability prescribed by reformers and powerful crafters of state power's geographic functions.

While for early US landscape scholar J. B. Jackson, the American vernacular landscape expressed the evolution of novelties imported and transformed in practice by (white) settlers combined with the environmental and economic imperatives of "open land" and "available" resources, accounting for Black vernacular landscapes requires an alternative understanding, given the history of forced emplacement and dislocation on earth rendered land through genocide and expropriation. Black vernacular architectures, infrastructures, and landscapes are often marked by impermanency, sometimes active only in and through the appropriation and commandeering of stolen space—and with it, the corollary of stolen time—in relation to dominant orderings of the city's spatial and temporal coordinates.[17] In thinking through Black vernacular landscapes and their relationship to the dominant features of geography, I draw on the work of Black geographic and ecological thought—Ruth Wilson Gilmore's critical abolitionist analysis of the ways that the state transformed the geographies of "excess" people, land, and power through the prison fix; Katherine McKittrick, writing in the context of Black women's unthought geographies; Clyde Woods in collaboration with McKittrick for the critical *Black Geographies* collection, as well as in his two monographs about the dynamics shaping the lower Mississippi region; Rashad Shabazz in his analysis of the geographies of confinement and masculinity in Chicago; Farah Jasmine Griffin's pioneering effort to examine literature, painting, and music through the prism of migration narrative; Davarian Baldwin's analysis of migrant's transformation of Chicago through the market of ideas with its spatial coordinates along the city's avenues; Jarvis McInnis's work to think critically about the "afterlives of plantations" through Black women's artistic engagements, as well as his efforts to recover US South-Global South diasporic writing publics; Justin Hosbey's work about the effects of post-Katrina Black expressive culture to contour time and place in New Orleans; K. Ian Grandison's theorization of post-segregation continuity in unequal geographies from the "wrong side of the track" through the "wrong side of the highway"; Marcus A. Hunter's engagement with Black city makers and the ways they shaped the city outside victimhood to displacement; Zandria Robinson's approach to the ways that the multiplicity and intra-regional variation shapes the South and the ways that Black southern identities shape race, gender, and class, regionally and beyond; Danielle Purifoy's analysis of southern towns as sites of enduring plantation spatial relations and her work on Black relations to forests; Hilda Lloréns's ethnographic engagement with Afro–Puerto Rican women's efforts to create livable worlds in the face of "matriarchal dispossession" and environmental catastrophe; Ashanté Reese's work to engage Black Washingtonians' food geographies outside the flattening description of food deserts; and Andrea Roberts's work to locate Black free towns in East Texas. These works underwrite my own here to think about how together, the histories and geographies of slavery, racial capitalism, migration, extraction, violence, segregation, urban reform, and resistance shape Black relations to the matters of space and place in the context of Philadelphia.[18] As well, I draw on the literature building from Nathan Hare's 1970 formulation "black ecology" to underscore Black ecologies, a formulation describing not only Black communities' relationship to the environment as victims of extraction, violence, toxic dumping, and climate change but also the relations of mutuality and resistance giving expression to possibilities beyond the delimitation of Blackness as living in vulnerability and death and taking seriously various cultural mediums of Black expression as vehicles of insurgent and practical knowledge in the face of environmental degradation, geographic dislocation, and territorial violence.[19]

In this work, I underscore how the illicit world of the sexual and economic undergrounds cocreated common epistemic and cartographic territory in dialectic with the set-apart, and how these two distinctive visions for the urban future underwrote a Black working-class vernacular landscape that served as infrastructure of connection, vitality, and "black aliveness" for the dispossessed. "Black aliveness," as Kevin Quashie develops, is a complex encompassing the fullness of living in a context in which Black people continue to be exposed to life-ending circumstances of the eventful and slow varieties.[20] For Quashie, "black world making" in poetry and in the poetic lyricism of first-person essays constitutes an "assemblage, an open collective of dynamism, of pull and tug and relationality" that registers as a distinctive relation of becoming and being.[21] As I describe, the cultivators of these spaces shaped the city from below through distinctive and sometimes conflicting visions of personal well-being or gain, "erotic sovereignty," and holiness—here encompassing the traditional Christian connotations as well as the non-Christian doctrines and practices of religious-political sanctification and distinction enacted through communities contoured by shared cosmologies, theologies, and practical changes in shared behavior, dress, and self-understanding.[22]

Connections within the sites constituting dark agoras, as well as encounters across them and movement between them, underwrote a distinctive Black working-class phenomenology of the city, the basis of what I term Black queer urbanism. Rather than simply attending to Black or queer experiences of the city, Black queer urbanism refers to a critical approach that views nonnormative forms of Black social-geographic life and the distinctive and often discredited knowledge produced in dark agoras as the conceptual resources and bases for an alternate vision for the future of urban life and ecologies outside the rubrics of gendered individualism, heteronormative familialism, and reproductive futurity, primarily through engagements with the sensuous encounters across these riven borders in Black city life. Experiences of encounter invoking indifference, embrace, or disavowal were often heightened in the juxtaposition of passage with the impassible, of movement or the transfixing suspension of encounter in spaces often defined by stillness as stasis or confinement. These experiences documented in Black expressive cultures and the archives of Black religious groups, as well as by the state, engaged in alternative worldmaking underwrote transformative ways of knowing and understanding the city. Though often, the formulations of Black sociality in dark agoras and their attendant formulations for the city and its future were demoted, especially in relation to the science of the city consolidated by planners, these modes suggest meaningful formulations of living and collectivity in the face of the spatial violence and regional demographic reterritorialization that were compounded by the consolidation of the postwar state.

My definition of Black queer urbanism draws from Cathy Cohen's pathbreaking theorization of queerness as a position with respect to power, as a relation to myriad conceptions of deviance, and as a social assembly rather than solely a sexual practice.[23] Along with Cohen's work, Black feminist literatures examining the processes of racialized gender, including work by Hortense Spillers, L. H. Stallings, Sarah Haley, C. Riley Snorton, Saidiya Hartman, and others, also press the limits of queerness beyond strictly sexual affiliation, opening questions of the spatially and temporally discordant in conjunction with nonnormative or antinormative sexualities as constitutive to a critical outsider position. I ground Black queer urbanism in a theory of queerness wherein queerness notes an outside or vexed position associated with conceptions of spatial-social deviance, heterodoxy, and abnormality. Black queer urbanism, embodied in the worldmaking practices of dark agoras as assemblies of the dispossessed and marginal names a mode of reproducing the city from the vantage of those condemned within Progressive and post-Progressive thought to a sinister future or to no future at all.[24] Within the derided spaces of "slums," in areas marked by planners, researchers, and the police as (sexually) disreputable and obsolete, and in social institutions considered strange and unproductive, Black communities engaged in efforts ranging from small acts of refashioning urban spaces to expressly confrontational and liberatory efforts to transform the social and ecological arrangement of the city. Traversing and straddling various worlds, South and North, disreputable and set-apart, Black people of the Great Migration and post-migration generations wrote a rogue phenomenology of the city, encountering and crisscrossing the threshold between the underground and the spaces of self-fashioned holiness and purity—those set-apart spaces of Black religious movements—to articulate heretical visions of the social, spatial, and cosmological order for life in the city, often grounded in hybrid imaginaries combining visions associated with rurality and the South yet possible only within the distinctive urban social and geographic formations of segregated migrant culture.

Émile Durkheim developed the concept of anomie to name the emergence of a kind of normlessness and to describe the evaporation of social forces acting as controls over individuals and regulating their behavior in industrial urban contexts. The loosening of moral and other intracommunal policing in the transition from "folk" rural society to complex urban socialities underwrites the derisive description of Black migrant communities defined not only by their proximity to the folk, damningly associated with the perverse tutelage of slavery and inhabiting a new stratum in the urban-industrial context—redundant worker, criminal, excess population. In the overlapping literatures of sociology, criminology, and social-reform movements that culminated in the 1940s consolidation of urban statecraft through the ascent of planning, the modern Black urban subject was defined not only by a degraded labor status associated with slavery and peonage but also by the cultural differentiation that was held to inhere in a fixed relation to extractionism in the context of the US South (and beyond) and that was lived as a modality of discordant rurality (in the vernacular, country-ness) that undermined integration into the labor and housing markets of the industrial metropolis. Black urban communities in Philadelphia and beyond came to cohere as the definitive margin, or limit, of urban social life and sociality that was defined in the ante- and antisocial life of delinquency, immorality, criminality, and cultishness. These categorizations, read back onto and through the prism of rurality and supposed affiliations with a peasantry and the folk, however overdetermined they were in literatures as the sources of Black poverty and death, are the wellsprings of Black queer urbanism.

As Louis Wirth defined it in the classic sociological formulation, urbanism is understood as "the complex of traits which makes up the characteristic modes of life in cities."[25] Wirth's foundational definition distinguished urbanism from the movement of populations into urban centers, rather underscoring the adoption of urban behavioral and social mores (or the lack thereof) as the definition of urbanism. Adding the qualifiers *Black* and *queer* to urbanism highlights the divergent modes of life derived through migration and subsequent transformation of urban and rural Black landscapes. Despite the similar work performed by both qualifiers, I use both because of the added effect of commotion engaged through queer as a continuum of alternative affective economies and social arrangements underwriting Black urban social worlds. To place *Black* alone names a dispropriative relation to kinship, the appropriation as property of affiliation and reproduction, as well as the vexation of these relations. But *queer* qualifies the projects for urban futurity that I am interested in as not only those seeking the resolution of the terms of imposition and exclusion but also as formulas that challenged the basic premises of capitalist urban futures that in planning discourse demarked Black life as a product of decay defined by proximity to imminent and future death. Placing these together is not an effort to render them interchangeable phenomena, reduce Blackness to a relation of sexuality, or purge queerness of all sexual connotation straightforwardly exchangeable with the terrain of Blackness in the city as it is marked in cartographies of dominance as deviant, disruptive, and deadly. Their uncomfortable, sometimes fraught, positioning brings divergence and breakdown to the fore, not only as in the production of problematic outliers like the delinquent to be tamed or dissolved but also as dynamic social emergences and dissolutions that press at our interpretation of twentieth-century Black urban life, culture, and politics.

In line with Black queer urbanism's fluid demarcation of temporal and spatial connection and visions of urban futurity, I should also note that when I describe migrant cultures and migrant communities, I am not simply reducing the phenomena described to a discussion of movement. Rather, I am seeking to excavate the ways that the cultural difference and outlooks born of urbanization and of lingering rurality and plot imaginaries informed collective outlooks about the city. Even people who were multigenerational residents of the city and those who could trace lineages to the city's colonial era had their institutions and cultural practices transformed by the influx of southern migrants during the Great Migrations, beginning with the era about which Du Bois wrote. As Black women, men, and children, reared in a displaced home, joined preexisting social institutions, they shifted their frequency. These reformulated institutions (in the broadest sense including churches and taprooms along one continuum) in turn incubated new generations in a hybrid cultural milieu defined by the translocation of the plot and its ongoing repression and regeneration. Underwritten by its geographic antecedents in plotting and the Black commons in the context of the rural and urban South and materializing through the dislocations of urbanization beginning at the turn of the twentieth century, Black queer urbanism names modes and practices of the city tethered to but not delimited by rural and regional translocation that register as outliers within prescriptive relations of governance, state function, and territoriality but that nevertheless served as a means by which migrants made sense of their traversals and engaged in forms of worldmaking often illegible to state officials, researchers, and reformers, except as that which must disappear for the institutions of "normal" conditions through the architectures and infrastructures of the biopolitical city.

To the historiography of twentieth-century urban social movements, *Dark Agoras: Insurgent Black Social Life and the Politics of Place* contributes the account of a trajectory of the Black radical tradition whereby ordinary Black city dwellers traversed the spaces of the underground and the set-apart spaces of esoteric religious life, tracing a rogue urban phenomenology and generating a challenge to key aspects of the pro-growth formula of social-spatial order prescribed by dominant urbanists. Part of this project's primary intervention is historiographical, as it queries the notion of the theorization of the Long Movement for Black freedom by analyzing actors relegated, even within this temporally and spatially capacious paradigm, to the edge of the literature because of their embrace of heterodoxy and the identities and modalities of community and futurity viewed as incommensurate with integration, leftist radical transformation, cultural nationalism, and other vindicated paradigms within the Long Movement historiography. This capacious framing, crystalized in Jacquelyn Dowd Hall's essay and in the work of scholars who anticipated it before the framework was ensconced in the historiography by Hall's naming, has opened the fields of civil rights and Black Power in ways unimaginable at the outset of these historiographies that centered on the classical period of southern-based activism and which often failed to appreciate Black Power as anything more than the declension of civil rights.[26] The Long Movement framework has produced a number of histories, those like Matthew Countryman's *Up South*, which moved to dislodge southern exceptionalism, highlighting what Jeanne Theoharis and Brian Purnell term the "Jim Crow North," and draw to light various local, regional, and national efforts to transform the political hegemony of white supremacy across space and time.[27]

The Long Movement framework has also drawn important criti-
cisms, especially Cha-Jua and Lang's characterization of this framework
as vampiric and their attendant claim that it erases geographic contex-
tual specificity and critical heterogeneity within twentieth-century Black
social movements, eliding and flattening while elasticizing time and
space within the accounting of Black social movements from the 1930s
through the 1980s.[28] I think there are uses and limits to this framework
that I do employ and even expand temporally. My quips with it mostly
have to do with the key exclusions that mark all but a small selection of
formal, institutional churches and the underground from the matrix of
twentieth-century Black urban social movements and life or that rel-
egate matters of spirit and religion (beyond institutional churches' civil
rights activism) to the edges and have disregarded groups not convenient in narratives, emphasizing instead well- established political lines,
because of their prickliness. I take geography as an analytic, perhaps in
ways that will not fully account for Cha-Jua and Lang's ringing critique
but that are akin to thinking through the prism of the Black radical tradition as Cedric Robinson understood it, as not a singular phenomenon
but the work of scholars to excavate various living tendencies and tra-
jectories in struggles for Black liberation within various local, national,
regional, and globalized contexts.

This route to Black Power's emergence in Philadelphia joins the long
river of the Black freedom struggle that Vincent Harding describes as
a rather queer tributary defined by its propensity to seemingly evapo-
rate, turn underground, and reemerge before joining the predominant
tributaries of post-emancipation struggles for collectivities beyond the
horizons provided by the planter and post-planter states. This book is
inspired by Ashley Farmer's important analysis of women's organizing
and activism during the Black Power era, especially Farmer's capacity
to find commonality and resonance along the various tendencies she
draws together. Keisha Blain's work to locate the complex intellectual
terrain of ordinary Black women activists and organizers in Black nationalist and internationalist traditions opens ground for this work as
well. Claudrena Harold's *New Negro in the Jim Crow South*, in thinking centrally about the complex intellectual terrain of the "New Negro"
and her geographic outlook and field of expression, serves as a critical intervention informing my approach. Treva Lindsey's history of the

transformations in public life and culture precipitated by the activism and intellectualism of "New Negro" women in Washington, DC, including "race women," blues performers, educators, and others informs my integrative approach to various archives of Black life in this book.[29] As well, Brittney Cooper's genealogy of Black women's intellectualism from the turn of the twentieth century to the era of Black Power, and Martha Jones's account of Black women's multi-century tradition of struggles against racism and sexism in relation to the franchise and citizenship, also inform my approach in drawing out a long genealogy of Black alternative worldmaking.[30]

In this work, the *insurgent* holds together two derided sets of spaces as significant and meaningful for engaging in the histories of Great Migration and post–Great Migration politics from the era of the New Negro to the era of Black Power, without seeking to tame them through "epistemological respectability" and in ways that center analytically the spatial registers of Black life and living as itself a movement against enclosure and violence.[31] In Rinaldo Walcott's extension of William Haver's concept "epistemological respectability," Walcott deploys this terminology in the context of late twentieth-century Black studies to challenge the enduring place of fixing historical injury and addressing the enduring precarity of Black studies in the academy. Walcott challenges epistemological respectability by calling for us to consider how Black queer subjects generatively challenge the limit in Black studies. Epistemological respectability in relation to Black migrant communities renders Black migrants subjects delimited by and defined in relation to wounding and injury and in need of salvific redemption, what Candice Jenkins in another context elucidates through her conceptualization of the salvific wish as "a longing to protect or save black women, and black communities more generally, from narratives of sexual and familial pathology" that are often associated with the histories of slavery and its haunting of the social present.[32]

The underground and the set-apart in the context of this work register formulations of sociality, politics, and geography that are neither pure nor uncomplicated, which gives additional significance of the use of *insurgent* as a header for drawing together these sometimes contradictory geographies into one polymorphic tradition. The underground in this analysis includes the fleeting and peripatetic spaces of the city's stoops, corners, gambling houses, buffet flats, and red-light districts, corners, taverns, row houses serving as unlicensed bars, gambling houses, and drug dens. Philadelphia's Black underground emerged and grew with the movement of migrants who arrived in neighborhoods that had long traditions of informal and underground economies, by-products of the social and political organization of the city beginning in the era of Republican-controlled Philadelphia after the Civil War. In 1890s Philadelphia, Black communities were engaged in more illicit and off-the-books businesses than in officially licensed businesses, already constituting "a separate city . . . with its own unique social and economic structures and social rules that greeted southern migrant's en masse during the First World War."[33] In the period of Republican political control that lasted from the late nineteenth century through the New Deal, this "separate city" remained integral to Philadelphia's political structures as "commercial vice was a longstanding, quasi-legitimate, and integral part of the urban economy, inextricably tied into district and ward-level politics."[34] Despite the previous presence of the underground as expressed by the centrality of the informal economy before the large in-migration of World War I and the interwar period before the Depression, the underground, as both a descriptive rubric attempting to contain the excesses of criminalized Black vitality and an index of Black vitality itself, was infused with new energy, investments, and meaning by the large migrations from the South. Rather than the underground's marking a territory outside of the law, it approximates, through the fogginess of the archives that index its existence, a site of unmaking, reversal, rescripting, and resolution, enacted through contests over the state's claim to the ultimate monopoly on violence—here the power to define market-state relations and their functional territoriality.

Given this complex relation, the underground is not a romantic space of outlaws challenging capitalism at every juncture. More often than not, the lines of flight rendered possible through it in the context of this book in twentieth-century Philadelphia recapitulate forms of state-sanctioned domination, especially along the well-worn grooves of patriarchy and economic exploitation, even when engaged outside formal markets and social-geographic relations. Nevertheless, Black working-class migrants used the underground to create individual and collective alternatives to drudgery and economic and social marginality, defying the overall precarity and their location within Philadelphia's economic architecture and social geography. The underground was often defined by the ethos of *werk*.[35] While often still privileging personal or familial gain or lines of flight over other modes of collectivity and politics, the geographies of werk were queered in terms of time, space, priority, leisure, productive labor, and social reproduction. Although for outsiders and the city, the indeterminable terrain of the underground indexed the degradation of rurality and urbanization at the margins of the industrial city, Black migrants used this semi-clandestine geography to give expressions to their own visions for personal and communal autonomy. Drawing on the early efforts of Sharon Harley to recover the agency of criminalized Black women who took up hustling, and following on the book-length works of Kali Gross, LaShawn Harris, Cheryl Hicks, and Sarah Haley, in particular, I examine ways that experiences with the semi-clandestine worlds of bootleggers, "prostitutes," numbers runners, and others whom Du Bois considered the "semi-criminal" or "vicious" shaped key aspects of the city's twentieth-century spatial contours and political trajectory.[36]

The set-apart in the context of thinking through Black queer urbanism includes varying sites of spiritualized identity formation and collectivity that are most often associated with Black Christian traditions and variants but are not delimited by these theological parameters, even by those replaying complex synchronizations that have never been easily dislocated from the larger field of Africana religious practice.[37] The form of the storefront, and the wider geography of the set-apart it indexes, represents a remarkable longevity in Black urban life and culture, owing, in part, to their aesthetic appeal and alternative formulations of authority and power, as Deidre Crumbley's ethnographic engagement with a contemporary Philadelphia storefront brings to the fore.[38] As Ashon Crawley develops astutely through his theorization and engagement with the ascetics of whooping, shouting, and tongues in *Blackpentacostal Breath*, the aesthetics of these worship experiences, which outside observers could only interpret as loud, discordant, unreasonable, and backward, underwrote what he terms "otherwise possibilities" to describe the "ongoingness . . . of things existing other than what is given, what is known, what is grasped."[39] Those embracing holiness and other rubrics of spiritual and religious distinction sought encirclement in collectives outside the corrosive violence, dislocation, and alienation of the outside world, as Anthea Butler illustrates in her engagement with the Women's Department of the COGIC Church.[40] Within the set part, Black women in particular built corresponding permanent and semi-permanent sites of communion and engagement with the divine and elaborated collective cartographies of the city that shaped their quotidian movements across urban space.[41] Here I draw on the complex geographic and spatial transformations that Imani Uzuri historicizes in her conceptualization of "sacred migration" through her recovery of Sister Gertrude Morgan's movements across locations in the South and within and across New Orleans animated by her spiritual practice.[42]

A critical part of the enduring possibilities within the aesthetic, social, and political traditions of this long twentieth-century urban formation, the set-apart, is the geographic dynamics of the form taken across its diverse collectivity. Taken in the widest aperture, the set-apart describes a motif of spiritualized and often politicized (if not directly political) congregation materializing within the quotidian Black geographies of northern industrial cities across the twentieth century, physically manifesting, or at least indexing, the roving and imaginative social, spatial, and political outlooks of the new cultural modalities that emerged through Black urbanization. As Judith Weisenfeld demonstrates, Black religious worlds that were derided as cultish engaged in significant contestations over identity and racial formation, shaping new formulations of spiritual and communal identity, as well as practices of place. Despite the reality of their temporal and geographic susceptibility in cities shaped by tides of racialized capitalist displacement, urbanized Black communities employed the storefront along a continuum of informal and formal religious communities to constitute the various worlds of the set-apart and the wayward and insurgent religious worlds of Black migrants in early and mid-twentieth century New York, Philadelphia, Washington, and Chicago.[43] The set-apart describes myriad rubrics for social, spiritual, and sometimes political distinction, including the Holiness, Spiritualist, and Pentecostal formations associated with the notion of the set-apart, but also including temples and mosques among groups like the Moorish Science Temple and the Nation of Islam.[44] Dispossessed Black communities utilized these primary social-geographic formulations to establish, cultivate, and defend autonomous social, cultural, and spiritual practices and sites across the twentieth century.

Just as the underground is not easily cleared of its messiness, the territory of the set-apart is also a complex terrain in which to investigate Black working-class worldmaking, given the preponderance, especially in the 1920s and 1930s, of the charismatic-led mass. As Elsa Barkley Brown develops in relation to post-Reconstruction churches, the transformation of Black politics in the wake of violent political retrenchment narrowed the field of democratic possibility within Black public and institutional life, sidelining Black women in the realms of Black church and political institutions.[45] The resulting restrictions on public forums for Black intracommunal democracy set the ground for, and conditioned the emergence of, formulations of power within Black communities privileging men, as Erica Edwards illustrates through conceptualizing the "charismatic scenario" to describe "a cosmology, mythology, and performative technology of African American mass mobilization," directing formulations of freedom that center individual capacity and authority, often god ordained, as the means of Black political advance and thus "hous[ing] black freedom dreams while also impeding their realization."[46] Many of the groups I examine in the context of the plot's transposition and transmutation in the urban context, including Father Divine's Peace Mission movement, were also characterized by what outsiders suggested were the excesses of the charismatic as gnostic formations. Gnosticism names a "prophetic-charismatic movement and its doctrinal system" with varying degrees of religiosity and organizational infrastructure, wherein adherents attribute to the current order of things the defilement of human life and existence.[47] Taken broadly, heretics of the gnostic tradition embrace the notion that through the esoteric mysteries of their faith and its unique epistemic and cosmological reordering, derived through their recalibration of order beginning with the purification of the flesh and the mind prompted often by a mystic's teachings, they can effect a catastrophic reordering of the cosmological-social order, thereby transfiguring the world from a place of violence, fluctuation, chaos, and cataclysm to one of order, perfection, and permanence. Gnosticism, especially in the wake of twentieth-century (and now twenty-first century) fascist movements, has taken on the stench of these deadly regimes, formulations of blind charismatic power tied to Hitler (and more lately to Trump), as well as of the charismatic religious figures of Jim Jones and the leaders of groups like Heaven's Gate that were associated with mass suicide/murder and authoritarianism. Gnosticism entails what Albert Camus referred to as "metaphysical rebellion," constituted through a dethroning of God and thus a fundamental reordering of the social-cosmological order, often in the hands of a charismatic figure who embodies the authority assigned to God the father in orthodox Christian divinity.[48] As Eric Voegelin has argued, Gnosticism and the heretical "[are] not harmless"; rather, they encapsulate a tautological loop wherein gnosis, or knowing, is the knowledge whereby an adherent interprets that they are "falling captive to the world" and at the same time are the singular "means of escaping" this captivity. According to Voegelin, the "gnostic's flight from a truly dreadful, confusing, and oppressive state of the world is understandable," and yet this flight to a new world through this order's destruction "will not destroy the world, but will only increase the disorder in society."[49]

Despite the strict appearance as top-down formulations of power for the groups I center in this work, these groups exceed this designation as a generic form of Gnosticism. They move beyond the topology of the "cult," understood as a charismatic leader followed by the hapless or duped. As Edwards accounts for in her astute analysis of the charismatic scenario mentioned above, and as Cedric Robinson analyzes through his study of Malcolm X's charisma, the charismatic figure coalesces a collective's aspirations and desires, drawing together and enacting and performing the collective's desires. Writing in a different context, Tiffany Florvil illustrates the ways that Audre Lorde helped galvanize the Black German movements during the era of national reintegration, in part through her own moving and sensual presence but also out of the ways that she embodied the aspirations of the emerging Black feminist writers and artists she encountered in Berlin and around the country. Likewise, Shana Redmond's creative engagement with the figure of Paul Robeson, in and through the form of his voice and (re)embodiment through the hologram, the stage, installations, and in geographies of urban transformation, also illustrate complex affective terrain materializing the charismatic figure and her or his afterlives.[50] I do not deny the charismatic function within the architectures of the spiritual communities I engage in this tradition but see it rather as a complex formulation of sociality and power derived foremost from the efforts of ordinary people's efforts at worldmaking, even if manifesting in disproportionately top down formulations of power.

Taking the spaces of the underground and the set-apart in their shared prickliness, in their conjunction in Black experiences of the city, and in their hybridization across space and time as elemental to Black queer urbanism is not to sanitize these spaces of their social and political complexity or to suggest that these spaces built by Black migrant generations recused their cultivators of the wider political ecology of violence and death. What interests me is the geographic materialization that these worlds index, draw upon, and forward in the context of mass urbanization, dislocation, loss, and renewed placemaking. As sites, they cultivated dissident cartographic-political outlooks that, while sometimes privileging the violent reenactment of other forms of unidirectional power and violence, also incubated an intergenerational challenge to ongoing modes of space-craft dependent on enclosure, exclusion, and marginalization. Centering rogue phenomenological passage between the criminalized worlds of the underground into the often equally condemned sites of heterodox religious-political formation on the part of migrants reveals the essential power of modes of discredited sensual connection in the reformulation of worlds devastated and abandoned by the dislocations of gendered racial capitalism, migration, and the resulting geographies of austerity and social murder that these processes articulated across the horizons in early and mid-twentieth century Black freedom dreaming and futurity.[51]

By taking as central the phenomenological arc traced by ordinary migrants and members of the post–Great Migration generations in their transformation within these respective sites and across the divide of the underground and the set-apart, *Dark Agoras* examines the generative worlds that migrants cultivated and spiritualized and the physical architectures—some fleeting and some permanent—that they employed to anneal the chasm between dislocated home and the city and between their visions for the future and the city's condemnation and removal of Black social worlds as the prerequisite of a living neighborhood. Both of these worlds centered ecstatics—fundamentally, a blurring of time and spatial coordinates—with the effect of individual or collective timelessness and aspatiality, a fleeting cosmic rupture, a radical disembodiment and removal from the sense of the self and the collective sited in a contained geography and at the same time a lightning-rod re-grounding of the self or the collective in the excesses of the body's emotive, affective, and physical energies.[52] In the ecstatic, feeling overburdens the mind's capacity to control, allowing for sensual and embodied connection, whether through the plain of the orgasmic or the unburdening of the shout.[53] The ecstatic is often associated with the erotic and is likewise feminized and racialized as part of Blackness and therefore demoted as a plane of knowing and understanding. Yet taken between these worlds of the dark agoras, the ecstatic is also an embodied map that draws together the coordinates of multiple worlds across disjuncture and dislocation. This work uses sites excommunicated from the rational civil body of the citizen, the underground, and the set-apart and their excessive ecstatic modes of living and vitality, shadowing and refiguring normative social relations in the peculiarity of migrant culture's affiliations to reexamine the transformation in governance and politics across the long twentieth century. Many of the cultivators of the set-apart traversed the underground, were intimate with it, and mobilized narratives of their embodied transformation from disfigurement within it to a set-apart world combining vitality and well-being. This transit and the modes of collective description it underwrote incubated dissident visions of social, ecological, and cosmological integrity.

As I illustrate in the first two chapters, part of the potential energy of these experiences and the transformations associated with the migrants' rogue phenomenology of the city, written in their passage and in the encounters between the underground and the set-apart, was grounded in these sites' shared origin in the imaginaries and spatial dynamics of the plot. In the original context, the plot describes Black communities' engagement with practices of place and alternative figurations of land and water in the antebellum and post-emancipation periods. In chapter 1, I historicize the work of enslaved, free, and emancipated communities to create a distinctive and often furtive social architecture rivaling, threatening, and challenging the infrastructures of abstraction, commodification, and social control developed by white elites before and after the formal abolition of slavery. Practices centered in the various iterations of the plot—the site of the body's interment, the garden parcel, a roving imaginary of the potential for connection in land and waterscapes outside of control, and hidden insurrectionary activity—fostered a vision of de-commodified water and landscapes as well as resources. Evolving in dialectic with mastery and dominion—or biblically justified total control—enslaved and post-emancipation communities claimed and created a set of communal resources within the interstices of plantation ecologies, constituting the Black commons.

The plot is not a static formation defined by straightforward reproduction in the context of urbanization. Rather, the plot suggests "the persistent materiality which underlies the home experience" for Black migrants in the context of interwar and subsequent postwar migration.[54] As I demonstrate in chapter 2, the plot and the Black commons served as enduring aspects of the symbolic universe of Black collective expression after the Civil War and Reconstruction. In the ephemera produced in two primary domains of leisure of post-emancipation Black cultural life, among religious communities, in sermons, during religious ritual, and equally within the carnal pursuits of sex, gambling, and drinking against which the saints set themselves apart, the plot served as the cultural raw material for visions grounding individual and collective futures outside the confines of slavery's specters and afterlives. The plot underwrote a multifaceted outlook on territory and sovereignty that was defined through enduring resistance to the violent geographic processes of fallowing, enclosure, and commercialization that defined racial capitalism's geographic-ecological operations from rural community to port town and metropolis. The plot functioned within the worlds that migrants erected as a touchstone between two or more locations in material and immaterial senses such that these worlds impinge on, bleed into, haunt, and reshape one another through various kinds of return—literal movement back and forth, but most strikingly in some of the narratives centered in this work, including extra-physical relocation.

The plot is characterized by a complex geographic and social outlook that privileged use value, collectivity, pleasure, sustenance, abundance, reciprocity, and other connections between people and across land and waterscapes outside mastery and domination. Translated to the city, this imaginary continued to underwrite a diverse array of visions for personal and collective urban social formation outside or beyond the dislocations of gendered racial capitalism. As migrant narratives and expressive cultures illustrate, the plot served as a primary substrate of

Black cities within the city-—the *transposition* of the plot, its materialization often in the form of the residual of the physical, social, and metaphysical underwriting Black migrant worldmaking.[55] These recuperated
logics, outlooks, and modes of placemaking riffed on the imagery of the
plot within visions of personal and erotic sovereignty, earthly transformation, and metaphysical reordering.

The plot haunted both the social outlooks and the practices of the
underground and the set-apart as they took shape in twentieth-century
Philadelphia. As sites of embodied sovereignty, these formations
evolved from the spatial practices and imaginaries of enslaved and post-
emancipation communities that were translated into ritual and other
formations transported by migrants in the context of violent urban emplacement. These spaces, which I take together as dark agoras, evolved
from the clandestine and semi-clandestine under slavery wherein these
functional retoolings of the interstices of plantation geographies underwrote the articulation of Black social worlds, including carnal, social,
and spiritual pursuits. Thus, despite their expression in diametric opposition in the context of the city, the charged transgressions and encounters across these worlds emerges from their replay and recuperation of
the ground of Black modes of place evolving through earlier plantation
ecologies, the rogue writings of territoriality, possibility, and futurity
that were constituted in the cosmologies and geographies of the enslaved
and freedpeople through the Black commons.

As I demonstrate in chapter 3, the worlds of the underground and the
set-apart, along with the overall inscription of the "Negro slum" by the
1940s ascent of planning to state power, helped galvanize the first major
transformations of Philadelphia's landscape after the 1880s. Within planning discourses, which drew on a long local tradition of charitable and
reform work, these social and geographic formations expressed part of
the grammar of the "dead neighborhood," or alternatively, the "Negro
slum." During the era of planning's zenith beginning after 1942, and
gulping at its last breath as the city's economic tides began to change
as a result of deindustrialization and the transformation of governance
by the 1970s, Blackness, and particularly the association of Blackness
with the South and rurality, was inscribed within the grammar of stability and growth, animating large state investments in urban transformation as the embodiment of instability and death.[56] Within the social

imaginaries that actuaries, statisticians, sociologists, eugenicists, and reformers coproduced after the 1880s, racial Blackness was conflated with sinister forms of "darkness," including risk, morbidity, mortality, and criminality. With the ascent of Keynesian statecraft as orthodoxy in the United States in response to the Great Depression, the conflation of Blackness and other forms of darkness helped articulate a fundamental social-spatial grammar for assessing value—here not only as the figuration of its metastasized form, price, but in all reinforcing systems of human productivity and worth rated along a continuum from normal and productive to degenerative. Black migrants as an amorphous mass helped define the spaces and populations requiring amelioration and intervention, and reformers worked to use housing and other related social-spatial technologies to tame the unwieldy social worlds of what they inscribed as the urban frontier. Urban planners, reformers, researchers, and the police were empowered in the age of federal urban reform to map, surveille, and insure urban social fabrics against darkness, poverty, blight, and criminality, conflated with Blackness.

Despite the interpretations of migrant culture as incommensurate with urban-industrial life and the inscription of their formulations of sociality with death and the area simply requiring razing, between the 1920s and the 1940s, these communities erected large-scale organizations materializing key aspects of an enduring Black spatial imaginary within emergent movements that served as sites of earthly transformation. In chapter 4, I pick up on the Peace Mission movement, an organization that rewrote the visions of the plot within elaborate ceremonial formations around the communion table, where they sought to remake social-geographic relations through shared abundance. They embodied the set-apart in its most elaborate formation through their early renunciation of the bonds of matrimony, the affiliations of parent and child, and all other familial and social bonds outside of their connections to their sisters and brothers, remade through their connection to Father Divine. I historicize the efforts of Father Divine's Peace Mission movement as bottom-up formulations, not denying the complex formulation of a sociality expressed in relation to a charismatic figure whom many outsiders denounced as charlatanic rather foregrounding the efforts of those who materialized Divine's charisma and attributed healing capabilities by joining each other. In particular, recentering the communion table and the group's religious feasts, I illustrate how migrants material-ized captive maternal futures in a flickering reassembling of the plot to articulate a vision of imminent heaven on earth. I examine the groups' fashioning of insurgent modes of social belonging wherein they de-fied customary and de jure segregation and violence and articulated a new vision of the future based in peace. I take together their hetero-dox visions of futurity and their odd spatial and temporal logics as a quintessential form of Black queer urbanism—again, various projects interrupting critical aspects of the dominant urbanist growth paradigm that emerged to reinforce gendered racial capitalism in response to the Great Depression. Adherents of the mission sought to remake property as a collective asset, disarticulating it from blood and familial transmis-sion. They embarked on a program of collective purchasing across na-scent metropolitan-scapes within deteriorating spaces in the urban core and—surreptitiously—in exclusive neighborhoods. The flock rehabili-tated and reorganized the real estate that they acquired for alternatively imagined use that was responsive and adapted to their cosmological and social outlooks, and through this process, they articulated reciprocal re-lationships between individual, community, and property under a novel paradigm of stewardship.

In chapter 5, I use arrest records to examine the temporary erection of the Black commons during the 1964 North Philadelphia Columbia Street Riot. This chapter illustrates the ways that the momentary syn-chrony of the underground and the set-apart precipitated the sudden activation and weaponization of alternative dimensions of territoriality in North Philadelphia, suggesting the ways that quotidian Black geog-raphies of semi-illicit leisure and sites associated with the underground were activated in the collective desire to disband property in response to the invasion of police forces seeking to disperse what they viewed as an insurgency. The riot evidences the temporary erection of the Black commons, expressed most pointedly by "receiving stolen goods" and alternative demands on the nature of proximity and use to collective authority to remain present despite mayoral order and violent police enforcement. "Receiving stolen goods" collectively suggested the direct assault on ownership, the reappropriation of commodities as resources for personal and collective use, and a fleeting injunction against the sacrosanct relations of ownership, commodities, markets, and profit.

"Looting," despite violent inscriptions as lawlessness by the state and reformers, in this context names a means of expressing Black futurity from the vantage of the Black captive maternal, including the appropriation of the means of care in a neighborhood defined by urbicide, joblessness, and hunger, to establish the means of a new urban horizon.

In chapter 6, I examine the emergence of MOVE after 1972. The organization, or the "powerful family of revolutionaries" as they understood their collective, drew on the earlier social-spatial grammars of the set-apart and on the tactics of the city's historical underground to build an explicitly decolonial vision of social existence in West Philadelphia. They directly confronted the growth paradigm and its dependence on Black living-in-death, incarceration, and debilitation, and they expressed a vision wherein adherents sought a return to a relation to living and life that would discontinue war and territorial violence and allow the expression and sovereignty of humans and nonhumans alike in their various locations. In a reversal of earlier expressions of plotting politics through abundance, MOVE embraced what outsiders might consider asceticism, replacing the feast with a respect for the natural rhythms of their bodies in the expression of hunger without reference to time and using exercise, especially running, to help recuse their bodies from the debilitating forces of the city and the underground. MOVE members understood John Africa not only as the man born John Leaphart but as embodied wisdom and a model for their own lives outside the system, with its twinned life-degenerating forces of anti-Blackness and ecocide. MOVE illustrated the enduring echo of the plot and of plotting in Black Power political aspirations defined by the desire and practice of an alternative territoriality against the backdrop of late-twentieth century's gendered racial capitalism's geographic transformation.

Figure 1.1. Blanfield Plantation Garden, Essex County, Virginia

1

Plotting the Historical Origins of Dark Agoras

Within the context of plantation ecologies that were constituted through a dynamic of intergenerational displacement, the calculated destruction of Black kinship—the confinement, extraction, exposure, overwork, persistent hunger punctuated by glut and a horizon of debilitation, mutilation, and premature death—the enslaved cultivated modes of unsanctioned placemaking that provided the cover for collective self-creation and belonging in excess of domination. To those barred by law and custom from the contours of the social itself, these early iterations of dark agoras gave geographic expression to the complexities of modes of worldmaking and placemaking "surpass[ing] the everywhere and every way of black death."[1] Facing the cyclical enclosures and fallowing of the mining-plantation complexes that consolidated the Americas beginning in the late fifteenth century, insurgent Black forms of assembly assumed their characteristic duality, their opacity, and their association with darkness as the absence of visibility or comprehensibility constituting a point of possibility and power among the condemned and at the same time embodying danger requiring preemptive epistemic and physical assault from the perspective of settlers and the planter state.

This chapter centers the complex negotiation of territoriality represented by dark agoras that were crafted by the enslaved to plot a present social world and a future beyond the horizon of social dissolution, dislocation, and displacement. The fugitive practices of plotting that enslaved, free, and post-emancipation Black communities across the littoral Chesapeake region shared between Maryland and Virginia, as well as in the broader region under the wrenching dislocations connecting the upper South to the old Southwest after the closing of the transatlantic slave trade and the violent dissolution of indigenous sovereignty, created possibilities for survival, connection, and spatial insurgency through the strategic renegotiation of the landscapes of captivity and dominion. This chapter recalls this history, examining Black communities' engagement with practices of place and alternative figurations of space, land, water, and futurity, primarily in the antebellum period. It follows upon the work of scholars such as Octavia Roberts Albert, Moscoe E. Lewis, Zora Neale Hurston, and others to record a body of US slave narratives alongside autobiographical narratives such as those of Harriet Jacobs and Frederick Douglass. These sources evidence the formulas of world-making on the part of slaves that served as critical antecedents for the social, spatial, and political relations that developed in early and mid-twentieth century in Philadelphia across the dislocations set off by the Jim Crow enclosures between 1890s and the 1920s and 1930s.

My formulation of dark agoras in the original context of their articulation depended on plotting, or the actions of enslaved, free, and emancipated communities to create a distinctive and often furtive social architecture that rivaled, threatened, and challenged the infrastructures of abstraction, commodification, and social control developed by white elites before and after the formal abolition of slavery. Following Sylvia Wynter, the plot and plotting name the various iterations of a cosmological, geographic, and social outlook with material and political manifestations, whereby captive Black communities renegotiated the terrain of radical exploitation and totalizing social control envisioned by slave masters and later Progressive and post-Progressive urban developers and boosters related to urban enclosure. As Wynter describes in the context of the Caribbean, the plot was constituted foremost through a parcel of land given to the enslaved by planters "on which to grow food to feed themselves in order to maximize profits." On the other hand, the provision ground in the US South, like its counterparts in the women's market societies in the Caribbean, rendered enslaved women the primary progenitors of a critical body of ecological knowledge that created epistemic possibilities for alternative modes of land and water stewardship. The plot allowed "African peasants transplanted" to the plantations of the Americas to transpose "all the structure of values that had been created by traditional societies of Africa" by which the "land remained the Earth—and the Earth was a goddess; man used the land to feed himself; and to offer first fruits to the earth; his funeral was the mystical reunion with the earth." In turn, the plot incubated "traditional values—use values."[2] The plot or provision ground thus offered "the possibility of temporal and spatial control" and functioned as a "semi-autonomous space of cultural production . . . imbued with both a sense of . . . burden and a sense of creative possibility."[3]

The plot/plotting has a number of distinct and overlapping registers in the context of this chapter's elucidation of the historical development and endurance of these alternative figurations of place and belonging. Foremost in this chapter, the plot signifies the space of the body's interment after death. Sometimes the site of the elaborate funeral, and more often the site of unremarked burial held in the memory of loved ones, the plot as a burial ground serves as an entry into the broader social architecture articulated by plotting. Plots for the dead signal a primary mode of organizing community, anchoring the present through the past within the grooves of a landscape. For people without the means to secure estates or other monuments to signify their importance or connection, the site of the plot is endowed all the more with significance. As well, funerals, in their seriality, marked time for rural and urban Black communities alike. Because they were one highly visible and thus commonly discussed manifestation of Black communities' efforts to maintain different visions for the interface between the social and spiritual realms, funerals served, perhaps ironically, as an index of the cultural complex that the area's Black communities used to negotiate alternative visions of life, the earth, and the divine. Derived largely from syncretized forms of West African mourning acts, enslaved Africans created new forms as their epistemological and cosmological frameworks were remixed and transformed to deal with disproportionate physical death as well as the condition of radical social alienation in the emergent geography of the North American colonies.[4] Funerals and the plot as a site of burial evidence the assertion of Black social life, despite the ongoing anti-Black environmental catastrophe defining plantation and post-plantation society in the region and more broadly in the extended project of transcontinental expansionism and competing imperialisms. In the context of the plot as a site of burial, local Black communities ritualized enactments of social life, refiguring death and the outdoors as sites for recalling ancestry and for unsettling white supremacist capitalist exploitation of both the land and Black people.

Second, the plot signifies the garden parcel, the gendered and gendering space in which enslaved Black women were required to perform reproductive labor critical to the maintenance of the enslaved population. On the one hand, the plot as garden parcel further taxed the labor of enslaved communities by forcing them to use the time after hard labor to augment their diets. Yet the plot as garden space served as a space for the enslaved to reproduce visions for land usage organized through use value—or as spaces sustaining biological and social existence rather than land or water resources to work for profit. As Dianne Glave illustrates, enslaved Africans tended gardens to stave off starvation and to cultivate independence in the face of master sanctioned hunger and lack, cultivating an environmental perspective and consciousness distinct from the formulations associated with slave mastery.[5] As illustrated by Angela Davis in her critical 1970 essay, "Reflections on the Black Woman's Role in the Community of Slaves," enslaved Black women's daily work to sustain communities through reproductive labor underwrote futures that were alternative to the horizon of social dislocation that defined slavery generally and antebellum society in the US context acutely.[6] The plot as a garden parcel reproducing use value and creating the raw materials of social reproduction in excess of slavery's expansion underwrote insurgent and unsanctioned modes of intracommunal care and provision that facilitated truancy, marronage, and open insurrection.

Third, the plot signifies the extension of these ongoing visions of use value into the ecologies of the forest and over the region's waterscapes. The maintenance of values and value in use to make biological and social existence possible incubated a vision of the wider landscapes whereby procuring extra food, independent of the food parceled by slave owners, bled into more subversive "taking of liberties" among the enslaved. Slaves extended the extra labor of hunting and fishing into subversive forms of leisure that often drew them into conflict with the logics of mastery and pushed them to remap plantation ecologies outside the landscapes of domination that otherwise defined these geographies. Knowledges and intimacies with the nonhuman species on plantations and in their interstices, including the trees, a range of plant life, fish, deer, rogue herds of cattle, feral hogs, snakes, rabbits, bears, turtles, and wolves, as sources of shelter, food, danger, connection, and information served as the basis for intergenerational knowledge transfers that could be enacted through intimacy with place as well as across dissolution through forced relocation.[7]

This leads to the final designation of the plot in this chapter and in the variegated forms it took in the context of the city that I develop in the remaining chapters. The plot signifies insurgent cartography whereby the enslaved, the free, and the emancipated used the various interrelated modes of plotting to articulate geographic identities laden with generative potential, beyond the theologies of dominion and outside the parameters of white dominance and control.

For enslaved communities and post-emancipation communities, these iterations of the plot often disrupted mastery and efficiency in terms of labor discipline, control, and dominion and required the articulation of a unique set of paths, hiding spots, and techniques of anti-surveillance and weaponization. The plot as hidden time and space expressed in the outdoors invokes the opacity of Black sociality in a world in which all forms of autonomous Black collectivity were rightfully feared by colonial and then American powerbrokers. By hiding in plain sight and developing social-geographic grammars that were unintelligible to outsiders, the enslaved created zones of ambiguously accounted for space and time, dark agoras as insurgent assemblies within landscapes of ostensible total control, mastery, and surveillance, providing the basis of the Black commons—an elaborate counter-landscape and Black ecology that stretched the delimitations of mastery and dominion to create social possibility. Dark agoras in this context represented unaccounted-for space and forms of Black gathering illegible as anything other than terror and danger, by which and within which enslaved communities created and perpetuated underground social life, while the Black commons represented the elaborated sense of place outside mastery, as expressed through human-to-human connections as well as in intimacy with the delicate ecologies of the wider biosphere. In the description of a Black commons, I draw on the work of Sarah Haley in her conception of "black girl commons." Writing about the context of the Jim Crow era's transformation of Georgia at the turn of the twentieth century, Haley underscores this conception of a commons as Black girls negotiation of a treacherous anti-Black anti-girl/femme terrain, their "traversal of the 'micropenality of everyday life,'" querying and challenging the "relations of household and property" seeking to confine them in a domestic carceral continuum.[8] My conception of the Black commons in this chapter centers the generations preceding the post-Emancipation ones Haley discusses but likewise underscores challenges or unaccounted-for relations within the social reproduction of plantation enclosure and slavery.

Taken together, the various interlocking aspects of the plot erected a Black commons in which enslaved, free, and post-emancipation communities extended their notions of value and values that ran anathema to racial capitalist enclosure and mastery. The plot/plotting in this is an especially powerful example of Black social life lived in dark agoras that is enacted in intimate relationship with death itself. The plot as a complex produced significant forms of Black sociality in the midst of an excess of loss, grief, and violence associated with death. The plot as burial site, garden parcel, and larger visions of de-commodified water and landscapes served as the basis of a local and migratory Black radical spatial-ecological tradition of which Black women, the elderly, and fugitives were the primary progenitors of epistemologies and cosmologies that subtly or explicitly challenged mastery.[9]

The Black commons formed out of the evolving manners by which enslaved Africans and their descendants created alternative modes of place through their cosmologies and forms of social life. They defied their simple thingification, reclaimed social bonds among those constitutionally configured as subhuman, reimagined the divine outside of mastery, and articulated the basis for a different mode of human-earth connection. Evolving in dialectic with mastery and dominion—or biblically justified total control—enslaved and post-emancipation communities claimed and created communal resources within the interstices of plantation ecologies. Migrants during the long twentieth century would later transpose the geographic operations of dark agoras as insurgent forms of gathering, articulate plotting as formulations reorganizing space around alternative values, and reestablish the Black commons as an elaborated motif of counter-territoriality stewarded in collectivity.

Plotting and Slavery

Given the centrality of disproportionate death as part of the mundane and quotidian effects of racial capitalism from its consolidation in the seventeenth, eighteenth, and nineteenth centuries, funerals and practices of mourning have served as dense sites of cultural memory through which Black communities engendered and transmitted their visions for an alternative interface among humans and between humans and the earth. Funeral rites, mourning practices, and spiritualized efforts to ward off death or to embrace it have signified the deep metaphors of human/earth reciprocity that Diasporans perpetuated as they grafted African cosmologies over the unfamiliar grooves of the North American topography. Together, the interment of the body in the ground and the ritualized mourning of funerals served as the primary elements of the plot.

As the literature in Black studies attests, death, mourning, and the stylized cultural event where these things come together—the funeral—have remained central to Black culture and politics in the United States and in the wider African Diaspora. In part, this reflects the intergenerational proximity to trauma and death that Black communities have faced. As Karla F. C. Holloway writes, Black "vulnerability to an untimely death in the United States affects how Black culture represents itself."[10] According to Sharon Holland, "In existential terms, knowledge of our own death determines not only the shape of our lives but also the culture we live in."[11] Writing about the Jamaican context, Vincent Brown posits that the dead always have "enjoyed an afterlife" in the cultures of the Diaspora, often animating what he terms a "mortuary politics."[12] For Nyle Forte, the funeral in Black culture represents "a ritual of death transformed into a 'celebration of life.'"[13] As Dagmawi Woubshet theorizes from spirituals, Black mourning practices belie the simplistic dichotomy outlined in psychoanalysis between normative mourning and its "pathological" forms, like melancholy. Black mourning is marked by what Woubshet terms "compounding loss" to underscore "the serial and repetitive nature of the losses [Black communities] confront," ultimately also transforming the grammar of life itself.[14] As Amaka Okechukwu develops in relation to the geography of twenty-first century transformation in Brooklyn, "Gravestone murals—as memorial, an archive of collective memory, a space of worldmaking, and resistance to anti-Black violence—suggests that death is not an end, but rather, people have a persisting collective relationship to the dead."[15]

As early as the 1660s, enslaved Africans along the estuaries that cut southern Maryland and Tidewater Virginia had begun to make alternative claims on the region's emergent social geography. In both the

1663 Gloucester County plot and in the more famous 1666–67 Bacon Rebellion, enslaved Africans joined indentured servants from Europe in seeking to overthrow Virginia's colonial government. However, it was in 1687 that enslaved Africans on the Virginia side of the Potomac River in Westmoreland County plotted the young colony's first all-Black rebellion. Explained in part by the increasing social separation between the enslaved and indentured servants that the Virginia General Assembly legally enacted after 1667, the assembly's legal response to the foiled 1687 plot draws us back to an originary moment in the articulation of a politics of life in the face of death among the regions' first Black inhabitants. As the respondent of the Executive Council wrote in the aftermath of the rebellion:

> And this Board having Considered that the great freedome and Liberty that has beene by many Masters given to their Negro Slaves for Walking on broad on Saterdays and Sundays and permitting them to meete in great Numbers in makeing and holding Funeralls for Dead Negroes gives them the Opportunityes under pretention of such publique meetings to Consult and advise for the Carrying on of their Evill & wicked purposes & Contrivances, for prevention whereof for the future, It is by this Board thought fitt that a Proclamacon doeforthwith Issue, requiring a Strickt observance of Severall Laws of this Collony relateing to Negroes, and to require and Comand all Masters of families having any Negro Slaves, not to permitt them to hold or make any Solemnity or Funeralls for any deced Negros.[16]

This passage refers back to Virginia's earlier Act of 1680 to "prevent Negro insurrections," which prohibited "feasts and burials" among the enslaved and illustrates that leading colonists developed paranoia about the social life of the people they tried to render into fungible commodities through social death.[17] The explicit naming of funerals in both 1680 and 1687 as a site of conspiracy also substantiates the maintenance of an alternative cosmological and political force among the enslaved.[18] Funerals served as sites in which traditional communal rites were remixed and repeated. The funeral was a site of self-conscious intergenerational communal fashioning enacted by the enslaved, whose existence was otherwise flattened into interchangeable, subhuman laborers in the service of the emergent Atlantic economy. Many aspects of Black funerals were derived from West African funerary practices.[19]

Funerals and death *grounded* Black cultural life in a set of often clandestine sites from the Chesapeake's origins as a part of the nascent European colonial complex. For example, archeologists have excavated a series of subterranean floor pits from the eighteenth century that historians describe as having been used to hide various delegitimized effects of transplanted African culture, including ancestral altars.[20] Africans in the Tidewater maintained covered and hidden earthen holes in the quarters that they may have used to honor the dead; this was part of the foundations of a kind of hidden—sometimes in plain sight—alternative Black landscape.[21] As historians of slavery illustrate, Black landscapes, comprised of a "system of paths, places, and rhythms that a community of enslaved people created as an alternative, often a refuge, to the landscape system of planters and other whites," created a "largely secret and disguised world," a kind of fugitive geography.[22] Spaces of engaging and honoring the dead were a fundamental aspect of the plot that helped articulate the grammar of insurgent Black social life.

The centrality and importance of death and funerals in a context of ongoing anti-Black environmental catastrophe and as part of the wider politics and episteme of the plot as a central place within a Black landscape grounded continuity in the region's Black cultural life and bridged the divide of successive dislocations related to expansion into the Old Southwest. Black communities continued distinctive spatial practices that undergirded Black communal survival and explicitly challenged the logics of racial slavery and plantation geography. This included the continuation of the plot and its extension into a Black commons and also orchestrated fugitive connections between enslaved people on both banks of the Potomac. For example, in his 1937 Works Progress Administration narrative, James V. Deane, a formerly enslaved resident of Baltimore, described life on a large plantation along Goose Bay, an inlet of the Potomac River, in Charles County, Maryland, where he was raised in the antebellum period. Deane described a distinctive Black geography that denies the bounded and strict cartography instituted through the regime of real property and chattel—"over 10,000 acres" and "a large number of slaves, I do not know the number"—that was the primary source of white patriarchal power. The Black geography of the plantation overlaid the dominant layout and infused it with other kinds of spiritual and social significance.[23]

According to Deane, there were a number of activities, unsanctioned by the owners of the plantation, that built a social world alternative to the edicts of dominion. The alternative Black landscape Deane described grounded other kinds of potentially dangerous practices that served as the infrastructure of a different order. As Deane relayed, the enslaved convened from plantations across the Potomac in Virginia: "When we wanted to meet at night we had an old conk, we blew that. We all would meet on the bank of the Potomac River and sing across the river to the slaves in Virginia, and they would sing back to us."[24] While this kind of connection through sound was not a call to arms against the enslavers per se, it did serve to create the potential for secretive and fugitive social connections that endangered the vision of total control proposed in the legal fictions of the enslavers.

Deane also charted continuity in the plot and its wider significance for materially anchoring the less tangible elements of an alternative Black landscape. According to Deane, the enslaved "had small garden patches which they worked by moonlight." Although there was an official physician charged with ensuring the health and productivity of the enslaved, as he described, "The slaves had herbs of their own, and made their own salves," which they grew in their plots.[25] While the record leaves no evidence of the full parameters of this alternative way of seeing the landscape, it is clear that the enslaved created and maintained a distinctive interpretation of space from a shared vision for social and cosmological integrity. Indeed, these served as an important counterpoint for the nascent biomedical prescriptions for health and the ideologically laden religion of the enslavers that confined them to a "slave gallery" in the church where they learned the "Lord's Prayer and the catechism."[26]

Deane also described another element of the plot as a site of the continuation of a different kind of cosmological and social vision and thus also a source of Black vitality: a vision for a *Black commons*. As he relayed, "My choice food was fish and crabs cooked in styles by my mother." Here, it is significant that Deane's preferred foods were products of the delicate watershed and brackish ecologies that constitute the primary contours of region and that it was prepared by his mother. Food that the enslaved independently procured from the waters of the

Potomac and similar estuary environs, as well as the labor of Black women in the processes of food production and preparation, served the currency for forms of insurgent Black social life and intergenerational affection in the face of dominion that rendered the master-class lord of Black bodies and resistance as sickness.[27] The small acts of feeding illustrate the maintenance of kinship in intimacy with the subaquatic and the wider water and landscape as a means of sustenance and possibility against the imperatives of slavery to atomize, starve, destroy kinship, render fungible, and justify sale across territorial expanse through chattelization.

Black communities forged around the products of a unique and threatened ecology a vision of social life, vitality, and cosmological integrity that prompts us to think about the significance of the commons and the reproductive labor of Black women in the forwarding of Black resistance. Generally, Black communities are either collapsed into the environment or pictured as unconcerned about the preservation of the biosphere. Enslaved Black people and their descendants, over whom the institution cast a long shadow, navigated the precarious line between acting directly as the agents of ecological destruction and working the landscape to carve out the contours of an entirely different kind of social order. As the enslaved asserted their vision for the commons, their labor was also forcibly mobilized for the rapid colonization of the land and the devastation that colonization wrought upon the rivers and streams that constitute the Chesapeake, rendering the Black commons that Deane described fleeting, tenuous, and contradictory. For example, when Washington, DC, was established as the capital in 1790, the Anacostia River was navigable to Bladensburg, Maryland, and was reportedly one mile wide and twenty feet deep at the place where it meets the Potomac. Within a century, land clearing and cultivation, effected primarily by the forced labor of the enslaved, drove rapid sedimentation and shoaling that transformed a river once teeming with life into a slow and increasingly toxic sludge in the twentieth century.[28] While the enslaved were among the primary agents used in the clearing of this land for cultivation and urban development, they anchored in the phenomena of death and the plot a vision of social and cosmological integrity that included the Black commons, a furtive and sometimes failed challenge to dominion.

On his journey through the region to the Cotton Kingdom farther south, noted writer and landscape architect Frederick Law Olmsted also observed the landscape he encountered between Maryland, Washington, and Virginia. Olmsted described a landscape of capitalist redundancy, environmental degradation, and ruination with parcels of land that had once been cultivated but had lapsed back into bush or forest. As he wrote, "Land may be purchased, within twenty miles of Washington, at from ten to twenty dollars an acre. Most of it has been once in cultivation, and having been exhausted in raising tobacco, has been, for many years, abandoned and is now covered by a forest growth." Olmsted advocated the return of this land to productivity, arguing that "by deep plowing [sic] and liming, and the judicious use of manures, it is made quite productive." While the kinds of technologically enhanced farming practices Olmsted advocated would not emerge in large measure until the twentieth century with the recapitalization of the region's agriculture as part of the truck-farm production for a growing market in Washington, these kinds of interventions would have disastrous effects on the estuary environments of the wider Potomac and Chesapeake basins.[29]

An outsider, Olmsted also unwittingly captured elements of a fugitive Black landscape: individual and collective renegotiations of the plantations' geographic parameters to carve out Black social life. Fugitive Black landscapes of the antebellum period were often confined, as Katherine McKittrick describes through her reading of Harriet Jacobs's escape narrative. Yet as McKittrick elaborates, they were also the points of possibility for acts of rebellion, including an effective escape.[30] We should view these fleeting geographic alternatives as part of a wider if not totally recoverable vision of social-cosmological integrity, cultural continuity, and futurity, as well as more eventful attempts to subvert dominion that outlasted the peculiar institution. On visiting a plantation in Maryland, just north of Washington, on December 14, 1852, Olmsted observed the dominant geography and also got a taste for the fugitive practices of Black culture in their "rudeness." "The residence is in the midst of farm," he wrote, "a quarter of a mile from the high road—the private approach being judiciously carried through large pastures which are divided only by slight, but close and well-secured wired fences." "The kept grounds," euphemistically disarticulated from the subjects doing the keeping, "are limited, and in simple but quiet taste; being surrounded only by wires, they merge, in effect, into the pastures. There is a fountain, an ornamental dovecote, and ice-house, and the approach road, nicely graveled and rolled, comes up to the door with a fine sweep."[31]

Once Olmsted reached the gate, an enslaved person who remained unseen interrupted the idyllic scene. As Olmsted transcribed, fabricating Black speech, "Ef yer wants to see master, sah, he's down thar—to the new stable." Olmsted continued: "I could see no one."[32] For Olmsted, this kind of Black obstinacy, the enslaved person's refusal to be seen and thus accounted for, was part of the ineffectiveness of the institution of slavery. Olmsted used these kinds of interruptions in social-geographic order as a point of comparison for the system of land tenure on the part of an "industrious German" without slavery. However, given the totalizing control over land and life intimated in the ideology of dominion, the ability to remain yet unseen was a point of possibility within a continuum of political action and within a fleeting but present fugitive Black landscape. As Simone Brown has developed in the context of surveillance studies, a politics of Black countersurveillance, or "dark sousveillance," resisted the optics of total control that masters fantasized was possible.[33] Through the refusal to be seen, by hiding in plain sight or doing things beyond the reach of surveillance, enslaved Black people opened critical and sometimes strategic gaps in the cartography of mastery. Black communities cultivated dark agoras, forms of Black presence and gathering defined by strategic invisibility or hiddenness that were practiced to create the possibilities for the Black commons and a wider-world *otherwise*.[34]

Moving south along his journey, Olmsted described a feature of Richmond's Black landscape that, as I describe above, remained an important site of Black cultural practice and continuity: the funeral. In addition to being struck by the "decent hearse," he was surprised to find that among the twenty or thirty women and men in the procession, "there was not a white person."[35] Upon his arrival at the grounds, Olmsted noted that the burial ground was already inhabited by another group of enslaved "heaping the earth over the grave of a child, and singing a wild kind of chant," and attesting to the ways that premature death continued to weigh on Black communities.[36]

Once the procession reached the final resting place, Olmsted observed Black communities engaged in a distinctive mourning that remained unintelligible to him as an outsider and which must be considered as part of the wider practices of a distinctive cosmological universe in and by which Black communities maintained the grammar of the Black commons. While there can be no return to the words and the full meaning of them within the universe of the mourners, the fact that they were closed to an outsider and were well rehearsed by insiders illustrates the continued importance of funerals as spaces of cultural defiance, limited self-fashioning, and furtive resistance in the face of processes of unmaking that commodifying humans presupposed, tying intergenerational early death to markets in people and land. Funerals represented dark agoras, not necessarily as invisible or hidden places but more as strategically unrecognizable collective forms unnamable in the purview of the gaze of an outsider that doubled as sites of resistance. Here, resistance signifies not open rebellion that threatens in total the civil and social order but rather the points and places of possibility for Black life and futurity outside the limiting definition prescribed by the juridical rendering of Black people as chattel. For example, when the well-dressed orator and officiator of the funeral rites began to speak, Olmsted was prompted to write, "I never in my life, however, heard such ludicrous language as was uttered by the speaker. Frequently I could not guess the idea he was intending to express." Later, Olmsted described the singing of a hymn, "a confused chant—the leader singing a few words alone, and the company then either repeating after him or making a response to them. . . . I could understand but very few of the words. The music was wild and barbarous."[37] Although space does not permit further exploration, I must note that the contrast between Black unintelligibility as a practice related to the plot and the Black commons, and Olmsted's architectural work to render landscapes more easily traversable and accessible as part of the ongoing practices of dominion and enclosure, are stark.

The ability of the enslaved to convey intelligible messages within the community and not to outsiders indexes the maintenance of an infrastructure in a fleeting fugitive Black landscape through the space of the funeral and through the rituals of the body's internment. Local enslavers tacitly acknowledged as much. As Olmsted observed, "No one seemed to notice my presence at all. There were about fifty colored people in the assembly, and but one other white man besides myself. This man lounged against the fence, outside the crowd, an apparently indifferent spectator, and I judged he was a police officer or someone procured to witness the funeral in compliance with the law which requires that a white man shall always be present at any meeting, for religious exercises, of the negroes."[38] While the songs and spoken words at the heart of the funerary rites practiced by the enslaved remained opaque to Olmsted, white Virginians recognized the continued threat posed in the fugitive sonic world mapped in the dirges. They had, as I have illustrated, enshrined the strict surveillance of Black funerals by white observers in the law during the colonial period. The inside world of the enslaved and the surveillance of slave mastery converged here at the site of the funeral, since masters understood the threat that the funeral rites posed even without having full access to the contours of the rituals and ceremony. Olmsted, however, remained a total outsider.

Frederick Douglass's accounting of the ceremonious movement of the enslaved who were granted permission to move between the Maryland plantations owned by his master provides the keys to understanding the subversive potential of the unintelligible cultural productions of the enslaved in antebellum Maryland and the broader South. As Douglass recalled:

> While on their way, they would make the dense old woods, for miles around, reverberate with their wild songs, revealing at once the highest joy and the deepest sadness. They would compose and sing as they went along, consulting neither time nor tune. The thought that came up, came out—if not in the word, in the sound;—and as frequently in the one as in the other. They would sometimes sing the most pathetic sentiment in the most rapturous tone, and the most rapturous sentiment in the most pathetic tone. This they would sing, as a chorus, to words which to many would seem unmeaning jargon, but which, nevertheless, were full of meaning to themselves. I have sometimes thought that the mere hearing of those songs would do more to impress some minds with the horrible character of slavery, than the reading of whole volumes of philosophy on the subject could do.[39]

The dirge and other sung forms, which Olmsted could only decipher as incoherent and which white southerners sought to contain, Douglass evidences as having their own coherency as a form of vital social and cultural production preceding what Clyde Woods terms "blues epistemology," a post-Reconstruction musical-ideological complex encompassing subversive social and political outlooks in the period of severe repression that remade the Mississippi Delta region after 1877.[40] As Douglass acknowledges, the dirge conveyed multiple social-ideological registers resonant to Black communal interpretation and was capacious in its ability to convey emotion, information, and critique— often in plain sight of whites. These forms that register as incoherent and threatening bear their own cultural idiosyncrasies forward, creating a reserve of cultural forms subtly and explicitly transmitted that later migrant generations drew on as they created new forms of gathering, dark agoras that terrorized the industrial metropolis and which at the same time generated their own visions of urban present life and urban futurity through the two distinctive forms of congregation centered in later chapters.

Within the context of death, depravation, and starvation, the enslaved drew on the resources of the plot as stolen time, as the garden parcel, and as the watery and forested commons of the region to supplement meager diets taxed by the physical intensity of plantation labor. As James L. Smith recalled in an 1880 narrative, slave owners allotted enslaved men a weekly provision of "a peck and a half of corn meal, and two pounds of bacon," while women and children were given "a peck of meal, and from one pound and a half to two pounds of bacon." According to Smith, slaves supplemented these starvation rations with fish, crabs, and oysters they fished from the region's various waterscapes, the meat of "coons and possums" they hunted at night, and sweet potatoes and other vegetables they grew in the small plots they maintained. On the one hand, slave masters' paltry provisions forced the enslaved to feed themselves, enhancing the abstraction of value from slaves by forcing them to absorb the cost in terms of labor and time of reproducing themselves.[41] On the other hand, working the plot brought slaves into direct confrontation with the vision of temporal order and labor discipline, what La Marr Bruce calls Western Standard Time, that enslavers sought to enforce.[42] As Smith recalled, "One night I went crabbing and was up most all night; a boy accompanied me. We caught a large mess of crabs, and took them home with us. The next day I had to card for one of the women to spin, and, being up all night, I could hardly keep my eyes open; every once in a while I would fall asleep." Crabbing to supplement the inadequate diet provided by slave masters in the first instance enhanced the exploitation and taxing of the life energy of the enslaved, yet the effort to live and to extend unsanctioned social existence brought Smith into conflict with mastery. Through these kinds of fugitive relationships with the plot, antebellum and postbellum Black communities forged alternative claims on land and water resources organized primarily around the Black commons and through the practices of what I term fugitive commensality—the unsanctioned and often illicit procuring, preparation, and sharing of food. Fugitive commensality required active imagination and work since under slavery and in its aftermath, starvation served as an essential technique of discipline, control, and punishment, while feasts served as a compulsory and coercive form of glut that enhanced the quotidian violence of depravation.

Generally, this caloric and nutritional content offered by masters as provisions to the enslaved were unsustainable for people required under the threat of the lash to labor intensely in agricultural work. Given the conditioning of hunger, theft of food was a form of pilfering central to the Black commons. From the colonial period in Virginia, for example, slaves faced steep punishment for the theft of food, especially meat. The fact that a number of men and women who were punished in colonial Virginia for hog theft were repeat offenders facing more disfiguring punishments for second offenses suggests the intensity of their hunger, as well as their disregard for planter authority.

Records from Essex and Richmond Counties in Tidewater Virginia make it clear that slaves risked physical torture and disfigurement to engage in fugitive commensality. The most common of the offenses related to food was "hog stealing," for which on the first offense slaves received thirty-nine lashes at the public pillory and for which on subsequent offenses, they had their ears nailed to the pillory in addition to public whipping and finally had their ears removed. As a number of cases evince, enslaved women and men pilfered hogs and the meat from hogs stored by colonial planters to augment inadequate diets and to reproduce Black social worlds around shared food. This second aspect of food theft is only indexed in colonial court records. For example, on

October 21, 1765, two enslaved men named Harry and Will stood trial in Essex County, Virginia, for hog stealing. They confessed to stealing two hogs, the property of one John Clements, and were punished by the court with the colonial Virginia requirement of thirty-nine lashes for the offense. Although we do not know the extent of their conspiracy to pick off Clements's hog—for example, whether it involved other people or if they simply divided the meat among themselves—the contraband pork animated an illicit social bond for which the court ordered the sheriff to torture both men. In October 1766, an enslaved pair, Flora and Tom, each received thirty-nine lashes in their public whipping for stealing hogs, also in Essex County, Virginia. Similar to the mention of trial and punishment for Harry and Will, the case of Flora and Tom leaves only the trace of an insurgent social existence born in pilfering food and sharing in the savory succulence of stolen meat. And yet in these double trials and coterminous punishments, there is evidence of a world of social and spatial autonomy that threatened property through theft.

In all likelihood, many of the people who were tried as individuals probably also indexed collectives, the stolen food animating familial and social life outside the purview of mastery. People who received punishment likely shielded the others who enjoyed the delight of pork with them and also drew the jealousy of others who bore witness to their transgressions. Even if individuals were acting alone for themselves to procure food not granted them by their masters, we can take their stories together to further evidence the space and significance of fugitive commensality. In 1765, a slave named Tom plead not guilty to the same offense of hog theft. Despite his plea of innocence, Tom was found guilty and ordered whipped at the public whipping post. During the summer of 1766, an enslaved man named Johnny brazenly broke into the meat storage building of one of colonial Virginia's most important landowners, Landon Carter, to steal bacon. On January 21, 1771, a slave named Abram was permanently disfigured for having stolen hogs more than once. For two hours, his ears were nailed to the public pillory after which, both his ears were cut off. Abram's case exemplifies not only the desperation of consistent hunger but also the persistence of resistance to the violent imposition of hunger as a condition of Black life under slavery (and after) that served as a pillar of the Black commons.

In spite of violence and coercion through nutrition, however, Black communities appropriated feasts—sometimes formal, sometimes furtive—to create a unique social grammar through formal as well as unsanctioned and illicit collectivity around food. If commensality provides the basis of human socialization and community, it is also embedded within a wider ecology—the landscapes and waterscapes people use and cultivate to make eating possible.[43] Blurring discrete lines between human communities, nonhuman species populations, and the ecological, commensality includes not only an interface between people but also between people and the wider biosphere. Through the technologies of fugitive commensality in relation to the Black commons, these communities partially indigenized their relationships with the landscapes and waterscapes, forwarding visions of use value despite enclosure and commodification. In quotidian practices of fishing, hunting, planting plots, and foraging in forests for curatives and other plant life with cosmological significance, tied with an imaginary that also pilfered hogs, these communities practiced the Black commons. Black communities created, inhabited, and manipulated dark agoras, forms of gathering shadowing and terrorizing the colonial state to create the conditions for Black social life whereby Black social life is understood, in the words of Terrion L. Williamson, as "fundamentally the register of Black experience that is not reducible to the terror that calls it into existence but is the rich remainder, the multifaceted artifact of Black communal resistance and resilience that is expressed in Black idioms, cultural forms, traditions," and geographic practices.[44]

Slaves used the plot as stolen time to engage in their own independent visions of self, family, and community.[45] In a system that sought to atomize slaves and to render them fungible, the plot as an insurgent relation to space and time brought the possibilities for an otherwise. Insurgent here signifies a spectrum of infra-political action, a continuum encompassing outright individual refusal and collective refusal as rebellion but practiced more generally in the efforts associated with reformulating social bonds in the face of kinlessness and the attendant formations of assembly and space underwriting kinship despite social alienation. While plotting, or the carving of stolen time and space for the insurgent assemblies of dark agoras, most often did not disrupt the larger institution of slavery like it did in Northampton, Virginia, during

Nat Turner's 1831 rebellion, it provided space for individual slaves and freed people to renegotiate the terms and conditions of plantation labor and discipline and tore openings in the artifice of master time wherein enslaved and post-emancipation communities created affirmative collective identities despite the violence, depravation, and social death that were the hallmarks of the institution and its afterlives.

As many who were enslaved during the antebellum period described, the plot as stolen time bled into the practices of the Black commons, creating the conditions for leverage along what Joy James calls "the Black Matrix," an alternative political fulcrum "shaped by triad formations in racial rape/consumption, resistance, and repression in a renewable cycle of fight, flight, and fixation."[46] As Angela Davis's early engagement with women's resistances provocatively suggests, enslaved women's quotidian efforts at reproducing slave life in excess of the confines of reproductive slavery sustained Black communities and served as the basis for communal forms of resistance.[47] As Jennifer Morgan describes, the effort to maintain kinship in the face of emergent logics of the market and political arithmetic seeking to render enslaved Africans interchangeable and exchangeable to the benefit of the state constituted a "foundational refusal" on the part of those in bondage around the Atlantic.[48] As Jessica Marie Johnson investigates in the context of the French slave trade between Senegambia and the Caribbean archipelago, including New Orleans, Black women and girls negotiated an uncertain terrain predicated on the rendering of them as fungible and consumable through the complex renegotiation of kinship.[49] Plotting the Black commons allowed enslaved communities to rupture the spatial and temporal logics of captivity to refuse the basic aspects of their social-spatial alienation. The political leverage that James describes as an aspect of the Black matrix derives from the Black commons as a mode of spatial-social practice along with its attending outlooks for the present, past, and future. Spatial leverage, marronage, and stolen time and space, which perpetuate themselves unto themselves but also terrorize the white state, not as a precondition of their existence and which, as one part of it, are the vital source of Black political kinetics, including "movements," those ideological and practical frameworks addressing violence and inequality and garnering direction and traction vis-à-vis the state that are taken seriously, if only momentarily, precisely because of their renunciation or their promise to contain inchoate rebellion.

The Black commons was a function of what many masters understood as "Ni**er day-time," or the space and time for activities ranging from those, like gardening, that were tacitly sanctioned by masters to those that were illicit, like gorging on a stolen hog.[50] Manipulating the optics on which mastery depended, slaves used the cover of night and the alternative knowledge of forested and swampy landscapes to forge an infrastructure of hidden paths and furtive geographies that helped give shape to the Black commons. Runaways, as well as individuals seeking alternatives to violent former masters in the wake of slavery's formal demise, weaponized the infrastructure of dark paths through the forests and swamps of the region to gain basic provisions in order to survive—the very precondition of other forms of geographic leverage.

Minnie Fulkes recalled the weaponization of enslaved peoples' knowledge of the terrain of captivity and their renegotiation through "darkness" of master time and the geographies of captivity to create fleeting autonomous spaces of prayer, ecstatic worship, and a radical reworking of Christian theology in the hands of slaves. She recalled the use of "a great big iron put at the door" that slaves used to dampen the sounds of their worship and to prevent the old "paddy rollers" who "would come and horse whip every last one of them, just cause poor souls were praying to God to free 'em from that awful bondage." Fulkes also recalled the worshippers tying

> grape vines an' other vines across th' road, den when de Paddy rollers come galantin' wid their horses runnin' so fast you see dem vines would tangle 'em up an' cause th' horses to stumble and fall. An' lots of times, badly dey would break dere legs and horses too; one interval one ol' poor devil got tangled so an' de horse kept a carryin' him, 'til he fell off horse and next day a sucker was found in road whar dem vines wuz wind aroun' his neck so many times yes had choked him, dey said, 'He totely dead.' Serve him right 'cause dem ol' white folks treated us so mean.[51]

Charles Crawley recalled a robust spiritual world among the enslaved as the people on his plantation "met and worshipped from house to house" and "talked to my God all us wanted." Likewise, Marriah Hines recalled members of her community "turn[ing] pots down, and tubs to keep the sound from going out" in order that they could "have a good time, shouting, singing, and praying just like we pleased."[52]

As Smith described, he along with other slaves in a twelve-mile or more radius used the cover of darkness and their intimate knowledge of the alternative pathways to hold prayer meetings and to engage in ecstatic consecration where, as Aliyyah Abdur-Rahman describes regarding another context, "the black ecstatic pervades expressive forms as an abstractionist practice of conjuration that foregrounds the importance, the timelessness, and exuberant pleasures of black communion."[53] As Smith recollected, "I remember in one instance that having quite [sic] work about sundown on a Saturday evening, I prepared to go ten miles to hold a prayer meeting at Sister Gould's" where "quite a number assembled in the little cabin, and we continued to sing and pray till daybreak." Smith described the lively worship experiences of these illicit prayer meetings as "almost indescribable" and in that intangibility as an "ecstasy of motion, clapping hands, tossing of heads, which would continue without cessation about half an hour."[54] While the ecstatic is not singularly liberatory, in the register of embodiment, whether in the sumptuous possibilities of unsanctioned or forbidden taste or in the collectivity built around communion with divinity, the ecstatic rends the temporality and spatial dynamics of mastery and dominion, opening a space for an "unruly structure and experience" that "operationalizes the limit, which it also perpetually violates and reforms."[55] Thus, while ecstatic prayer meetings did not necessarily dovetail into outward rebellion against mastery, the effect of timelessness and indescribability that Smith recalled temporarily suspended the subject-object relations governing plantation ecologies, edifying a competing schema for connection outside abjection tied to the plot and the commons.

The ecstatic encompasses an epistemological and experiential danger in relation to white spatial and temporal order, especially under slavery. The ecstatic in this context often included millenarian and non-Christian outlooks that drew the enslaved to reject the conditioning of slavery on earth and to embrace metaphysical rebellion. In using *metaphysical rebellion*, I depart from Albert Camus's strict association of the term with the collapse of reason and the rise of fascism. Black metaphysical rebellion is instead the desire for a radical reordering of the world in total, including the hierarchy of being itself. Spirit oaths, spirit possession, and other forms of transgression between the demarcation of the spiritual or metaphysical and the physical in the experiences of the enslaved represented challenges to the dominant order of being articulated by enslavers, in the context of the paternalist ideology of eighteenth- and nineteenth-century slave masters who viewed themselves as ordained by God to govern slaves, land, and other subordinates. The falling of the spirit represented a challenge to this theological premise, bringing the possessed in direct communion with God or with some spiritual entity outside the paradigm of slave mastery. The ecstatic harbored outlooks defined by the spiritual cleansing of the world of white domination and exploitation. Although the religion of the enslaved produced outward signs of docility, reinforcing mastery in the public transcripts, the experiences of the Black ecstatic that was facilitated through the plotting of the Black commons could also align with explicitly liberatory visions of the landscapes and waterscapes wherein the enslaved and the freedpeople saw these spaces as animate, with power sufficient to end white domination. As Fulkes recalled, these hidden spaces of the Black ecstatic were capable of producing theologies that if given full expression could take the negation of slavery to potentially revolutionary ends. While the post-1831 repression of enslaved and free Black people in Virginia and beyond limited antebellum rebellions, these spaces of hidden ecstatics continued to buttress a vision of the landscape that was anathema to mastery and dominion wherein God and nature served as arbiters of cosmic justice outside of white domination. Fulkes maintained this vision through emancipation into the 1930s, when she revealed part of this vision to the Works Progress Administration interviewer. According to Fulkes, the sublime—the landscapes wherein one might contemplate God, divinity, and nature—could also be invoked to destroy white oppressors. Fulkes told her interviewer quite candidly, "Lord, Lord, I hate white people and de flood waters gwine drown some mo."[56] Here, an appreciation for the watery landscape doubles as a means of cosmic justice whereby white people would drown for the evils of their violence against and violation of slaves, former slaves, and ostensibly free people.

In the context of plantations, the spaces of formally recognized Black social life were articulated within a complex terrain of deprivation and glut channeled and shaped by the calculations of exaction and extraction. Slave owners punctuated quotidian starvation with eventful feasting. Feasting, like other moments of merriment, helped planters exact further productivity and thus served as a tool of discipline by which enslavers could manipulate and draw nigh the affection of their slaves despite the violent power they otherwise wielded. In the lower Chesapeake, these spaces also served as spaces of Black gatherings, spaces "full of Colored people," as Mrs. Fannie Berry recalled in later recollections of her wedding and reception in the parlor of a white mistress on Crater Road near Richmond, Virginia. Weddings and receptions that were acknowledged and supported by slave owners did not ensure the power of a legal contract to protect the relationships slaves built. Further, they evidence the matriarchal and patriarchal paternalism in response to the international discourses of abolitionism. As Berry remembered, "Wasn't no white folks to set down and eat before you." "We had everything to eat you could call for," and they could sing and dance square dances of their choosing. As Berry recalled through the refractions of memory, "Lord! I can see them gals now on that floor, just skipping and a trotting." Although it is an expression blurring the lines between Black social life and the forced merriment Saidiya Hartman describes, the visions of fullness and abundance drew on the plot and the Black commons to articulate the feast as a fundamental, if vexed, grammar of Black social-ecological life in the plantation context and outward into urban migrant communities outside the South.[57]

Simon Stokes, a former slave in Matthews and Gloucester Counties in Virginia, told an interviewer in 1938 how he and others used the woods to hunt at night to procure food for a feast. As he remembered, "In the fall when the simmons was ripe, me and the other boys sure had a big time possum hunting." This collective of Stokes "and the other boys" took to the woods and captured possums alive. Rather than simply eating them right away, however, Stokes and the other boys sought to "fatten" the possums with their rations of cornmeal hoecakes. When they were ready, Stokes's mother "would roast them with sweet potatoes around them" until they were "all . . . nice and brown with the sweet potatoes in the gravy." The savory tastes provided through meat that slaves had procured through hunting and growing sweet potatoes indexes the plot as a counterpoint to the violent sumptuary regulation through starvation or eventful, coercive merriment, a practical means of attaining satiation and fulfillment on one's owns terms. This meal is a different terrain from the fields of plantation enclosure, of endless tobacco, wheat, sugar, and cotton. It indexes in taste and in memory the social worlds of care, an excess beyond simple social reproduction, that Stokes's mother and the other enslaved young people provided against the backdrop of the monotony of the hoecake. The taste's prominent role in memory indexes the power of the ecstatic as a sensorial complex that privileged difference and the dispensation of pleasure through various forms of tasting and feeling community, beyond the delimitations of the legal demarcation of chattel, as constituting the nonsocial basis of society.

Sweet potatoes and possums are here products of the same earth; they swirl together in this recollection as metaphors of community, underscoring intimacy between Black and nonhuman life, beyond simple predation and consumption. Despite ravenous hunger imposed by inadequate diet, the enslaved young people divided their meager rations of hoecakes with the possum. Fattening here is also more than a metaphor of enhanced consumption; this relation to the possum as more than prey opens the possibility for enhanced Black social life, the capacity to share more meat and gravy over the sweet potatoes.

The Black commons inspired alternative epistemologies, unfolding and forwarding vernacular wisdoms about daily life in relation to nonhuman species, natural events, the divine, and the wider features of the watery environment defining the region. Many of these remain embedded within the epistemic universe of their progenitors and do not necessarily correspond to modes of engaging the features of this landscape in ways directly accessible to people outside the parameters of these communities. As post-emancipation oysterman and fisherman Robert Slaughter recalled:

> I tell you what I did once. My cousin and I went down to the shore once. The river shore, you know, up where I was born. While we were walking along catching tadpoles, minnows, and anything we could catch, I happened to see a big moccasin snake hanging in a sumac bush just a swinging his head back and forth. I swung at 'im with a stick and he swelled his head all up big and rared back. Then I hit 'im and knocked him on the ground flat. His belly was very big so we kept hittin' 'im on it until he opened his mouth and a catfish as long as my arm (forearm), jumped out jest a flopping. Well the catfish had a big belly too, so we beat 'em on his

belly until he opened his mouth and out came one of these women's snap-per pocketbooks. You know the kind that closes by a snap at the top. Well the pocket book was swelling all out, so we opened it, and guess what was in it? Two big copper pennies. I gave my cousin one and I took one. Now you mayn't believe that, but it's true. I been trying to make people believe that for near fifty years. You can put it in the book or not, jest as you please, but it's true. That fish swallowed some woman's pocketbook and that snake just swallowed him. I have told men that for years and they wouldn't believe me.[58]

The Black commons expressed a vision of Black resourcefulness that was manipulated by slave owners to maximize the profitability of water and land resources but that was also often capitalized on toward ends that were at odds with the sense of social-spatial order on antebellum plantations. For runaways, whether engaging in full-scale marronage or the other smaller acts of running away whereby they renegotiated the conditions of their labor and living, the Black commons represented a tenuous, fleeting, and dangerous re-commoning of what the ownership class held to be their property. Runaways "lived in the woods of tak-ing things such as hogs, corn, and vegetables from other folks' farm."[59] This was quite dangerous, as it risked the possibility of transport to the emerging plantation ecologies of the Deep South. As Harris recalled, "Well if dese slaves was caught, dey were sold by their new masters to go down South."[60] Although fugitive commensality was dangerous, the en-slaved engaged its forms and thereby manipulated and weaponized their intimate knowledge of the geography of plantations, especially of the spaces between them, to subvert the dictates and discipline of property and profitability and to express a vision for the land and water beyond dominion.

When interviewed by Octavia Roberts Albert as part of the 1890 *The House of Bondage*, Charlotte Brooks recalled the trauma of slavery as ongoing, embodied for her as insomnia and persistent physical discom-fort. In Brooks's memory—here an intersubjective archive, the vehicle of personal and collective meaning-making about the past rather than a simple reproduction of past events—her pain and her inability to sleep resulted from having worked in conditions that sapped her vitality. On the plantation, her master demanded that she and the others "go out before day, in high grass and heavy dews" where she "caught cold" and "lost all of [her] health."[61] As Tony Perry writes in relation to exposure on plantations in Maryland, "Cold weather uniquely informed slavery in the US, touching the lives of the enslaved far beyond inhibiting agricultural production during the winter."[62] Indifference to suffering or the active weaponization of the weather, including the cold, structured the debilitating regime of slavery, extending the caprice and violence of Brooks's master, who also "sometimes . . . would get mad about something going wrong on the place, and . . . beat every one of us and lock us up in a jail he made for us." As her recollection suggests, the elemental torture, everyday exposures, and likely outcomes of physical exhaustion and depletion structured emancipation and post-emancipation life.

The effects of physical debilitation were amplified by the dislocation and displacement of insulating familial and social relations. As Brooks noted, she had been sold from Virginia to Louisiana, and between the three masters who claimed ownership over her before slavery's demise, she had lost everything. For Brooks, this was devastating, as she "never seen or heard" from her siblings or mother after her forced relocation to Louisiana in her teenage years. Brooks's familial loss after her sale from Virginia was compounded by the social and cultural isolation that she experienced in the context of Louisiana's sugar plantations. While her mother had taken her and her sisters and brothers to "church every Sunday" and was visited regularly by a traveling preacher when she "came to Louisiana," she did not go to church anymore, because "everybody was Catholic." Catholicism remained strange to her since she "had never seen that sort of religion that has people praying on beads." Additionally, her master spoke Creole, rendering basic communication nearly impossible.

Against the backdrop of social dissolution and isolation, Brooks found a new source of possibility in fleeting forms of unsanctioned collectivity among the condemned. Four years into her permanent dislocation from Virginia to Louisiana, Brooks heard that "the speculators brought another woman" from Virginia to a plantation near the one where she was enslaved in Louisiana. Uncontainable in her anticipation that the woman "might be some of [her] kinsfolk, or somebody that knew [her] mother," Brooks used the first available opportunity to search out the woman. Despite her masters' prohibitions against leaving the plantation and his working of her and the others even on Sundays, she stole a free moment to find this recent arrival from Virginia. "I went to see who the woman was," she remembered, "and I tell you, my child, when I got in the road going I could not go fast enough." Despite her anticipation of a possible direct familial connection with the woman from Virginia, Jane Lee was "no kin."

Notwithstanding the lack of an identifiable blood or social kinship, Brooks and Lee found great comfort despite their losses in their cultural connection reformulated and reconstituted from memories of fugitive Black social life in the context of plantations and farms in Virginia. They found shared comfort upon their initial meeting, when the women "talked and cried . . . till nearly dark." Like Brooks, Lee had lost everything in her forced relocation through sale to Louisiana. Lee's "old marster got in debt, and sold her to pay his debts," destroying her connection to her children, including her five-year-old, her youngest. Comforting one another in the sting of their losses, Lee "prayed and sang" for Brooks, which caused Brooks to "think of [her] old Virginia home and [her] mother." The hymn's line "Guide me, O thou great Jehovah, Pilgrim through this barren land" drew Brooks back to Lee after an extended period of absence, dictated by the demands of "rolling season" on the sugar plantations, when everyone "was so busy working night and day" and when her master most often used the "jail he made" to confine her and others to ensure that his crop would not rot before processing.

Despite the prohibitions of both of their masters against prayer meetings and other forms of unsolicited gathering, Brooks and Lee formed a rogue spiritual congregation defined by ecstatic consecration, shared collectivity centering affective states and experiences defined by the momentary breaching of the twinned violence of confinement and forced movement, with sometimes disorienting intensity, pleasure, and an overwhelming embodiment blurring the edges of space and time dictated by slave mastery and dominion. While Lee's master sometimes permitted her to go and see Brooks, this was not nearly with the frequency she desired, so she sometimes "slip[ped] away from her place and come to see" Brooks without sanction. The clandestine congregation that Brooks and Lee built illustrates that dark agoras were foremost a creation of Black collectivity, an interior world carved into the spatial and temporal relations of dominion through acts of theft and fugitivity.

Brooks and Lee reimagined the social worlds of those they were forced to leave behind in Virginia, codifying these practices through hymns and rituals to remap those worlds over the contours of the unfamiliar terrain of sugar plantation ecologies and to replicate a mode of sustaining collectivity grounded, perhaps ironically, in another landscape of captivity, Virginia. These were already hybrid formulations, combining African cosmologies with emergent Black protestant ones. As Brooks remembered, all those who gathered with her and Lee would sing and "march around and shake each other's hands" as part of their clandestine ceremonies. Nostalgic in her recall of these stolen moments of collective engagement with the divine through singing, moving together, and touching one another's hands, Brooks reminisced "how happy [she] used to be in those meetings although [she] was a slave." Productive nostalgia here signifies a critical cartographic technology that facilitated Brooks and Lee's collaborative transposition of the intimate hidden worlds of slave assemblies in Virginia to the unfamiliar terrain of sugar plantations in southeast Louisiana to reclaim the interiority and sociality that were banned among slaves.[63]

Though derived from internal desires for a return to the familiar, these formulations were also materialized acts of defiance in the unfamiliar social ecology of a new region. As Brooks recollected, though her and Lee's masters explicitly prohibited these secret meetings, "we would have our little prayer-meeting anyhow." For the planters claiming ownership of Brooks, Lee, and the others constituting the secret congregation, this clandestine congregation represented at once a threat and something incomprehensible, illustrating the ways that these assemblies were shaped by the imperceptible demarcation erected by the planter state and successive regimes to repurpose their fundamental logic that all Black gatherings were fundamentally dangerous or radically unintelligible. As Brooks recalled about an instance in which her master broke up one such meeting, "We were all having a prayer-meeting in my cabin and master came up to the door and holler out, 'You Charlotte, what's that fuss in there?'" *Fuss*, as a penchant for excessive excitement, discursively neutralized the unsolicited gathering and rendered it from the vantage of mastery little more than incomprehensible noise. Although dark agoras in this context derived their primary contours from the desire to create fleeting social bonds anchored in an alternative relation with divinity, recognition that their clandestine meeting registered as fuss or worse as a dangerous breach of discipline impinged on Black collective interiority and shaped the aesthetics of these clandestine gatherings. As Brooks remembered, "We would put a big wash-tub full of water in the middle of the floor to catch the sound of our voices when we sung . . . and we would sing easy and low, so marster could not hear us."[64]

Plotting as the action to garner unaccounted-for spatial and temporal dynamics in the context of the plantation enclosure constituted forms of social gathering marked outside the territory of acceptable connection among the condemned, the assemblies I term dark agoras. These practices helped create and to partially realize an ephemeral Black commons that, while unstable and antagonized by the state, provided an alternate set of relations outside of mastery through which slaves and the self-liberated free people in the years after the Civil War continued to create unsanctioned collectivity and possibility in the face of violent dislocation.

During the US Civil War, key sites of the Black commons' reproduction were partially destroyed, along with the wider infrastructure of plantations, roads and bridges in Virginia and vast swaths of the South, as Du Bois documents in his 1935 *Black Reconstruction*. The Potomac and the other waterways in the Tidewater were fortified and weaponized, further delimiting, if not fully foreclosing, the historical relationships of these sites and reterritorializing the interstices of plantations as sites of more intensive danger and violence. Near the zones of open conflict, former slaves faced down war as "murder, force, [and] anarchy" to free themselves.[65]

As Du Bois writes in his field-defining chapter on "The General Strike," "Wherever the army marched and in spite of all obstacles came the rising tide of slaves seeking freedom." Du Bois homes in on the decisive significance of this movement for the redirection of the war, with the redistribution of former slaves' critical labor from the Confederacy to the Union as cooks, servants, fort builders, and later as soldier serving the decisive role in the war's final resolution. Du Bois goes on to describe successful experiments, led by the Union Army, in Black free labor and self-governance. While this influential thesis is significant and rightfully opened the path for understanding the ways that slaves freed themselves, it draws these communities into the fold of the Union's preservation diminishing Black collective life in excess of a shared desire to return to labor in the service of solidifying a nation founded in the extirpation of Black social worlds through the imposition of chattel status.

Du Bois's formulation of the general strike elides the horizon that some former slaves recalled in the period of immediate Emancipation. For example, although he later renounced the belief as foolish given the hindsight of the Reconstruction and post-Reconstruction years, Charlie Davenport, a former slave in Mississippi interviewed by the Works Progress Administration, remembered that the immediate approach of freedom signaled a horizon abolishing labor. He remembered believing that running away to freedom would end his entanglement with the tedious plantation regime, giving way to a time where he and others wouldn't "have to chop cotton no more," could "throw that hoe down and go fishing whensoever the notion strikes," and could "roam around at night and court girls just as late as you please" where "ain't no master going to say to you 'Charlie, you's got to be back when the clock strikes nine.'"[66]

While Du Bois's is a strategic historiographical move in the "problem-space" presented by the 1930s economic crisis of the Great Depression and the New Deal order and the predominant racist historiography that sanitized slavery of violence and rendered it irrelevant as a part of the matrix of the Civil War, his effort to render running away into not only a strike against the Confederacy but the organization of Black labor on behalf of the Union forecloses other possible engagements with this moment from outside the contours of ensuring the nation-state's survival through ongoing service through labor. As David Scott suggests in thinking about C. L .R. James's powerful *Black Jacobins*, it is not that Du Bois was/is wrong so much as the rubrics of the general strike formulation delimit other formulations of history that remain vital in the present.[67] Du Bois's framework, as Thavolyia Glymph illustrates, obscures the role of women within the overall transformation and overwrites the complexity of the gendered politics of the "contraband" for the expediency of labor politics.[68] As Saidiya Hartman questions, what happens to the "scheme of the general strike . . . [as] a placeholder for the political aspirations that Du Bois struggles to name" if we center the "sex drudge, recalcitrant domestic, broken mother, or sullen wet-nurse"? Moreover, "how does the character of the slave female's refusal" a "minor figure" "augment the text of black radicalism?"[69] As Glymph's and Hartman's critiques, and those of Alyss Weinbaum, suggest, building Du Bois's emphasis here on the rapid movement from slavery to the successful experiments in federally supported free Black labor through the rubric of a general strike seeks to tame a complex field of mass resistance into a formulation of power generated by the worker in the Marxian sense without fully attending to the complex territoriality and historicity of reproductive labor under slavery.[70] Although Du Bois underscores how the movement of slaves to the Union lines destroyed the South's capacity to reproduce itself, the connotation of a "general strike" truncates that shredding of the South's social and economic tapestry to the transfer of labor to the enemy.

The continuity of the forms of social life were articulated at the edges of the livable itself, an amorphous zone usually actively dissociated from the realm of political significance because of its lack of the identifiable sovereignty associated with patriarchy. As Du Bois writes, citing firsthand accounts, the "hordes" exhibited "no plan in this exodus, no Moses to lead." And yet they came, "many thousands of blacks of all ages, ragged, with no possessions, except the bundles they carried . . . assembled at Norfolk, Hampton, Alexandria, and Washington." These "landless, homeless, [and] helpless" people came some in families and others in "multitudes." As Tera Hunter illustrates, former slaves used the breach in plantation power enacted by the Union forces' incursions to seek family and loved ones, which in part explains the distinction Du Bois forwards between identifiable collectivities of families and less cognizable formulations of sociality in apparently frenetic motion.[71]

Du Bois's desired subject of leadership projected backward as an absence; "no Moses to lead" evidences his own investments in patriarchal power, but more importantly, his intellectual development within the milieux of Black politics during the era of bloody repression and Jim Crow consolidation. The multitude without a male leader, read differently and beyond simple haplessness, signifies a sociality fashioned among those seeking to reconstitute collectivity and belonging outside of slavery that overlaps but is not totally coextensive with the project of the state to preserve the Union, which is the thrust of centering labor as the decisive break and the family as the only meaningful and legible unit of collectivity. This formation of collectivity inscribed as a leader-less horde preceded and exceeded the state's reformation of force into a vast soldiery of laborers, fighters, spies, cooks, and trench diggers. The formulations of collectivity inscribed between the multitude or horde and the legible laborers that were organized in legitimate units of social and familial life mark a complex continuum of Black social forms that emerged from the reformulation of plotting within a geography of dislo-cation, violence and hunger and that built on the rubrics of stolen space and time in the context of plantations.

Du Bois's emphasis on labor rather than reproduction decenters a more robust analysis of the active role of everyday Black sociality and placemaking on the part of the "captive maternal" and organized fore-most by the desire to erect and extend the social worlds enmeshed, re-produced, and edited through plotting, in shaping slaves' decisions to flee and the worlds they began to build even in the tattered landscape of total war. Dark agoras, as a description of Black assemblies' shapeshifting forms—the there that is there—shaped by a dynamic of outside inscrip-tions of meaninglessness, backwardness, or danger, suggest formulations of kin and connection inspired within the contraband camps that reso-nated with the queer potential and affect of the intimacies forged in the hull of the slave ship, a bodily politics of connection exceeding the log-ics of dissociation, atomization, and forced congealing associated with slave or "refugee" status. A "contraband" woman named Affey who was recorded by teacher Elizabeth Botume, who went to teach former slaves in South Carolina after the Union took control of the region, exempli-fied the enduring possibilities of the visions of integrity and integration grounded in the Black commons and set in motion, as a kind of mobile Black relation, under the pressure and heat of war. Along with her chil-dren, Affey had under her care a young girl who called herself Pleasant Riddle. Affey found the young girl abandoned and wandering the roads with no caretaker, what Farah Jasmine Griffin describes in another con-text as "thrown-away child," after everyone had fled the surrounding plantations.[72] Affey took on Riddle as her own. While Botume could only note this relation as curiosity, she also inadvertently documents the cultural logics of a Black futurity that exceeds labor. Botume inscribes in curiosity the remarkable ability to absorb the abandoned into networks of care and support critical for survival and futurity that precedes and exceeds the formulations and rubrics predestining the insurrection as revolutionizing only of labor and that mark it as outside the normative rubrics of associational and political life through the patriarchal family.

This capacity to absorb what Du Bois described as the multitude rehearsed what he had earlier lamented in *The Philadelphia Negro* as the chance relationships of migrants from the South in the post-emancipation generation. Affey's connection and instant incorporation of what she might have viewed as a drain on limited resources suggests a formation of power and a source of it that exceeded the benefit of the Union's strategic largesse and the everyday violence of "contraband camps." It is not a state but rather a vision of mutual well-being, especially for the vulnerable, born of the social-spatial relations of plotting the Black commons as a fugitive formulation of social connection and meaningful belonging. In this context, the plot was nearly uprooted with the approach of war. Yet fugitives and contrabands decided to abandon familiar spaces for the camp as the potential sites of liberation.

2

Crossing the Thresholds between Worlds

Toward a Black Migrant Phenomenology of the City

In the period between Radical Reconstruction's fleeting promises and the full erection of Jim Crow during the turbulent 1877s–1920s, Black communities built out from the central ethos of the Black commons to partially realize a vision of social and familial integrity that materialized the possibility for collective sustenance and social reproduction centering the plot. In the Tidewater, Black agriculturalists and aquaculturalists combined strategies of small-scale production that could sustain and build the material requirements for self-determination. In one small Tidewater community in Essex County, Black Virginia families combined agricultural and aquacultural production on their small holdings, illustrating the enduring legacy of the visions of cultivation articulated in relation to the plot. Black farmers and aquaculturalists operated primarily along the Rappahannock at a scale commensurate with a strategy of subsistence and, in times when harvests exceeded the burden of taxes and the speculative rent on riparian land, perhaps even small excess, consistent with the visions of self-sufficiency that emerged as a central theme in post-emancipation life. These families sought stability and basic social and familial soundness and not necessarily massive wealth derived from an ever-expanding holding.

The Fauntleroy family was exemplary. Lawrence was born in 1837 in Virginia, likely in Essex County, as a slave. Nearly thirty years old at the outset of the Civil War, by age forty-three, in 1880, he owned a small parcel of land—just over fifteen acres—near the post office at Center Cross, eight acres of which he tilled, with half an acre dedicated to either an orchard or a meadow; the remaining seven he left as unimproved timberland.[1] Fauntleroy lived on the farm with his wife, Emily, his daughter, Willie, and his two sons, Richard and Moscoe. According to the 1880 census, though still residing on his parents' farm, nineteen-year-old

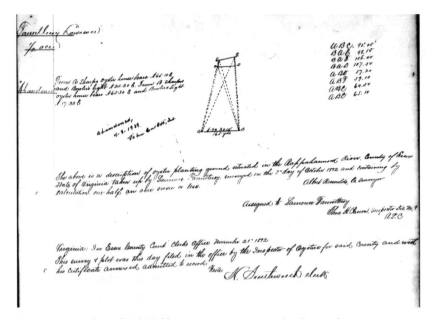

Figure 2.1. Fauntleroy family half-acre riparian river rental, Library of Virginia

Richard listed with the census taker that his occupation consisted of oystering. As is evidenced in the notation by the census taker, Richard spent a little more than three months idle when oysters were not in season for harvest, suggesting that during this time, he contributed his labor to his parents' farm. In addition to his farm land, in 1892 Lawrence rented one-half acre of river bottom for oyster planting, likely as part of the diversification of his small holding and in collaboration with his oysterman son.[2] Oystering for the Fauntleroys allowed them to enhance their family's stability and perhaps to render small profits between harvests on the then extant natural oyster beds in combination with artificially seeded ones that cost the family one dollar per annum and for which they held enforceable rights akin to ownership.

Census takers noted Henry and Hettie Tunstall, a young couple in their twenties who in 1880 had been married for just two years, as a "mulatto" couple. Together, they worked their small farm, also near Center Cross, Virginia, in Essex, along with their nephew, twelve-year-old William. Henry and Hettie, who owned approximately thirteen acres of land, six of which they farmed and seven of which remained in timber, lived on the adjoining parcel with Henry's brothers, Walter and Julius, and a young sister, Mary Tunstall.[3] Walter and Julius listed their occupations in 1880 as oystermen. In October 1892, brothers Henry, Walter, and Julius began, like the Fauntleroy's, to rent a small parcel of river bottom from the state. Together, they leased four and a quarter acres of riparian land for seeding and harvesting oysters.[4] The Tunstall family mobilized a strategy similar to that of the Fauntleroys, combining farming and oystering across the seasons to maximize stability as a small family operation. Although the Tunstalls rented a significantly larger parcel of the river bottom, the scale suggests a combined labor strategy rather than the desire for maximizing profitability.

These oyster plats represent the tenuous nature of the Black commons and the visions for autonomy and social reproduction it underwrote. While they underscore the continuity of these formulations among former slaves, the record itself is part of the repressive regime that consolidated in this period. The state sought to tame the complex and "messy reality of local common property rights" into a manageable system of extraction, taxation, and governance as part of the consolidation of Jim Crow. Although symbolically underwritten by nostalgia for the pre–Civil War plantocracy, "Jim Crow modernity" emerged through an unprecedented sexual-social-ecological enclosure, combining a regional system of legal exclusions from political and social power enforced through sadistic racialized rape and lynching violence.[5] Jim Crow's legal and extralegal architectures reinforced the speculative privatization underwritten by cyclical rural displacement, urban enclosure, and carceralization.

The nascent regime threatened to displace Black modes of living and to dissociate Black communities from the plot and the Black commons, decoupling their historical territorial coordinates as insurgent assemblies, or dark agoras, forged in the interstices of the historical plantation enclosure through the imposition of these ways of knowing and being as "folk." A new regional power bloc combining the political legacy of Whigs, the symbolic Democratic leadership from the antebellum and Confederacy periods, and private capital from both Britain and the US North conspired to restrict what had been open spaces for fishing and hunting to racially exclusive, privatized leisure and amusement, a move that coincided with the massive commercialization of rural land and waterways by railroads and other speculative interests.

Despite displacement from the means of reproducing the Black commons, the rise of peripatetic Black life associated with these generations that were dislocated from the southern countryside and towns did not dissipate the power of plotting; rather, these continued to serve as regional and transregional cultural imaginaries, transposed to mill town, urban, and metropolitan contexts shaping new sensibilities about the desired relationship between space and time, labor and leisure, the past, the present, and the future. As a collective, migrants hybridized rural and urban aesthetics and forms of collectivity to create unprecedented consciousnesses and worldmaking practices across the disruptions in the historical Black commons in the face of Jim Crow enclosure. They transposed these historical practices, rewriting them and recombining their syntax to the new conditions of urban enclosure defining the legal Jim Crow of cities like New Orleans and the de facto Jim Crow of northern cities like Chicago and Philadelphia.

Black communities used music and other forms of collective production, especially the rich repositories of the spirituals and the blues, to subtly note these transformations in their watery worlds. In a 1928 recording for Paramount Records, "Old Country Rock," Virginia rag guitarist William Moore opens the recording by calling to "Bear," "Let's take them for an old country rock." He grounds this sound, the sounds of an old country rock and its attendant movement, in the watery contours of Tidewater Virginia: "Let's go back down on the Rappahannock, Tappahannock way." Next, Moore calls for "everybody to rock." Recorded in Chicago, the song's prideful invocation of displaced home in a watery Virginia town announces a new kind of mobile, migrant southern subject in the age of the peripatetic blues and rag. Moore's sound and the subsequent dance he invokes operate through a longing for home and its affiliations—"them boys cross the river"—and its attendant movements—"that old country rock." The invocation of a rural southern place identified by its river with which he is intimate grounds Moore's innovative style and the cultural transformation in which he took part.

Moore's longing for his watery home is a structure of longing and a relation to place that was, as we have seen, itself in transit, unstable, and fleeting. While since slavery, Black communities in Tidewater Virginia utilized the area's various waterways, its streams, ponds, marshes, creeks, rivers, and the Chesapeake Bay, for self- and collective creation and plotting, the commercialization of the region after 1880 threatened these delicate ecosystems and endangered the soil, forests, marshes, and rivers and actively relegated Black experiences with the water and with fishing to tedium and drudgery. By the time of Moore's recording, the water's centrality to Black cultural life, including in work and leisure, was in rapid decline.

Although Black families used the area's oyster reefs and other fisheries to create stability and an ethos of partially indigenized cultivation, by the turn of the twentieth century, the transformation of the Chesapeake's oysters through commercialization relegated Black people, who had harvested the area for small commercial gain and to eke out a living from the bounty of the commons, to proletarianized laborers working for large fishing operations or as oyster shuckers and crab pickers. Moore's invocation to the "boys cross the river," his nostalgia for the old country rock animating his innovative guitar work and an associated movement riffing on a particular water and landscape with which he is familiar and that he understands as marking a "home," documented the fleeting possibilities of the affiliations around waterscapes for Tidewater's Black communities in the face of ongoing processes of conquest, racial capitalist geographic transformation, and the transition of people's interface with the contours of the Tidewater from an orientation along wharves and boats to one increasingly dominated by extraction and mobility. Here I want to think with Ashanté Reese drawing on Lorena Munoz's term "productive nostalgia" to describe "a process in which nostalgia is not just memories or imaginations but instead calls for the embodiment and enactment of practice."[6] Rag and the blues represented forms that galvanized various sentiments, like that evoked by the water, to draw Black geographic subjects through their own paths of desire, connection, disbandment, mobility, and affiliation, despite the forces rendering their communities displaceable, condemnable, and subject to the gratuitous violence under white supremacist governance of Black life and the subaquatic.[7]

As Carter G. Woodson documents in the *Rural Negro*, the rural South's local and regional waterscapes endured seismic transformations in the cultural lives of Black people living after emancipation. While ongoing large baptisms in creeks, rivers, ponds, lakes and at the seashore signified enduring spiritual and social connections to various kinds of

waterscapes across the region, commercialization and enclosure threatened more quotidian uses of and attachments to the various waterscapes. According to Woodson, Black people were increasingly "turned
away from the bathing beach which was once a free-for-all swimming
place . . . not admitted to the private game reserve which occupied the
old fishing and hunting grounds" and prohibited from having "any parties on the placid lake where they once rowed their canoes without fear
of disturbance."[8] As Woodson documents it, the dis-commoning of waterways and the erection of racially exclusive commercialized leisure
undermined Black people's abilities to access water and gave powerful
significance to Jim Crow's early twentieth-century spatial consolidation, of Jim Crow modernity. In the US context, despite slaves' overthrow of the antebellum regime during the Civil War and the flickering
possibilities of something otherwise given expression during Radical
Reconstruction, Jim Crow, along with the terroristic violence of continued systematic rape and lynching across the color line enforcing a
labor regime of excess profitability and political hegemony, was marked
by the territorial reorganization of the Black commons, the enclosure of
southern places, which set off the dislocations of the Great Migration
and the concomitant reterritorialization of Black ecological practices
and knowledges reduced to the folk or inscribed as dangerous.

In this context, the worlds that dispossessed Black communities
crafted across demographic, political, and economic transformation—
including spaces of disrepute—represented resources and knowledges
for navigating catastrophe and displacement with meaningful insight
about how to imagine and create means to collective futures in the face
of enclosure. Of the variety of the formulations for sociality and futurity
arising from the translocation of dark agoras, plotting, and the Black
commons, the often radically opposed poles of Black life in the city—
the underground and the set-apart—are my primary focus for the remainder of this book. As poles within interwar migrant thought into
the 1970s, they together constituted a spatial value system, not the direct
replication of the Black commons but its transposition and reexpres-
sion. Around movement between and through these sites, Black communities organized collective maps, not as the products of transparent
or linear plotting as in Western cartographies of domination but rather
as a more circuitous or queer formulation relayed through recollection,

through memory as intersubjective archives shaped by loss, continuity, and nostalgia, and documenting, through expressive culture and other forms of rendering possibility, new bases for sociality across experiences of unmooring and dissolution. Migrants' reproduction of unsanctioned assembly constituted a large-scale practice of Black alternative urban worlding that combined forms of cultural representation and the reproduction of expressive culture connecting urbanized rurality and rural urbanity. These practices of assembly and their cultural registers replay and remix the Black commons and its precondition, plotting as stolen space and time, articulating a set of alternative idioms of being associated with the city with attendant practices of place and collectivity. Together, these forms of assembly and the ideologies and cosmologies of collectivity they inculcated among the displaced articulated a shared working-class Black spatial consciousness that formed hybridized modes of place illegible to the rationalizing forces of urban enclosure as anything other than the folk, the derelict, or the antisocial.

Despite their sometimes vehement opposition, these modes of place-making, represented in the transmutation of dark agoras through urbanization, and the resulting coarticulated consciousness about the city—Black queer urbanism—shared an orientation toward an indeterminable horizon associated with ecstatic consecration. Although I employ this terminology in chapter 1 to describe the social worlds that enslaved people created through insurgent formulations of place and belonging, in the urban context, this formulation takes on a related meaning as a description of the affective territorially that migrants constituted across the continuum from the disreputable to the respectable. Ecstatic consecration names the shared affective orientation of the forms of insurgent Black assembly and collectivity. In part, the effective power of both of these often opposed worlds is the experiential power of the temporal and spatial fold, or pocket, that mark these worlds as outside the routinized lifeways and territoriality of gendered racial capitalist social reproduction, giving the sense, even if only fleetingly, of a world of eruptive pleasure, mystical possibility, intimacy, abundance, and transcendence.

The ecstatic in the urban context suggests an atemporalizing and a despatializing affective or emotive collectivity blurring edges between distinct persons and, in the case of the set-apart, often between people and divinity. This formulation defies the subjectivity of racialized individuality or globular demarcations of "the Negro," as well as the gendering nuclear familial unit theorized as the meaningful basis of an urban future in Progressive and post-Progressive thought about urban rationalization and the enclosures it underwrote in full force later through urban renewal. The intentional opacity of the underground and the epistemological opacity of the Black esoteric facilitated forms of Black urban life defined by such intensive embodiment and instantiations of collectivity in place as to produce disembodiment and an excessive and productive disorientation from the dominant coordinates of place marking the neighborhood as a site of extraction and confinement—the slum, and later the ghetto. Ecstatic consecration in this context names a politicized affective structure rather than a cogent liberatory political agenda. It is underwritten by mutual recognition and the melding of bodies, not necessarily in the sense of sexual or sexualized contact but rather through one of the many sensuous possibilities for community off the grid—literally and in terms of intelligibility out of the coordinates or off the frequency of the surrounding world. Ecstatic consecration facilitates forms of sociality expressed on a horizon of indetermination, and in that, given the horizon of expected impairment and death through slavery and its afterlives, underwriting generatively disruptive potential and kinetics.

In the remainder of the chapter, I analyze the architectonics of Black migrant worldmaking, emphasizing the hybridity of urban and rural forms and the important boundary work embodied in the erection and transgression of the underground and the set-apart. I emphasize the nature of Black urban geographies across diversity and heterogeneity, showing through continuities in encounter, experience, and transformation between the interwar and postwar periods and into the late twentieth century the phenomenological basis of Black queer urbanism. There is a complex sense of Black place that I want to draw out. Foremost are the direct encounters across the city's underground and its set-apart, as well as the more quotidian features of time and place these modes of assembly and collectivity shared. Experiences seeing or hearing or otherwise recalling members of these other worlds punctuated collective memory of traversal and transformation. Another feature, relayed often in direct response to these encounters across dark agoras, are the ongoing cultural raw materials of plotting and the Black commons shaping the meaning derived from experiences with the city.

Just before the Great Depression of the 1930s, "Mrs. W," a Black woman in her early thirties, moved from a rural community in Virginia to Philadelphia. One day, while still new to the city, she discovered a group of men gambling in front of her stoop. Mrs. W was dismayed by her encounter with the world of the city's underground, here materializing as mobile and temporary instantiation of the illicit economic order outside sanctioned exchanges. Perhaps it frightened her because she had witnessed or heard about the potential for physical violence and coercion in unregulated, speculative financial exchanges like dice games. Perhaps her rearing in the church of her upbringing in the South set specific prohibitions against gambling that she maintained after her relocation. Whatever the nature of her alarm, Mrs. W recalled how her experience with the crap shooters prompted a prophetic vision and an experience with the formless but transformative holy spirit: "I felt myself lifted high on a mountain . . . so high I could look and see over the world." The sun, which "was going down right at [her] back," cast a transfiguring light over the urban landscape. Suddenly, the endless rows of dense housing gave way to open fields. "It looked like it does in the country . . . like if you went to the end of the field you could touch it," she recalled. "This represents the son of God," a voice rang out to her. The disembodied voice went on to charge her with an earthly mission. "You must warn men and women to be holy," it demanded.[9]

As she recalled, Mrs. W took to heart the work of spreading holiness—for her, an ecstatic feeling, "just like an electric shock," and its attendant doctrine of purity and sanctity in anticipation of the immanent second coming of Jesus. By the time Black folklorist Arthur Huff Fauset interviewed Mrs. W in the early 1940s, she had made her spiritual home as "an ardent worker" as part of a "holiness group" praying for the end of the world. Through her spiritual mission, Mrs. W elaborated a vision for transformation, interpreting the displacement of an agricultural field as a sign that she must work to draw more people into the fold of the set-apart, for her, a temporal and spatial pocket defined by proximity to divinity, healing, and righteousness, a world of anticipation, a state yet to come yet already practiced in her community among the other members of a storefront Holiness church.

Mrs. W's narrative of transformation and her vision for the transformation of the world into a space of righteousness, bodily well-being, and community in direct communion with the divine demonstrates the ways that the articulation of the set-apart depended on charged pedestrian encounters between and across the worlds of the underground and the set-apart in the urban neighborhood. People moving between work and home, engaged in leisure, or seeking semi-illicit fun along with their normal course of drinking in tap rooms, unlicensed drinking sites, and other sites structuring the semi-clandestine underground, sometimes happened upon street revivals that forever transformed their lives, drawing them out of the worlds of the underground and into the set-apart. *Fallenness* suggested this transit in reverse. Some who had been born and raised in the set-apart "fell" into the worlds of the underground, either as inadvertent victims of its organizers' designs or as willing revelers freed from the constraints of rural communal life. Place marks these transitions and passages between and within specific spatial segments of the city—the clandestine geographies of illicit gambling, drinking, substance use and the red-light districts and storefront congregations. Encountering gambling men in front of their stoops along their course on the street dismayed Mrs. W and others like her and transported them into the spiral of a prophetic vision, leading them to become further entrenched in the worlds of those distinguished by their adherence to an embodied theology that differentiated them sartorially, spiritually, and practically, in the sense of how to approach the living of one's life. The various movements animating a sense of the desire for spiritual transformation and the work to build collectively toward that goal was often narrated through an interdependent set of tense encounters across geographies of labor, leisure, and the illicit. Together, these sites and the navigation between them underscore dark agoras as charged sites of Black working-class and migrant self-creation, forming the basis for distinctive cartographies of the city.

Mrs. W's memory is not a linear reproduction of territory cohering through the organizing logics of dominant ways of mapping and viewing the city. The multiple social, geographic, and temporal registers operating within Mrs. W's recollection provide an opening for outlining the complex cartography and geographic practices Black migrants built of the city and the distinctive phenomenology constituted in their efforts at worldmaking within and between dark agoras. Foremost, the encounter with the gamblers punctuates her cognizance of the competing modalities of living in the city, shaping both her identity formation and the narratability of her experiences and drawing her to a line of flight intelligible only within the features of Black migrant urban modernity. Mrs. W's movement between two Holiness congregations housed in storefronts following a marked repulsion though encounter with the congregation of the underground underlines the significance of practical and spiritual information gained through the daily practice of movement shaped by the largely unrecorded coordinates of Black vernacular landscapes within and crosscutting neighborhoods. In particular, the architectonics of her memory-scape suggest the meaningful nature of this juxtaposition of dark agoras in charting movement and transformation, bringing into focus a line of sight and a social axis unaccounted for from the vantage of dominant urbanism mapping the city from the modes through which urban landscapes are rendered governable, the birds-eye view or the vantage of the beat patrolmen, the social worker, the social scientist. Her encounter with a specific mode of collectivity and communion identified in the peripatetic institution of the craps game propels her toward the insulating collectivity of holiness, itself knowable and realizable along the contours of pedestrian encounter and experience.

Mrs. W's recollection of her vision evidences the duration of the plot as a complex and open symbolic terrain animating variegated projects for self-actualization and spiritual and spatial autonomy in and across migration, giving meaning to this charged encounter outside the purview of white domination and spatial control. Within her memory Mrs. W is transported into the shadowy zone of a prophetic vision in which the slum was cleared for an open field, recombining this flickering image of a landscape left behind with her vision about the future of the urban landscape. The plot, here in the portable form of the vision, serves as a touchstone of memory and sensation that helps her to derive coherence from the turbulent experience of dislocation, movement, encounter, and transformation. Like Brooks and Lee before (see chapter 1), Mrs. W sought familiar terrain associated with Black spiritual assemblies and in the process helped constitute new forms of urban social life associated with the storefront. In the ephemera of post-emancipation Black cul-

tural life—work songs, sermons, recorded religious rituals, and visons—
and equally within the carnal pursuits of sex, gambling, and drinking
against which the saints like Mrs. W distinguished themselves, plotting,
as the seeking of fugitive spatial and temporal coordinates off the grid of
the city's dominant infrastructures, expressed the cultural raw material
for visions that grounded individual and collective futures outside the
confines of slavery's afterlives. Here, plotting and the Black commons
are matters of place produced through translocation, wherein one place
articulates, haunts, and gives shape to the experiences of another.

From the interwar period through the end of the Great Migrations
by 1970 and into the 1980s, encounters between the underground and
the set-apart underwrote transformations like the one Mrs. W narrated.
The outlining within memory of encounter and passage between these
two worlds served as a collective cartography composed in the face of
a dynamic constituted through chosen movement and forced confinement, displacement and worldmaking, that shaped the experiences and
interpretations and uses of urban landscapes on the part of interwar
and postwar Black urban residents writing the city from below. This recollection indexes the dense phenomenological and affective worlds of
Black migrant and post-migrant generations, analyzing these collective
spatial experiences and knowledges as expressing a Black migrant form
of urbanism I describe as queer. Here, *queer*, as a qualifier to Black urbanism, expresses a formation not only of sexuality but of devalued outsider producing demoted knowledge about the city. I employ it to locate
a distinctive form of Black working-class practice and knowledge-base
about the city written in the transregional and everyday movements of
the "wandering" generations. Attending to Black queer urbanism opens
capaciously, if not transparently, the worldmaking practices of working-
class migrants and residents. It establishes these communities as hybrid
formations creating cultural worlds and praxes annealing community
through disruption and articulating coherency and possibility in a world
of displacement, contingency, and the always uncertain resolution of
placelessness for Black people.

Mrs. W's and other narratives challenge a firm and stable delinea-
tion between Black working-class respectability and disreputability associated with the set-apart and the underground. I follow the important
prompt provided by Ahmad Greene-Hayes in his extension of Hartman's

notion of the wayward to account for the rich, often non-normative cultivation of a life or a collectivity found in formally religious sites defined
by respectability.[10] Attending to the spatial dynamics of these modes
of being, collectivity, and worldmaking that were constituted in the assembling of dark agoras reveals the underground as a collection of po-
rous and intertwined communities, resisting facile or narrow readings
of those deemed respectable. Respectability associated with the set-apart
in the context of this work more accurately names a chosen set of spatial
affiliations inverting but intimate with those of the underground. Taken
in this way, the underground and the set-apart served as modes of belonging in space and time that co-constituted a shared grammar of territoriality that centered ecstatic consecration as a mode of belonging and
collectivity and that, rather than emphasizing formal labor and its linear
reproduction, centered modes associated with the epiphenomenal production of sociality and immanence. The underground and the set-apart
as dark agoras represented shapeshifting social-geographic formations
that allowed migrants to cohere into transient but significant comings
together against the backdrop of dislocation, atomization, and forced
territorialization in the confines of the enclosed urban neighborhood.

Taking the underground and the set-apart together under the conceptual umbrella of dark agoras, as forms of assembly and collectivity
shadowing and terrorizing state formulations for Black flesh and disposability, dispenses with facile distinctions between the disreputable
and the respectable in Black working-class urban and rural life. The
shared social-spatial grammar centering the ecstatic coarticulated between the underground and the set-apart suggests the phenomenological connections traced in movement from the quotidian geographies of
confinement to the possibilities of individual self-expression, belonging, collectivity, and placemaking outside the normative and routinized
temporal and spatial grooves of twentieth-century industrial modernity.
Even in instances of outright denunciation, disavowal, and rejection, adherents of the set-apart worlds in Black neighborhoods continued to
give expression and meaning to the worlds they charted through their
esoteric worldmaking through prior and ongoing intimacies with the
underground.

For outsiders, the relations underwriting dark agoras were defined by
their transitory nature. According to Du Bois, "Away from home and op-

pressed by the peculiar lonesomeness of a great city, [migrants from the South] form chance acquaintances here and there."[11] Chance acquaintance resides in the philosophical condition associated with immanence as opposed to transcendence associated with Hegel and universalism. Black migrant life is marked as fleeting, and potentially as nothingness or meaningless because of the consecration through the rubrics of quick gratification and rapid fulfillment followed by equally swift or hasty disintegration, but what Du Bois dismissed as rather queer forms of Black migrant sociality—defined by rapid passage into and back out of connection—facilitated the remaking of social worlds among the condemned, forming part of the basis for working-class Black migrant worlds within the world, including the spaces of the dark agoras. These modalities of social existence born of the dissolution and reality of death and social alienation generated dissonant modes of living and expressions of vitality, discordant and disruptive, within the temporal and spatial logics of the industrial metropolis. What Du Bois could describe only as sexual and moral impertinence or frenetic and irrational connection, and what later social scientists and reformers codified as Black pathology born of slavery and plantations, indexed small-scale rebellions in the realm of intimacies, the reappropriation of care and other forms of labor to cultivate dynamic worlds within the world, a renegotiation and sometimes rejection of the restrictive visions of affiliation through blood, sex, and property.[12] House and storefront congregations, temples, and mosques, along with other unsanctioned social spaces like those of the street and the tap room, constituted Black vernacular geographies that challenged the predominant vision of orderly urban life that was channeled through the normative home, the patriarchal family, the institutional church, and the institutions of (legal) secular civil society.

The connections between these distinctive modes of urban assembly bring attention to their shared antecedents in plotting and the commons and the displacement of these modes that shaped the ways that migrants transposed and refashioned practices of place and collectivity in the urban context.

Carter G. Woodson's analysis of the processes of social transformation of Black rural life from emancipation to the 1920s is critical for attending to these shapeshifting assemblies built across rural and urban life and their connections during the interwar mass migrations that coincided with reversals in Black landownership and the economic transformation of agricultural communities, with permanently lower prices after the consolidating dislocation of the 1920s. Woodson's analysis serves as a primary basis for the conception of Black queer urbanism and critically predates Louis Wirth's influential description of the general processes of urbanism by nearly a decade, as referenced in the introduction. Woodson noted that forms of social life associated with urban life also gave shape to the rural terrain opened by railroads, steamships, and, in the decade before his publication, automobility. Woodson observed the gambling at gas stations, the movement of using cars from rural segments to the city for night life, and the enduring rhythms of the rural church (despite the construction of small-town dancehalls) as evidence of hybridity, urbanism, as the reterritorialization of ways of life associated with the city and the rural, their strategic blending in the navigation of a treacherous political ecology.

Woodson's analysis of leisure in rural southern Black communities also underscores the place of ecstaticism as multifaceted and sensual experiences in the lives of what he described as "peasants"—landless agricultural workers who formed the source of migrant populations flowing into the urban South as well as into Washington, Philadelphia, New York, and Chicago. According to Woodson, baptism in the Holy Spirit defined only one aspect of the ecstatic culture centered in rural Black life. Although during the rural revivals of the period between the 1880s and the 1920, preachers emphasized purity and a restrictive vision of saintliness that proscribed indulgence, dancing, gambling, sex, and immoderate drinking, these spaces drew in many who were not members of the specific congregation but who came to rural picnic sites or church grounds for the revelry and charged atmosphere. Held in July and August, when rural Black communities who built these congregations had the most money and food, they were characterized by a vitality lubricated by feasting, talking, sex, and laughter alongside praying, singing, preaching, and the raising of collective funds for burial and mutual aid.[13]

Rural Black communities used revivals as a collective form of leisure after the significant exertion of harvesting, sometimes traveling in consecutive weeks to other churches, holding their revivals in coordinated succession. In addition to feasting, attendees met new people across geographies that many in the era before automobility did not regularly traverse because of distance and the difficulty of travel. Despite the emphasis on chastity and sexual purity during sermons, these sites doubled as places for locating sexual partners, according to Woodson, and therefore of another kind of ecstatic related to the plane of the orgasmic. Woodson's emphasis on this hybridity of forms, ones consecrating religious edicts in the cascade of holiness, pleasure in shared feasting, and even in prohibited sex, complicate accountings of migrants like Mrs. W's "returns" to the church and the worlds of the urban set-apart as singularly determined by the sublimation of the sensual into sexual moralism. The experience of return to the ecstatics of that old-time religion in the form of the storefront, but also non-Christian-based religions created by migrants, have various sensual registers, many of them asexual but also some of a sexual nature, that help us better account for the power of this mode of collectivity, the bottom-up resources of social and geographic life that ordinary urbanized communities expressed to create possibilities in an alternative horizon of urban futures bound to—not predetermined by, but shadowed by—the plot and rural dislocation.

According to anthropologist of Black life and religion Allison Davis, Black rural, town, and urban communities in Louisiana created forms of community that elasticized and ritualized key features of the plot within their doctrines and practice and help us understand the means by which migrants transposed elements of the plot in the set-apart geographies of industrial northern cities. Embodied movements, common vocabularies of mourning, and the centrality of various forms of alternative affective connection carried forward in migrant consciousness shaped the social and geographic expressions associated with migration. In addition to features including embodied worship that he described, Davis highlighted the unique funerary services of these congregations in rural and small-town Louisiana, which included the collective viewing of the body and participation among congregants in the sermon and the prayer, creating the effect of a "highly communal service with violent demonstrations such as shouting and 'getting happy.'"[14] In the towns and in the city further removed from the countryside, funerals continued to serve as a collective formation of grief and a technology of futurity connected to but not bound by death. The stylized ritual of twentieth-century Black funerals, no less than those in the nineteenth century, regrouped simul-

Figure 2.2. Storefront Community Church, Chicago

taneity in the alienating dislocations of rural and urban traversal. Thus, while it did not necessarily serve as a site of explicit and planned rebelliousness against the reach of Jim Crow's tentacles, it drew together people into the rhythms of the old-time religion and service, allowing for the replication of cultural knowledge and an archive of mourning and grief that underscored the fragility of life and the repetitiveness of death while also invoking connection to one another and to the divine across the divides of the earthly and spiritual plains, across living and ancestral embodiments.

Alongside the ritualization of aspects of the plot in the enduring formation of the funerary rites, Allison also documents what he seeks to contain as backward social formations born in rural life and transferred to the urban contexts of New Orleans and beyond to Chicago but that exceed this simplifying geographic analysis. In their broader "highly communal service[s]," these congregations held on to "shouting" and "getting happy," competing sometimes and in response to the musical and sonic elements of the minister, who according to Davis used some combination of a "sobbing technique" and "a triumphant laugh in preaching" along with "elaborate physical dramatization" to whip the congregation into a frenetic knot, quaking and loud or subdued and opaque. These rituals involved

Marching of usher board of church or of visiting usher boards, around seated congregation up to chancel, where donation is made by each member of usher board. Repeated several times, while both usher and board and congregation sing . . . Intoning, or at times the singing of sermon or prayer by minister. Use by minister of sobbing technique, or of triumphant laugh in preaching; walking into congregation or elaborate physical dramatization of sermon by preacher" culminating in a collective defined by "ecstatic jerking and yelling of members.[15]

This means of culminating what social scientists like Davis characterized as a cathartic release required the erection of a dense affective circuitry coproduced by the charismatic minister and the shouting congregants, through the haptic sensorial experience of touching and being touched, reexpressing a grammar of healing, mutual aid, and abundance associated with the plot and the Black commons as grammars of worldmaking exceeding the plantation enclosure. Ecstatic consecration helped to replicate the ethos of the plot in the embodied cultural vocabulary of these communities facing the enduring relations of their violent dislocation as the precondition of racial capitalist value production.

Additionally, these spaces continued in stylized form the expression of the Black commons staged in "dramatized baptism in public setting" in urban and rural waterways, "a river, creek or (usually in Old City and its environment) in a hog-wallow." "Dramatized" baptisms served as public rituals, held in waterways that were increasingly subject to privatization under the restrictive edicts of Jim Crow segregation. As Woodson noted that while the ongoing large baptisms in creeks, rivers, ponds, lakes, and at the seashore signified enduring spiritual and social connections to various kinds of waterscapes across the region, commercialization and enclosure threatened more quotidian uses of and attachments to the various waterscapes. According to Woodson, Black people by 1930 were increasingly excluded from the territory of the older uses constituting the historical Black commons and were prohibited from having "any parties on the placid lake where they once rowed their canoes without fear of disturbance."[16] As Woodson documents it, the dis-commoning of waterways and the erection of racially exclusive commercialized leisure undermined Black people's abilities to access water and gave powerful significance to Jim Crow's early twentieth century consolidation. In this context, the baptism, loud and, for Davis, associated with backward rural life, distilled forward the memory of spiritualized and nonmonetized relations to natural environments, serving as a complex cartography invaginating older formations of space into the present context of dislocation.

Although these forms were associated with rurality, key aspects of these formations mirrored the inverse formations of the urban underground, suggesting not only the one-way transposition of the plot to cities but also its partial supplantation in rural communities through what Woodson described as distinctively urbanized forms of rural life. These transfers disrupt the teleology of social and spatial tropes of rural innocence, urban corruption followed by redemption that many migrants forwarded themselves to make sense of vicissitudes of geography in a violently segregated landscape. The reality is that migration and urbanization transformed the ritual life of urban and rural religious communities and created new forms of exchange and interface across the divides constituted in missionary storefronts associated with urban settings. Alongside "narration of 'visions' or 'travels'" to animate and enliven religious conversion, elaborate "communion services," defined by "marching and collective prayer, and antiphonal singing as a body," associated mostly with rural traditions, was the infusion in urban and rural working-class churches, especially of new Holiness and other formations of the "use of drum and jazz music" along with "sacred dancing, rolling in a sawdust pit in the state of ecstasy, tambourine playing, the reading of the future, healing of the sick, use of images of saints, foot-washing."[17] Jazz and the presence of modern drum sets dislodges the unidirectionality of migrant consciousness from rural to urban; along with developing technologies of recording and transferring sound, they allowed for the grafting of what Davis considered lower-class urban forms onto Black rural culture, creating a two-way form of hybridization and constituting a distinctive feature of Black geographies as spatially transgressive in the face of regularization and fixation associated with normative schema of urbanism.

According to St. Clair Drake, the storefront represented a feature that materialized later in Chicago given the largely interwar nature of Black Deep South urbanization. It was a feature of the cityscape that emerged directly through the inundation of the city by rural and southern migrants. Despite its later appearance in Chicago, however, the form held many of the features that Du Bois described in Philadelphia by the mission churches that began to crystallize at the turn of the twentieth century with the urbanization of upper south communities into Washington, Philadelphia, and New York. In particular, these sites served as refuges for peasants turned migrants, who in their new contexts often fell within the category of unemployed or poorly compensated working-class Black communities segregated on the West End or in the Southside. What Drake described as these storefronts' "'folksy' air," which included a preponderance of youth as well as "plenty of rough humor before and between services," assured the adherents of these new faith traditions of their welcomeness in distinction from the marginalization and policing poor migrant Black communities experienced within many large, more-institutionalized churches. While migrants were often viewed as a horde overwhelming the serene worship services amid the concerted efforts for political and cultural uplift of more established churches, the storefronts that popped up in Chicago allowed those committed to their faith to worship unhindered by the watchful eyes of those who considered themselves social betters. And despite the derision that pastors and attendants of larger churches ascribed to the poorly clad and impoverished migrants in the city's small mission congregations, these forms represented dynamic, hybrid forms. According to Drake, many of those who did join the larger institutional churches also continued to maintain affiliation with smaller storefront congregations, usually characterized according to Drake by memberships around thirty parishioners, as a means of accessing community when they could not dress according to the unspoken standards of the larger churches or when they could not afford to tithe.[18]

Additionally, Chicago's storefront churches, especially those that consolidated in the interwar period, also sometimes transitioned into large, powerful congregations that competed with the more staid churches for their memberships. A classic and significant example of this is Pilgrim Baptist, which not incidentally, along with Charles A. Tindley's church in Philadelphia, served as another site incubating modern gospel music's formation and consolidation. According to an account that Drake drew heavily on in a footnote in his memo, Pilgrim, as well as other churches that grew to prominence in the postwar era as large churches, "filled up and the storefronts began getting up." As even these began to fill, given the city's rapid inundation by migrants from the South, "the people sought tenement places and any other available place to hold services." While most of these remained small and eventually dissolved or merged with other formations, churches like Pilgrim, St. Luke Baptist, Little Rock Baptist, and Liberty Baptist "made good" and expanded to become some of the largest congregations in the city.[19]

Like similar congregations that formed in turn-of-the-twentieth-century Philadelphia, the congregations that remained small remained "concentrated on run-down, low-rent, business streets and in generally undesirable residential areas." Nevertheless, despite the often squalid conditions of interwar Black migrant housing and living conditions imposed by segregation and economic isolation in Chicago, their interiors—the inner sanctuary, temple, or sanctum—served as a marked contrast to the austere or sullied backdrop of the larger "world."

The movement between the outside and the inside enhanced the storefront's affective power by heightening distinctions between interiority and exteriority as a palpable difference in cleanliness, care, and upkeep. These interior spaces are often opaque, in the sense that the ritual worlds of Black migrant spiritual communities often hid parts or all of their inner workings from outsiders; even those that appeared to be more open often enacted and engaged in belief systems and formations of cosmology whose full meanings were hidden from non-believers and non-practitioners, as was the experience of being set-apart marked by the aspatial and atemporal experience of ecstatics. Again, these features enhanced the experiences of transformation by emphasizing rather than underplaying difference and distinction. According to Drake, "Members volunteer[ed] to come on Saturday an on Sunday mornings to scrub and dust" the sanctuaries. They utilized "white covers" placed on "officer's chairs" and "frequently a rocking chair or sofa" to "grace" the pulpit creating "a sort of throne for the pastor and visiting dignitaries." Here, like the organizations that transformed into mass movements during this period congregants within these communities strategically deployed their reproductive labor in new social forms associated with the peasantry-turned-lumpen to create sites of refuge and a collective sense of well-being within these formations that constituted the Black "excluded denominations"—formations and congregations of the condemned serviced by what outsiders interpreted as backward theologies and spiritual practices reminiscent of what they considered archaic southern and rural lifeways that doubled as "rackets" for charlatanic pastors.[20]

In addition to a kind of worship that was considered riotous and unbecoming of modern urbanized Black communities and the New Negro, as inscribed within literatures as moving away from slavery and its shadow, these formations harbored formulations of the cosmological and social future that was considered politically extreme, apolitical, otherworldly, and irrational. In particular, according to Drake, these congregations, like their forebearers in rural and urban southern locations, incorporated literal interpretations of eschatology into their dogma and myths. Moreover, the means of conveyance of these formulations of spiritual and cosmological integrity, preceding from an understanding that the end of the world was just over the horizon, were conveyed not through what observers considered an artful or intellectual sermon but rather through the "pictorial and imaginative recounting of Biblical lore" often to warn of the "wicked world" beyond and threatening to ensnare the faithful lest they commit fully to the purity of holiness.

Among the most popular biblical passages associated with Chicago storefronts, as it was in congregations in the South, was the story of the three Hebrew boys thrown into a fiery furnace. This kind of message, despite Drake's derision, emphasized the realities of a deadening world that threatened to encompass migrants and to consume them but for their faith in a forthcoming radical transformation that was promised in eschatology and knowable through an acute attunement to, but distinction from, the world beyond. Hell, despite its common implication within sermons, was, according to Drake, often excluded from direct "lurid" description, especially during revivals.[21] In part, this was because many who had escaped the hell of sexual, economic, and social violence in the South now found themselves within a fresh form of hell, the fiery furnace of the industrial metropolis, and the reality of their lives in narrow kitchenettes or subdivided rowhouses under conditions of economic marginality was, without their interventions to remake place through their purposeful labor and collectivity, already a hellscape.

During one sermon by an unnamed Baptist storefront minister whom Drake relied on, the pastor enacted the Hebrew boys in the fire. "He came out of the pulpit, took three men and had them represent the three Hebrew children," while the pastor himself "represented the fourth person who was seen in the furnace" usually associated with the Son of God's early appearance in the Old Testament. "The four strolled across the floor" out from the pulpit, while the pastor continued to preach, when suddenly, the pastor "ran upon the pulpit and sat down in a chair and preached about waiting upon the power of God and having faith." As Drake documented, these pastors used the epidictic dynamic pedagogical approach to draw in people to a message assuming their shared experiences with the torment of living under the violent domination of American society and significantly, their shared desire for God to deliver them immediately (and miraculously) from the confines of their scorching. Here I draw on Ersula Ore's formulation of epideictic rhetoric which as she writes "denotes discourse persuades through modes of display, exhibition, and demonstration."[22] While Ore writes about this modality of communal formation in relation to lynch mobs as part of the rhetorical enactment of a perverse form of communion, this formulation is also part of a critical redeployment in Black institutions to dramatize the biblical references in ways that conveyed an analysis of life in the industrial city.

While it is easy to dismiss these formulations of freedom given tentative expression in the otherworldly sermon or the emphasis on the physical or other aspects of the pastor's mode of messaging as bound by a form of base charisma, as degenerative and apolitical, the reality is that these spaces incubated generations within the enduring aesthetics, poetics, and embodiments of the plot—a desire for a horizon beyond the debilitation and death associated in continuity between the relations of rural countryside, small towns, southern urban communities, and the northern industrial metropolis. This is a form of longing, materializing often as the desire in Christian-based visions for Jesus's Second Coming, that also gave shape to pastoral power and again revealed ministerial authority as in part the congealing of bottom-up formulations for a new world. Central to this new order was the acknowledgment of the forthcoming "Millennial kingdom" in which the "dead will arise" and

"Men will beat their swords into plowshares, their spears into pruning hooks, and will study war no more."[23] The quiet but sometimes barely contained desire for an end to violence, war, pestilence, and evil and the emergence of a world defined by abundance rendered through the redirection of the energy and resources for killing to the symbols of the plot through the sword-to-plowshare illustrates the ongoing cultural grammar of the plot, its incessant if remixed shaping of Black migrant imaginaries for the urban present and future.

And despite the overall condemnation of "the world," these spaces, like those in Philadelphia, enjoyed their growth in part through the phenomenological tracing of migrants from the underground to the set-apart. This was partially recognizable in the specific prohibitions outlined in many of these church communities against adultery, drinking, and gambling, among others. One pastor documented by Drake in Chicago called out "lazy kidney-kneed men" whom he considered "too lazy to work" and who, he lamented, dedicated themselves to "stand[ing] around the corners" for most of the day "being 'sissies.'"[24] The sissy here served as a designation of effeminacy deriding poor Black men for loafing on corners, for joining the ranks for the lumpen as hustlers or as men relying on women for their bread. The sermonic and other formulations of distinction in the geographies of the set-apart relied on their removal from the underground for their sense of coherence.

In 1919, Sherrod C. Johnson began what would become the national network of campuses constituting the Church of the Lord Jesus Christ of the Apostolic Faith by preaching fiery sermons in the back room of his North Philadelphia row house. These sessions combined music, biblical interpretation, and sermons. His core message centered the strict doctrine of holiness wherein converts were expected to transform themselves from the world to join the set-apart flock of Johnson's followers in the growing congregation. As one headline in the *Tribune* following Johnson's 1961 death described, adherents of the faith renounced smoking, drinking, or the use of makeup. This specific formulation of the set-apart moved through its negation of the worlds of sociality embodied in these three acts imagined and projected as having been shaped by the underground. Proscription around smoking and drinking to achieve holiness and purity acted as a direct negation of the world of the taprooms and the semi-clandestine worlds that encircled them. The prohibition against makeup for women adhered to the biblical association of personal physical enhancement to prostitution. The congregation helped gain its coherence through the inversion of the worlds that surrounded members in their neighborhoods. This was a physical and embodied transformation, as well as a shift in outlook.[25]

Migrants who suggested that they had never been subject to the corruption of the illicit dark agoras at the edges of the city described pointed experiences and encounters in the spaces associated with illicit Black social life—the tap room or a boarding house in the red-light district—to highlight and distinguish the parameters of their set-apart existence. Louise Smith, a migrant interviewed in 1984 about her migration to Philadelphia and the region, recalled her prior commitment to righteousness and the set-apart before she encountered the corrupting spaces of the underground. According to her, commitments of faith and to "the church" prevented her from getting "with the rough crowd." Rather, she "stayed in the church" and avoided the "places where the girls used to dance and they throw money on the floor at them, on the stand at them." Despite her stated distance from the underground, it is only in light of her encounters with it that her expression of an unwavering commitment to "the church" cohere within her recollections. "In Atlantic City there was a bunch of them from Virginia that I knew," Smith remembered. One night, they convinced her to go out with them and "have a big time." The others whom she knew from Virginia took her "to a beer garden and they were drinking beer and they were singin.'" When they attempted to force her to drink and "One girl had a hold of [her] hand" while "the other was trying to pour the stuff" in her mouth, she "kicked over the table," demonstrating her commitment to her Christian devotion.[26]

Back at her rooming house in South Philadelphia, Smith also encountered and distanced herself from elements she considered disreputable. While she was staying in a place maintained by a Mrs. King, Ida, one of the other women with whom she shared her double bed, brought in "a guy and all these girls was on their cots—summertime—some of them had their nightgowns up." When she demanded that Ida kick out her guest, Ida slapped her across the face and used her superior age and size to attempt to subdue Smith. In the end, Mrs. King demanded that they both leave, and Ida and Smith found a room together on the "Avenue where they had the red light district, they call it." Ida attempted to fleece her and avoided paying rent. Nevertheless, one night, while Smith was out, Ida brought two men back to the room they shared and for which Smith paid from her earnings. When Smith returned, Ida expected her to engage the other young man in a sexual manner. When Smith refused, Ida again attempted to coerce her with her physical strength. Smith fled and got another one of the older girls to help her enter the apartment and retrieve her things from Ida's possession.

Later, despite avoiding the snares of the red-light district and the violence of older girls in a similar social situation to hers, Smith's ultimate profession of faith had an intense moment of affirmation at precisely the moment that her actions led her to look almost directly like one of the characters she held to inhabit the disreputable worlds she left behind through marriage. Confronting her cheating husband, "One night [she] attempted to kill him." She "went to the store on South Street and bought the gun and had taken the money out to pay the man" for the gun when "something spoke to [her] just as plain, and said 'Vengeance is mine. And I will repay sayeth the Lord.'" [27] Trembling and nervous about having almost purchased the weapon, Smith decided to attend church. She happened into a Tuesday prayer meeting of one of Philadelphia's most significant Black pastors, Reverend Charles A. Tindley.

As Smith recalled, Tindley's message on the night she had considered murdering her husband for his indiscretions miraculously spoke to her situation directly. As she remembered it, he preached that "the Devil gets you in trouble but he never know'd nobody who the devil got out. . . . And after the Devil gets you he showed how he pranced." Tindley embodied his sermon, his physical presence on the pulpit serving as a touchstone in Smith's memory of the sermon that saved her from life in incarceration. "And when he got through I went to him like a child and cried on his shoulder and told him he was talkin' to me, cause I had just attempted to get a gun," Smith remembered. According to her, Tindley then embraced her, closing his eyes and placing "both arms" around her whispering to her "Daughter, I want you to go home tonight and get on your knees and ask God to take him out of your heart cause he ain't worth you getting yourself in trouble for." Shaken by what she considered the specificity of Tindley's sermon to her situation and heeding his advice, she returned to her home at Fifteenth and Catherine Streets in

South Philadelphia and got on her knees, "prayed to the lord," and then cried and prayed for half the night. Like many other migrants experiencing ecstatic transformation of their spirits, often recalled as being saved not only from the world but also from the clutches of the underground, Smith described the confirmation of veracity for her spiritual encounter as an experience of physical constraint followed by radical freedom: "Every time I went to get up it was like somebody pushed me right back. I stayed down there until the burden was lifted and when the burden was lifted I felt like I had wings, I could fly."[28]

Smith's recollection of transformation derives from distinctive sources—from pedestrian movement as well as an otherworldly and disembodied voice, that which she attributes to the spirit or voice of God. First, note how she maps her experience through the close and uncomfortable intimacy of the boarding house, the red light district, the chance encounter with her unfaithful husband, knowledge about where to purchase a gun, information about where she might find a church and a word. This is Smith's vantage of the city through recollection, a retracing through seeing, encountering, walking past, or having heard about that in turn shapes her movements up through the climax of her turn to the church. The attribution of an external voice intervening in her determined march toward destruction, and specifically toward Tindley and his perfectly timed message, together intensify the boundary between the worlds of the disreputable and the respectable, charging the border with physical and metaphysical potential.

Part of Tindley's appeal was his ability to recall and recombine the plot imaginary directly and authentically from a condition approximating slavery, forming an elemental aspect of his charisma. Tindley's capacity to compel away from actions associated with death and the world derive from what Hortense Spillers terms the Black sermonic tradition's "strategy of identity for persons forced to operate under a foreign code of culture . . . offer[ing] an equipment not only for literacy, but a ground for hermeneutical play in which the subject gains competence in the interpretation and manipulation of systems of signs and their ground of interrelatedness."[29] Although the published versions of his sermons do not convey the embodied dynamics of sermonic performance, Tindley's proximity to the violence of exposure associated with slavery, helped to charge his presence with a kind of transcendence lending credence to his temporal and spatial metaphors of transformation, which explains in part his appeal among migrants. Though born to a free mother, he lived under conditions similar to the enslaved in his Maryland home following her death when he was a toddler. As he remembered, the slavers to whom his father was forced to hire him out subjected him to hunger, exposure, and violence, and given the status of his father, there was little sense to protection. He interpreted his enduring faith in God as the thing that brought him from conditions approximating slavery to becoming the pastor of one of Philadelphia's largest Methodist congregations, with nearly five thousand members by the 1920s and 1930s. Tindley, most famous for his hymn compositions and for his civil rights era anthem "We Shall Overcome," used his own grounded experiences with slavery, death, and the plot to articulate a claim against the violent materialism of the early twentieth century and to heighten spirited awareness of the temporality of a social-political order founded on exploitative violence.

For Tindley, the devil personified the evil of the corrosive relationships of commodification and materialism. Specifically, Satan could transform the "government of human lives" through the defilement of what Tindley considered humans' God-ordained appreciation and desire for nature as stewards. As Tindley described in a published version of a sermon he titled "The World's Conqueror," the devil "ruled the world because the ruled the world's rulers." In turn, governance through evil transforms the gifts God bestows on people in the form of an inclination toward appreciation for natural wonders like "gold and silver, [the] finest raiment, fruit and grain, wood and fields, birds and beasts, flowers and beauties of all kind" into an avaricious appetite manifesting in exploitation, and domination. According to Tindley, the devil "knew the inseparable nature of mankind and these things which were made for mankind, and how impossible for a normal, sensible and live being to exist without the desire for them; he knew also that desire was the state of the being . . . therefore he took possession of all the beauties and pleasure-giving and appetite-appeasing things." No longer were humans restrained by the respect for the ordering of the natural world, thus "the nature and imagination of its people were corrupted; the natural phenomena were disposed by them on the side of the ruler of fallen nature, the devil." For Tindley, this fundamental corruption into exploitation of human desire for nature left the world in a state of chaotic fluctuation and a fleeting peace drawn from the "cannon's mouth or the sword's point" that was heard in the "crack of the rifle" and seen in the "gleam of [the] steel" sword.[30]

Yet for Tindley, this order was ultimately temporal, a blip on the scale of eternal time, just over the horizon from the emergent possibility of the transfiguration of the world into a state of eternal spring. Drawing on Isaiah 64:6—"We all do fade as a leaf"—in a published sermon titled "The Frailty and Limitations of Mankind," Tindley emphasized the temporality of this order, underscoring the fragmentation and disintegration of everything material. Drawing his point through the ages to illustrate how the great classical cities, nations, and empires of the West had given way to dust, he forcefully drove his point home in the passing of slavery. As he noted:

> The colonial master of Virginia, of the Carolinas of all the Southland, ride no more the well-bred stallion over the plantation amid half starved, back scar[r]ed and frightened slaves. The fox hounds of slave masters have stopped yelping, the blood hound lost the trail of the old slave and gone to the kennel of dust. Slave markets have been turned into meat markets, and the auction block has been chopped up for fire-wood. Jefferson Davis has left his capital at Richmond and Henry W. Grady, southern orator and pro-slavery champion has forgotten his speech and left his platform.[31]

Tindley embraced in explicit reference the trajectory of the plot, its vision couched in familiar rubrics of Christian theology of ultimate annihilation of the given order defined by the corruptions of human desire and the commodification of the bounties and wonders of a natural order. "The earth must be destroyed in order that we may possess that new heaven and new earth wherein dwelleth righteousness," he wrote. With the promise of the millenarial return of a spiritual force higher than the government, the "treacherous, vicissitudinous and precarious time" would "give place to eternity where no changing seasons or waning days shall disturb the continuity of inexpressible felicity which shall constitute our state" and where the order would be flipped, transforming "Peasants to Princes" and "servants to Kings." Tindley's embrace of the plot threatens in its full expression to wipe away the order he defined as corrupt for a new breach of the terrestrial and cosmic planes that would destroy death, greed, and corruption and install the exploited as the powerful.

Tindley beseeched his audience to turn their "eyes of faith from the chilly West where leaves are fading and falling, flowers are withering and dying; birds are hushing their songs; cattle are shivering on the leeward side of barns; ponds are glazed with ice; clods of the field are frozen and the snort of blizzards are frightening pedestrians from the streets, from the fields to the cover of homes and the protection of fire." He implored them instead to look to the East in order to behold an alternative horizon in which "the rain [is] over and gone; the flowers appearing on the earth; the flight of happy birds with song and the glad springtime of eternal life that all the nights have passed away, sorrow and sighting shall be no more."

Spring serves as a consistent metaphor for Tindley of an approaching horizon of earthly and celestial translocation. The physical transformation of winter, the signification of human temporal vulnerability and death, into spring signified the possibilities for the radical reversal of contemporary human society. As he noted in a sermon titled "The Rose of Sharon," the message came to him "one day as [he] walked in the fields of Maryland." Looking out over the desolate winter landscape, he "saw the tip of a green sword-like spear pointing skyward above the dead grass and leaves that covered the ground" and heard a "shrill, tiny command: "Forward!" Drawing on the biblical text from Solomon 2:1—"I am the rose of Sharon, a lily of the valleys"—he professed that flowers manifested the presence of divinity in "the valleys," which included the "valleys of poverty" and the "valleys of affliction." According to Tindley, "Three-fourths of the human family are in these valleys of poverty." Flowers represented a portion of divinity and perfection that had proceeded the fall of the world and thus also they signified evidence of the immanent return of God and a righteous order without want on the horizon. Moreover, drawing from the "valleys of afflictions," Tindley affirmed that God reigned on the side of those suffering with "trembling hands." Indeed, as opposed to the cast-off lot of the unworthy and the unproductive, Tindley suggested that through afflictions, "God presses the keys that make music" and thereby created the possibilities for collectivity and regeneration after the long winter of the West, in harmonies sufficiently efficacious to help draw nigh the spring.

Tindley's messages, in the spoken-sung versions that preceded his formal inscription of written sermons and formal hymns, drew in migrant Black Philadelphians by the hundreds and thousands after he assumed the role of pastor at a church where he had previously served as building attendant. Tindley's invocation of the familiar landscapes of dislocation, like the field in Maryland, his adaptation of hymns from his own experiences of grief and highlighting redemption from alienation, and his explicit personification of the forces of unchecked desire corrupted as greed, exploitation, and vengeance as Satan registered powerfully among migrants, who brought elements of saintliness with them from their southern homes. This complex terrain of Tindley's sermonics engaged and expanded the territoriality of the plot to help ordinary Philadelphians make sense of the dislocations of urbanization.

Tindley's embodiment and performance of charisma appealed to Smith, drawing her, with many others, away from the dangers of the illicit and into a congregation transformed by the influx of migrants in the early twentieth century. Smith's recollection alongside Tindley's sermons suggest that at least part of his and others' charismatic appeal emerged out of her desire to make sense of the dizzying experiences of the city. Her desire to access the respectability of holy matrimony, driven by her encounters with the illicit subjects of the rooming house and the wider red-light district, led her nearly back to the violent world she sought to avoid.

It is in the figure of the charismatic pastor, mobilizing and remixing the imaginary of the plot, that Smith locates her return to her senses and to the set-apart, here in the form of a church remade by migrant cultures of music and worship. Tindley materializes her desire for protection, sagacity, and a direct spiritual connection to hear beyond her impaired judgment clouded by jealousy and revenge. He indexes the fleeting simplicity of an honest clergyman, partially through his sermonic enactments and metaphorical uses of plotting and rural imaginaries, and thus the embodiment of her desires, for familiarity and possibility in a new and uncertain world. He draws her into the immersive affectivity of the sung sermonic that enlivens, after the crescendo of his message, the release of tears on his shoulders, draining her physically and metaphorically of the tensions created in the frenetic worlds of the metropolis.

Perhaps this can be read as a displaced desire for patriarchal fulfillment, Tindley serving as a stand-in for her husband as much as an embodiment of godly wisdom and knowledge. Whatever its nature, the transformation facilitated her capacity to lead an independent life in the city, a path of her own making, separate from her husband and without the sting of his embarrassment.

While many narratives in this book take the form of traversal from the underground to the set-apart, to suggest that this passage between the worlds of the set-apart and the underground is unidirectional or more aptly not a mutual hybridization would be to miss the instructive ways that the underground drew on the rituals of the rural and urban churches and the wider vision of leisure on Sundays, resonantly the key day of the plot's maintenance and expression across much of the upper and lower South beginning with slavery. The sexual and economic underground, punctuated by labor and its lack, adhered to the tradition of leisure on Sundays to cultivate forms of congregation clandestine between friends' houses, where migrants enjoyed sex, alcohol, and other experiences of strategic temporal and geographic removal. They replicate the traditions of visiting on Sunday critical to the plot's expression in the contexts of migrant "return."

Leon Grimes, who moved to Philadelphia sometime in the 1920s, remarked to a researcher that the underground was easy to locate in Philadelphia: "Well, you soon find the wrong things in the city." After moving to the city from the South, Grimes "found and did everything around Philadelphia that [he] shouldn't have done."[32] Despite the insistence of his mother, with whom he had moved to return to school, he "got involved in all kinds of things like gambling and sporting and running around and what you." "Well, you would go from house to house on Sundays" as "everybody was bootleggin' in those days," migrant James Plunkett recalled. According to Plunkett, "There weren't no tap rooms or nothin' like that," so Black migrants improvised illicit social worlds rewriting the countors of the street and housing. "Every house you went in was a bootleg house. . . . We'd just go into this house and buy a drink and go to the next house" and "sometimes they would have five or six houses on Sunday."[33]

For Plunkett, the bootleg houses doubled as sites of illicit sexuality that he and other migrants associated with what they considered a new formation, "women sittin' back there, all dressed up . . . sportin' types of women all dressed to kill." Migrants from the interwar period sometimes referred to these women as "up-to-date girls" (as opposed to old fashioned) as a common fixture in these and other illicit sites of drinking and congregation of the dark agoras. Up-to-date girls were distinguished superficially in their sartorial expressions and more damningly for many in their embrace of the sensual pleasures of the ecstatic. As opposed to "old fashioned" southern girls, these figures centered pleasure, sensuality, personal gain, and leisure. As Grimes recalled, "Up-to-date girls" "broke [him] in" after he arrived from the South. Although his mother wanted him to pursue his education to insulate him against the vagaries of industrial labor, sex was "all I wanted," he recalled. When he returned to his rooming house one night, he found that the other tenants were having a party. Tired, he went to bed, only to wake up to the pleasure of two beautiful "up-to-date" girls lying naked on both sides of him. His ability to pleasure both women elicited from these women a nickname in which he took great pride, even as an old man who had joined the church: "the young bull." This moniker indexes lingering temporality of the plot's grounding of Bogan's "Til the Cows Come Home," the "up-to-date" girls name the parameters of their illicit pleasure in the ecstasy grounding a modern and urban form of sensual leisure in the ongoing possibilities afforded by the plot to lose oneself in ecstasy and illicit desire on the traditional church calendar and as a form of passage between houses common of bible study and congregational life. To these "up-to-date" women, he attributes a rogue form of urban becoming and tracing whereby he was no longer "dumb" or "scared" of passion but rather could express desire and enact it.

While Grimes narrates the up-to-date girl as part of his self-discovery, Blues performer Lucille Bogan's recording history acknowledges the complex continuum of drinking and illicit sensuality in the peripatetic worlds of the Great Migration generations, giving voice to an "up-to-date" woman. The subject at the center of Bogan's "Drinking Blues" is caught in a seemingly self-defeating cycle—drinking away the blues while the issues amplified by drinking, such as consuming her rent money for the bottle, exacerbate her instability, cause her to drink more.

Despite the direct association here of whiskey with further instability, it is the hazy zone between recognition of the detrimental effects and their ephemeral easing that Bogan's "Drinking Blues" resides within that is suggestive of the appeal of alcohol in the context of social misery, displacement, and dislocation. Drunkenness provides an atemporal and aspatial zone wherein anxiety, sadness, and loneliness are undone, if always fleetingly, and perhaps even in self-defeat.

In her 1933 recording "Til the Cows Come Home," Bogan suggests a similar opening of temporal and spatial indeterminacy provided through her embrace of sexual openness, even going so far as to embrace nonmonogamy, referring to two lovers who know one another, implied by Bogan's admission that "they are tight like that." Bogan's subject in this song takes pride in the sensuality of her body's curves and acknowledges her own and her fellow women listeners' capacity for illicit forms of pleasure: "I gotta big fat belly/I gotta big broad as And I can fuck any man/With real good class." She demands pleasurable reciprocity, acknowledging that she will perform fellatio after her partner engages in cunnilingus. "If you suck my pussy, Baby I'll suck your dick," she notes to listeners. Bogan centers her relationship with the city as a space allowing her sexual autonomy, referring three times in the song's middle stanza to the fact that "I'm a bitch from Baltimore." Likewise, the song's refrain and title "'Til the Cows Come Home" signal the possibilities opened in zones of temporal and spatial fuzziness, similar to if not coextensive with the sensibility of the drunken subject but also through a direct recourse to the temporalities associated with the plot. This reference and recapitulation of an indeterminant temporal marker associated with rurality for a distinctive and unprecedented, sexually liberated sensual subject, locates the "up-to-date woman" in a horizon of intensive embodiment, orgasm, and pleasure over the course of the night. Taken against the demands for a horizon of work, the recourse to a night of self-appreciating, non-monogamous, queer erotics represents the chords of the insurrectionary in the realm of gendered racial capitalist reproduction.[34]

Bogan voiced through the bawdy potential of the blues an unprecedented vision of physical and social autonomy available in the motion of Black life into urban terrain, yet one that draws on the epistemic resources of the displaced landscape, its temporal and geographic distinctions, as the bases of bodily and sexual autonomy in the city. For her audiences across the urban up south as well as those in rural and mill town communities the agricultural landscapes of a displaced home index an enduring source of epistemic dissonance in relation to urban geographies and underwrite the possibilities of a new urban social order, not delimited by tradition but rather suggesting the ways that tradition in the robust sense represents the messy and unpredictable forwarding, recuperation, elision, and eclipsing of often idiosyncratic modes of ideological interpretation, practical response to conditions, and broad visions for earthly transformation defined by two plains of the ecstatic that imbricate and cocreate cognitive-spatial territory.

Bogan's "'Til the cows come home," taken discordantly alongside Mrs. W's vision of the field as well as the other narratives, refers to a dissident temporality and cartographic imaginaries underwriting twentieth-century Black urban geographies—here the complex terrain of material, affective, and social relations defined in part by segregation and violence but as well by roving, autonomous visions for the present and future of the city, small and large, effectual and fleeting. The reference point to the farm landscape in relation to the lost-in-space-and-time ecstatic states associated with a liberated sexual subject tied to the city or a new religious identity defined by ecstatic worship, another timeless zone of prostration and sensual supplication, index a complex intellectual terrain ordinary Black communities used to negotiate what was new and old about the city, ones equally heated and frenetic, if in everyday life diametrically opposed.

These represent differing vantages for seeing the city outside the rubric of labor and racial capitalist reproduction offering alternative temporal and spatial world outlooks for reproducing the city outside of the demands of Black sequestration, debilitation, and death. The illicit sites of the street and the underground, as well as the set-apart, are dialectic social-spatial formations bound through the experience of indifferent encounter, avowal and transformation, or antagonism and disavowal. Mrs. W's encounter with an illicit congregation of the city's informal economy prompts a turn toward a set-apart of holiness and purity, while Bogan embraces illicit sex as part of the terrain of the city in and through which she claims "erotic sovereignty." These two lines of flight together defy the dominant ordering of Black urban life to death or dissolution through the processes of sanitization and biopolitical citizenship through the clear lines of social and spatial existence imposed in modernist architectures of reform theorized and actualized in the performative demarcation of Black neighborhoods as dead, expressing racial blackness as part of the rubric of decay, dissolution, and death and hiding in plain sight the effects of racial capital's ongoing dislocations of blackness to the periphery of value—as the enduring precondition of capital's motley regime of retrenchment and expansion.

The transposition of the plot imaginary shaping the social formations of dark agoras across the illicit sites of underground and the set-apart illustrates the ways that Black migrant communities in the interwar and postwar periods created hybridized geographic resources across multiple worlds of dislocation to express and enact autonomous visions of territoriality and temporality.

For many in these generations, the sexual subjectivities that Bogan and Grimes narrated marked the inverse of generative living, a foil for living shared even before beginning a journey to the city. Martha Allison remembered that her family in the South told her, "Don't do like Mary" when you go North. According to the story, Mary went to New York City, a "beautiful place, but she tried to be up to date and she got with the wrong crowd." She began to attend night clubs and "went around and was almost a prostitute." The joy Mary claimed in the freedom to do "everything she thought was enjoying herself" left her destitute. One day, somebody told Mary, "Come with me and go to my church." Burdened and already having experienced the life of an "up-to-date-girl," and having skirted and narrowly avoided sex work, Mary decided to go: "I've tried everything else, so I'll try that." When Mary went to church, she "became a Christian and ended up being an Evangelist." According to Allison, the story of Mary that was conveyed to her before leaving the South came with the final lesson that she could be *somebody*, a respected evangelist in the church, without going to "the lowest ebb of life" first. As Allison conveyed, the message was for her to "try to end up in good company with the Christian people" and to attend church before she could succumb to the influences of the underground's corruptions.[35]

"Mary" served as a key to the map of the city in migrant discourse. She names a transregional gendered signifier of the potential for pitfalls of the city, her name enlivening her as a collective characterization of biblical figures, placing her somewhere between the Virgin Mary and Mary Magdalen. Her transit away from and back to the set-apart and her narrow escape from the snares of the red-light district represent a collective map of the city—again, not as a literal plotting of place in a two-dimensional representation but rather as an intersubjective knowledge of place as relational, shifting, and potentially dangerous. In this map, received before she made her own journey, Allison underscores the ways that proximity and intimacy between the underground and set-apart, imparted in the familiar language of the fallenness and salvation, shaped migrant spatial orientation and consciousness.

Non-Christian Theologies

The world that the set-apart indexes is not delimited as a form to Christian-based theologies and practices. People also traced a rogue phenomenology into set-apart worlds that they cultivated that did not ground them in Christian theology but nevertheless replicated and remixed the vision of the plot as an enduring ethos of abundance and distinction. Akin to these spaces in their shared social-spatial outlook, while governed by varying and often opposed theological and cosmological premises, were the temples, mosques, and other landscapes that members of the Moorish Science Temple, for example, built across urbanized Black communities. The Moorish Americans embraced a different and important variant of ecstatic consecration defined by new affiliations under Allah that nevertheless embraced the wider elements of food sharing, mutuality, and social connection. For them, the visiting of and connections between different places that the community facilitated embodied this vision of community defined by peace and love and that in the name of Allah distinguished them as Moorish. Thus, while they did not speak in tongues or pray to Jesus, they found the consecration of their theology in shared meals and the delights of laughter, sartorial distinction, and singing in ways that suggest the continuity of the relations associated with the storefront beyond Christian theology in the wider cultural transformation unleashed by Black migrants through the set-apart.

In a January 1967 "Letter from the President," acting leader of the Moorish Science Temple of America (MSTA) Reynold N. El described "the vast community of love and mutual aid" as "the very essence of Moslem Society."[36] As part of this, the brothers and sisters of the MSTA traversed urban geographies, passing between Newark, Brooklyn, Philadelphia, and beyond to reinforce the shared bonds of sisterhood and brotherhood and the alternative basis of national identity. Sister Carrie El, an adherent of Noble Drew Ali's teachings in Augusta, Georgia, traveled for three weeks between December 1966 and January 1967 to Brooklyn accompanied by her son, Brother Benjamin Royal El. The members there invited her automatically, as one who recognized her true identity, into a network defined by "the hospitality of the members."[37] Just before January 3, 1967, two representatives of "The Moorish Order of Royal Bankers," Brothers T. Allen Bey Sheik and A. Martin Bey, accompanied by Sisters G. Martin Bey and Curry Bey, visited the headquarters of the organization to sell their "lovely art merchandise [they] put on sale for the benefit of the organization." In return for their efforts to advance the Moorish Nation, Sister W. William "gave a lovely dinner for them" just before they left to return home.[38]

The Moorish Americans purchased a "colony" or "home" set on a large farm in Southside Virginia, where many of the members from Philadelphia, Chicago, and New York took leave for holiday weekends or even for longer respite from the rhythms and entrapments of industrial metropolises. In 1942, members of the Anderson Temple of the Moorish Science Temple of America, including Sister J. Young El and her sons and Sister F. Moore Bey drove from Anderson, Illinois, to Indianapolis. There, the group stopped and enjoyed the hospitality of other members of the MSTA, Brother and Sister C. Frazier Bey, before boarding a train to Chicago. Once at the MSTA's home office in Chicago, they were again greeted with the hospitality of other Moorish Americans. After an evening in Chicago, the women and the two young boys joined "Sultan," the group's "supreme grand advisor and moderator," Colonel C. Kirkman Bey and the other members of the organization's home office to make a "pilgrimage" to the organization's "colony" South of Petersburg, Virginia. Making a grand statement amid the smaller early-evening crowd on a Sunday at Chicago's Grand Central Station, they were a "beautiful sight to behold," clad in "their beautiful headdress of turbans and fezes, crescents in the sisters' foreheads, emblems and traveling badges displayed with the Sultan quietly and efficiently supervising each movement." Members of the MSTA enacted the set-apart through their strategic deployment of an alternative sartorial repertoire as well as in their exhibition of collective discipline. After a brief layover in Washington, DC, members continued their trek south to Petersburg, where they switched from a train to "Big Bertha," the "Moorish National Truck." Along the way to Petersburg, Brother Barker Bey pointed out "historical landmarks of interest to the travelers" before they reached their final destination, the organization's "colony," or the Moorish National Home, which they described as the "ancient hunting grounds of our revered forefathers."[39]

A central part of the MSTA's "Home Land" was the dining hall and "high Barbecue pit," built just before the 1942 Fourth of July pilgrimage and positioned "a little southwest of the dining hall, by Brother O. Boseman Bey, R. Lattimore El, K. Lanke Bey, and B. Jones Bey under the direction of [their] Supreme Grand Adviser and Moderator, Col. C Kirkman Bey, who personally supervised the preparing of the first batch of meat from the Barb-q-Feast for the Moors." The barbecue pit centered the Moore's social engagements during their summer pilgrimage to their homeland, suggesting the ways that Black migrant communities of the set-apart continued to enact alternative imaginaries of collectivity, place, and belonging in acts of return to the plot—a farm reimagined as a site of authentic communal connection in the recognition of belonging and collectivity outside the confinement of urban statecraft and ongoing violence through extraction and ecological and economic marginality.

As one author, reporting though the group's organ the *Moorish Voice,* described how "on Friday night a group of Moors kept an all night vigil by the light of the camp-fire around the barbecue pit while . . . Col. C. Kirkman Bey, attended the barbecue, laughing and tolling [sic] jokes."[40] As successive groups came to the "Home Land," such as a group from Detroit who arrived in the middle of the night, they "were greeted by the brothers and sisters who remained up that night. They sat for a while at the fire and warmed themselves while Sister Nelson Bey and Sister Boone El prepared a place for them to rest." Later, a group arriving from New York brought news of a group arriving from South Bend, Indiana, who needed a ride from the train station in the national bus. Eventually, the group amassed by the fire reached an ecstatic state defined first by sleeplessness and a crescendo of uncontrollable laughter that confirmed, across their urban locations of residence, their connections as brothers and sisters.

In a strategy of collective landownership exhibited across Black religious, the Moorish Homeland reconstituted the plot imaginary on collectively purchased land and enjoyed a reciprocal relationship with work of the women's auxiliaries in urban contexts to raise money and other resources to support it over time. As Priscilla McCutcheon's work illustrates, these kinds of rural land experiments have continued to shape Black spatial imaginaries and collective stewardship of place, as well as Black environmental politics.[41] On June 6, 1942, the women of Philadelphia's Temple Thirty-Three, constituting the Ladies Auxiliary, "gave an affair for the purpose of the helping their Moorish National Home." Sister E. Clarke Bey, a "faithful member" of Temple Forty, also in Philadelphia, left in July from Philadelphia to become a permanent resident of the Homeland colony in Prince George, Virginia. On June 9, 1942, members of Philadelphia's third temple, Temple Eleven, sat as a collective "awaiting the appearance of the Moorish Truck," which contained their "Field Representative Brother C. Barker Bey and his co-workers." When the truck came, it aroused a great deal of excitement as members of the temple eagerly packed "packages of various sizes" that they "donated to the Home" in Virginia. For some, the homeplace became a permanent site of "return." Sister E. Franklin El and her daughters Doris and Winnifred joined Sister Greenidge Bey and her daughters, Pauline Greenidge Bey and Sister R. Yancey Bey, and her children, Princess and Yvonne, in leaving Brooklyn and the Brooklyn temple of the MTSA for the Moorish National Home in Virginia, where they all decided to take up permanent residence.

Abel Respes, leader in the mid-1960s of a Black Jewish set-apart congregation known as Adat Beyt Moshe (community of the house of Moses), described his past relationships with poverty and an intimate knowledge of Philadelphia's underground and its corruption of his familial life as a critical aspect of his religious and political transformation. As a youth, Respes lived on the nine-hundred block of Adler Street, just below the historical center of Philadelphia's Black underground along the back alleys of South Street. As he recalled from the time when he was six or seven years old in the 1920s, those "were reckless days," his childhood home surrounded by "red light houses" where "people they drank, they gambled" and there "were shootings on several occasions." Later, when he lived in a rooming house farther to the south on the sixteen-hundred block of Warnock Street, the homeowner ran "games in her house, gambling." By age six, Respes reported that he had "learned to gamble" and knew "all the gambling games." "But at 15," he reflected, "I started to shoot dice . . . and I learned to play poker when I was hanging around these corners." As Respes recalled, he used gambling to circumvent the economic precariousness he faced as a Black youth in Depression era Philadelphia: "I'd have a job for a while and then I'd get laid off. . . . And after some time when I needed some money I'd gamble, shoot dice, play poker, or some other card game and try to win some money." Eventually, when he was around seventeen years old, he came to work for a "numbers banker, a guy who writes numbers." The banker had "a house where you used to turn in the numbers," and Respes worked their writing leads. The numbers banker had grown his illicit business to the point where he was "a pretty big numbers banker in the colored neighborhood," and he "owned a night club" that Respes used to attend because he "was tall for his age." Although he never achieved the financial security enjoyed by the numbers banker, Respes recalled having "a pretty good spot" in the organization, and although there was no salary, he collected a percentage of the leads he wrote, which "would come up to $15.00 a week, $20.00 something like that." Seeking to get further ahead, he and his friend, who also worked in the illicit numbers game, "devised a scheme where [they] could make more money." In the end however, they went bust and "had to pawn [their] clothes to pay [the numbers boss] off."[42]

The economic precarity that Repses and his wife faced following the birth of their first child in 1940 pressured him "back to the corner again." As he remembered, "I started to hang out around the poolroom again with the fellows. I started to shoot pool and bet pool." Betting pool in an attempt to turn around his economic situation proved dangerous. After he "gambled the only $5.00 we had and lost it," his young family was pushed to the brink of hunger. Again, the fugitive forms of commensality and reciprocity associated with the historical plot continued to ensure visions of the future against the odds of starvation. Respes and his wife relied on his grandmother and aunt, who supplied "surplus food, some beans or something." Although there is no evidence to affirm whether Respes's grandmother or aunt provided beans and potatoes from plots they worked or purchased these goods at a food market, it is clear that visions of ethos of collectivity extended from southern communities working to hedge the starvation of those vulnerable across the dislocations of financial downturn and enclosure.

Respes had two experiences that for him exceeded the natural and that together punctuated his eventual spiritual transformation. The first occurred when he was thirteen years old. While playing tag with white children from his surrounding neighborhood, a bolt of lightning struck him from the dark clouds that had formed in the sky. Respes recalled that after being struck, all around him was dark and he "couldn't see anything, as though" he was "in a vacuum." Respes ran home to his grandmother, who was "superstitious about thunder and lightning." She had scolded him repeatedly as a child to sit and listen to thunder as "that's God talking." When he came into her house with his clothes scorched, she "was angry" and "socked" him with her fist, telling him, "Next time you sit down or next time God will kill you!" This first preternatural experience with having been struck, having his clothes burned around his body, feeling as if he were in a dark vacuum, followed by his grandmother's admonishment, led him to seek holiness.

Reared among southern migrants, he "believe[d] in omens" like "if a picture falls of a wall, somebody is going to die" and if "the door would shut and nobody shut the door, that's a bad omen." Although on occasions such as Easter and Christmas he had attended church with his cousins, he hadn't been raised as part of any religious congregation. Yet he felt from his experience that he needed church so that "maybe God [would] be merciful" to him. First, he joined a predominantly white "little mission" church. Next, he followed his brother, who had joined another small mission church. Despite his efforts to invite the holy spirit at the churches' "mourner's bench" where they would "get down and pray, and tell you to call on Jesus," "Jesus would not answer." Following the lead of the other men of the church, he began to "jump and scream and yell" and to call on Jesus until his "mouth was dry." Eventually, craving the transcendent spiritual experiences of the other members of the mission church, he "one day jumped up and started making some kinds of funny noises." It was a "farce" he recalled, since he "was pretending." He remained in the mission church out of fear that he "was going to die" following the lightning strike and in response to "these people of the Holy Church" who went "up and down the street saying 'Look, the day of judgement is at hand.'" Eventually, seeing what he considered the disingenuous nature of a girl he considered holy reveling at her birthday party, Respes quit the church.[43]

Respes's encounter with the missionaries is notable, suggesting the central importance of the knowledge and understanding derived in recollection of sudden encounter across the underground and the set-apart in shaping Black experiences with the city. A familiarity with gambling and the pool hall, the highly traumatic and symbol-laden experience of being struck by lightning, and living within the migrant consciousness of his family and community, his encounters with missionaries' loud public proclamations of hell and the unseemly activity of the girl at her birthday party in the street punctuate his memories of spatial and spiritual traversal, transformation, and reversal.

A second supernatural experience punctuated his eventual decision to follow the Jewish faith and to create Adat Beyte Moshe. In 1949, after returning to the streets and generally spending "all weekend gambling," Respes reported that his life in Philadelphia's illicit world began to "drain" his health. "Sometimes" gambling "all day and night," it became "very taxing" on his body." One night, when he was "half way asleep," "someone walked into the room" that he and his wife shared and in a loud whisper commanded him to "Seek God!" Although the voice "sounded like a whisper . . . it filled the atmosphere." The disembodied voice "floated down to [his] ears" and "had a tingling effect," waking him fully from his stupor. Afraid, he covered his head with his comforter to avoid whatever presence had floated into his room. Shirking the superstition that he associated with his grandmother and other migrant elders, he "didn't really believe in ghosts," and yet the spirit "brought terror" over him. Regaining his composure, he sought to remove the blanket, but it "seemed to be held down by a pressure like a force of wind." Although he "used all of the strength that [he] had," he could not take the cover from his head. For nearly a month following his encounter with the spirit telling him to seek God, when he looked in the mirror each morning, he appeared closer and closer to death. His "face seemed to take a powdery-dead look." He concluded, "Maybe I'm going to die." At first, recalling his earlier disingenuous encounter with the Holiness mission churches, he felt "there was no God." Nevertheless, in ways that are intelligible through his references to his rearing in the context of migrant religiosity, he began to read the Old Testament and to recall the stories of Daniel and Jacob, who by that time he already "felt were not white." Eventually, as a result of the "revelation" in his bedroom, he told his "wife we would have to start living—read the Bible, sing, pray." They gathered discarded phonograph records, and they "would listen to these negro spirituals" and "read the bible." They also stopped eating pork.

For weeks after his second supernatural encounter, Respes had dreams that drew him further into a desire to transform his life. In a series of three dreams, he encountered "flashes of lightning in succession across the sky" that "took the form of a fiery seven." After the lightning, he saw "a huge Bible open in the sky and heard . . . a very loud voice . . . saying 'Every word that is written here shall be fulfilled!'" Following the first series of dreams, he had another in which he saw three men with "the features similar to a colored person" but without "the skin texture." Afraid to look on the men who he thought must be angels or priests, he looked down at the ground in his dream. After working up enough courage to face the man, he could "detect his features," but "his face was bright, shining" and hurt his eyes.[44] During another vision, the racial order was transformed. In the dream, Respes was in charge of "making preparations to take colored people" to Israel. Attended by four or five assistants, he gave orders to "see that the white people were taken out of the Pullman" and placed in "the freight cars."

Eventually, Respes was convinced by another "fellow working at Campbell's" with whom he "used to discuss many things" to attend a meeting of a group that "called themselves Israelites" at the "Israelite Bible School in Philadelphia." The group, as he recalled, was composed primarily of those oriented around "black nationalism" and had emerged as "an offshoot of another group that had come along a generation before my time." Given his oratorical and public reading skills, Respes began to speak before the Israelite Bible School and eventually became the third speaker in line during their study sessions. He eventually also took to their post at the corner of Twenty-Second Street and Ridge Avenue, where they proselytized, leading "mainly with the international situation." Although he was in accordance with their variant of Black nationalism and their attention to the Jews of the Bible as Black, he eventually rejected their ongoing nonobservance of the Sabbath and their continued eating of "unclean food." When he began to question some of the leaderships' practices that were at odds with Old Testament teaching, he was expelled from the group.

In anticipation of the return to what he now considered the original home, Respes eventually formed the congregation Adat Beyt Moshe, which by the mid-1960s had purchased several acres of land in a rural section of South Jersey and erected a set-apart community defined by its strict adherence to their own food prohibition, internal cohesion, and a lack of antagonism. Carving the space from what was considered barren land, they cultivated a world they hoped would be a harbinger of their earthly return to a displaced homeland in Palestine. Although the majority of the members continued to work in Philadelphia, they lived set apart from the vice, corruption, and excess that defined Philadelphia's underground, its red-light districts, gambling dens, and other enticements that drew the faithful away from their earthly mission to reestablish a connection to their homeland.[45] The set-apart world Respes crafted, along with the others working to establish this independent Black Jewish community, relocated away from what they viewed as the corrupting influences of the city and with which many of them, including Respes, had intimacy. They extended a collective vision of rural land ownership and tenure as a rehearsal for their future anticipated return to an elsewhere.

Conversions and transformations across worlds of the socially, sexually, and economically disreputable to the worlds distinguished by holiness, righteousness, piety, faith, sartorial distinction, and differentiated eating practices remained grounded in transposed plot imaginaries activated along the livewires stratifying the urban neighborhood and shaping experiences between the underground and the set-apart.

Late Twentieth-Century Continuity

Despite the transformation of political economy and geography across the twentieth century, interactions and encounters across dark agoras shaped Black spatial experience and knowledge about the city into the late twentieth century. While the next chapters examine the transformation in the geography of the city through the rise of planning's governmental legitimacy between the Progressive era and the consolidation of postwar Fordism, and subsequent chapters add significant substance to the key changes in working-class Black spatial thought and placemaking, this final section suggests, in a preliminary way, that transit across the underground and the set-apart continued to shape Black becoming and collectivity in the post-industrial city.

In the October 17, 1986, edition of *He Lives*, Earl and Juanita Jefferson described their movement from lives of unholiness and meaninglessness to holiness primarily through a narrative of fallen sinners redeemed by the baptism of the holy spirit that would have been strikingly familiar to residents of the city in the interwar and postwar periods. The primary structure of the story traces the "miraculous" movement from their "sinful" cohabitation, or "shacking up," to "Holy Matrimony." As the caption of the accompanying photograph reads, Earl and Juanita "were once drifting separately, toward total self-destruction. Today they are man and wife, saved, filled with the Holy Ghost, and contagious with the overflowing love of Jesus Christ in their lives."[46]

Earl's narrative places his fall in the context of the Vietnam War, a common refrain to encounters with destruction, as we have seen with others embracing esoteric religious traditions as movements out of the underground and which I will develop further in subsequent chapters. According to Earl, "At 18 years old I was sent to Vietnam, and there was introduced to heroin." He recalled that he "sniffed heroin for the next two years along with drinking wine and smoking hash." Earl's own growing heroin use also drew him into further illicit activity as he "sold and transported drugs from one foreign country to another" for six years, according to his testimony. Eventually, he began to inject heroin "to be sure it was pure." Earl attributed the hold that heroin grew over his life to "just how much Satan had [his] mind." Although the narrative of personal redemption strains against the subtle critique of war, part of what Earl describes as driving his habit was his inability to sleep: "I began living from day to day just for a high. I had to take drugs at night in order to sleep, and it took drugs to wake me up in the morning." Earl does not directly attribute the demonic force of Satan's control to Earl's time in the military, but his adoption of use in the context of the bloody Vietnam conflict and his inability to sleep suggest the debilitating effects of the war on his mental and spiritual well-being. Further use drove Earl when he returned from "overseas" deeper into the abyss of the underground:

From 1976 to the time I met Juanita [1978], my life was steadily going down hill. I was taking more drugs than ever. I was drinking two to three quarts of wine per day, plus the heroin. I was eventually mixing speed and heroin together, not knowing what I was doing to my body . . . I stole from my family, stole from any source possible, just so I could get my high.[47]

Although subtle, Earl's narrative places the degenerating force of war at the center of his narrative of unmaking, emplotting the course of his life of stealing and other petty crime back to the matters of US empire.

Juanita, on the other hand, described the humdrum nature of her job as a cardiac technician as the starting point for her "descent" into an unholy life. Like Earl, she does not attribute her turn to "taking a little bit of everything: uppers, downers, and smoking and drinking" directly to the conditions of exploitation, because the narrative's point as a recollection of a "miracle" was personal redemption. However, as she emplotted her miraculous story, she employed a key temporal designation that framed her turn to drugs and alcohol: "After work, I would take Valiums and drink cognac." While these began as pleasure-seeking ventures, as ways of getting out of her mind and body after monotonous work akin to the care labor of generations of Black women before her, they eventually developed into "a necessity." As she noted, "I was very unhappy. I did not have a future." Juanita went on to note another origin of her misery in the violence of sexual abuse: "As a child, I was a rape and incest victim, and I was to the point of seeing a psychiatrist." Indeed, she ended up moving to Philadelphia seeking an out, a way "to find something better." Here, disclosure about sexual violence and the quotidian violence of care labor in the health-care industry combined to create depression and sadness.[48]

After they met in a bar in 1978, Earl and Juanita began to "shack up," attempting unsuccessfully for a time to hide their addictions from one another. Caught together in what they both understood as a downward spiral into the abyss, or in Juanita's words, "killing themselves," they happened upon a miracle one night while on their "way to get a fix." According to Earl, it was as they walked to find drugs—pills for Juanita, heroin for him—that they encountered "a street revival led by Elder Earl Carter, then pastor of New Life Church of God in Christ at 59th St. and Haverford Ave." Earl remembered in his testimony for "Miracles" that "young people were testifying as to how God had delivered them from the same things we were hooked on, and they were talking about healing and deliverance from drugs, prostitution, etc." Earl's relay of the events leading to their eventual "redemption," or his overcoming of the debilitating effects of racial capitalism and empire, depended on a cartographic and phenomenological mapping whereby the geographies of the life spiraling out of control and the spaces of "deliverance" overlapped. Earl and Juanita were "pinned or just glued" to the top of a car, just meditating "on what they were saying for about an hour and a half." Eventually they left, and according to Earl, he "still bought drugs anyway." Yet for them, "nothing was the same anymore." The disruption of their normal activity of drug seeking in the crevices of the underground were interrupted by the force and power of the young people's testimony they heard at Fifty-Ninth and Haverford. It proved disorienting, and it left them feeling like "strangers in a strange land," in the neighborhood they had previously traversed like second nature for narcotics.[49]

Juanita and Earl's narrative of miraculous transformation does not occur through the regularization of life schedules, embodiment, and social-cosmological order according to the rubrics outlined by standard living. Rather, it illustrates the ongoing rich phenomenological basis of Black urbanism from below, including the chance encounter with a street revival. For the couple, the encounter marked a profound moment of transformation, indeed transcendence—or movement beyond the spiritual and material limitations outlined for their lives by "the world" beyond that otherwise scripted them as fungible cogs in a war machine or in a care industry dependent on Black women's drudgery in Philadelphia's 1980s political economy. Following their encounter with the testimonies of the youth at the street revival, the couple "decided to go to that church where we saw the revival." As Earl remembered in his testimony, his memory of the service was "blank until the altar call." To enhance the effectiveness of the temporal reordering punctuated by the miraculous, he and Juanita denied discussing going forward before the congregation. Indeed, when the altar call began, they took "separate aisles to the altar," where they received the pastor's prayer. For Earl, the experience gave him "such a high, such a natural high and God had somehow miraculously drawn the poison out" of his system. "I was high but not on drugs," he remembered. Rather than immediately abandoning his old life in the dark spaces of gathering associated with drug use, like the members of MOVE before him as I develop in chapter 6, he returned to his old hangout to share his transformation and, in a sense, to evangelize: "I even went back to the dope house and shared what happened to me at church, with the brother who I had just finished getting high with Saturday night. I told him how I came out of that place straight. I was so straight, that it took me three or four days to realize that the craving was gone." The proximity between the spaces of Black gathering associated with sinister and corrupting forms of darkness evidenced in the uncanny encounter with the street revival on the way to use drugs, and the return to the "dope house" after leaving the church illustrate the ongoing phenomenological basis of transformation and transcendence both individually and collectively.

Juanita's ascription of meaning to the encounter with the street revival was punctuated with the intense bodily sensations she experienced during a bad trip. As she described in her testimony, "Thursday night before the revival I had almost overdosed." Describing the use of uppers, downers, marijuana, hash, and vodka, she began to experience paralysis and a "tremendous pain" in her chest. "I then realized I was dying," she noted to readers. Despite having departed from Alabama to escape the pain of her sexual trauma and the boredom of her job as a medical technician, during her near overdose, Juanita remembered the words of her coworker who had told her to invoke Jesus whenever she was in danger: "That was when the Lord used the nurse's voice and said to call on Jesus." She remembered feeling Jesus's "presence there," and this induced her to begin a conversation. She begged God, "Do not let me die and if you let me live, I will live for you, but you must help me because I cannot do it alone." Suddenly, "I began to feel a tingling in my legs, hands and arms and I lived," she reminisced in her written testimony. After her scare with an overdose and her direct and miraculous encounter with the divine, and her and Earl's happening on the revival, she, like Earl, felt forever transformed: "We went to the club but I felt completely out of place, to the point of not being able to stay. I even tried to dance, but eventually we left and went home." Like Earl, Juanita remembered nothing about the sermon before the altar call: "I do not know what Eld. Carter was preaching about, but I was waiting for the altar call." She then went forward, and "at that moment . . . felt a change within. . . . It was like a burden had been completely lifted." Like Earl, Juanita used her experience with the miraculous and the holy not to completely remove herself from the geographies of the underground but rather to work along with her husband "as a team to reach other young people who are drug addicts."[50]

Again, although the geographic and political-economic context of Earl's and Juanita's transformation were distinct from those of earlier migrants, their narrative illustrates the endurance of a familiar set of pedestrian encounters between the peripatetic worlds of the city's underground and its set-apart worlds, in the form of the street revival, as the basis for creating a new sense of relationality, place, collectivity, and belonging in the city.

Reverend Eugene Rivers served as founding pastor of Azusa Christian Community, an independent Pentecostal congregation, in 1984 in Boston's Dorchester neighborhood, where he helped organize local leadership. Before moving to New England to pursue his education, he came of age in Philadelphia. Although he was born and spent his earliest years in Chicago, it was the geography and culture of Black Philadelphia that shaped his path to the ministry and his approach to power and politics. Like many others inhabiting segments of the city dominated by twentieth-century migrants to Philadelphia, Rivers's experiences were shaped by the active movement between and across dark agoras. As he recalled, when he first moved to Philadelphia, he was drawn into a local gang known as the Sommerville Gang through his associations and through his need for protection. While "gangs were not so pervasive in Chicago," they were a mainstay feature in Philadelphia. "I learned about gangs in Philly," he remembered. As he recalled, he was drawn into the world of the gang circuitously through an initial moment of awe that he felt observing the congregation of the street emerging from the charisma of one of the gang's leader. Seeing a younger boy called Little Oscar, who commanded a group of other boys, "handle" a much larger boy named Jimmy, who had previously bullied Rivers himself, Rivers recollected, "I had never seen such a bodacious display of bravado."

Rather than keeping what he had seen to himself, Rivers told other schoolmates, which ran him into trouble with the larger boy who had bullied him and who had also been put in his place by Oscar. Jimmy and his gang caught wind of Rivers's reporting and one day caught him in the bathroom and attempted to "drown" him in the toilet, giving him an ultimatum: "Either join the gang or just get beat." Rivers subsequently joined the Sommerville Gang and began to act in concert with the other boys, hanging out, fighting with other street gangs, and engaging in illicit sex in the 1960s. In the context of the underground congregation that formed his experiences with Philadelphia in the mid-1960s, he recalled two forms of initiation that he found repugnant and refused. These together suggest the complex terrain within an oral history of the memories of the underground, gender formation, and violence that shaped his later work as a minister and that helped to give that work its coherence, cogence, and force.

Foremost, Rivers remembered being commanded by one of the other members of the gang to shoot and kill another teenager. As he remembered, he had known the would-be victim and his family from his mother's church. Although he and the other boys tracked the boy they wanted to kill like "a marauding pack of hyenas," he diverted the shooting, refusing to commit the act and fighting the other boy who insisted on the killing. In the second foundational memory of this moment, Rivers recalled an incident marked by "a sexual nature." Some of the other boys in the group were engaged in sexual acts with one girl, or "pulling a train." In his recollection, Rivers resisted participation because he found it "repugnant," and after he fought another boy who ridiculed him and attempted to force this sexual initiation, the joke about him was that he was "cock-strong" because he was engaged in boxing and gymnastics and wasn't interested in "pulling a train." Although he later distanced himself from these forms of violence, the double figuration of "bodying" people that shaped him, the recalled repugnance, did not result for him in a radical distancing. Like many before and after him, it continued to shape the nature of his work and his outlook beyond his passage into the otherworlds of the set-apart.

In 1966, at the age of sixteen, Rivers was drawn away from the congregation of the street into a large evangelical ministry headed by Benjamin Smith Sr., "a working-class black pastor" who, as Rivers noted, "pulled [him] off the street and got me into the church." Although Rivers did not recount the particulars of his conversion experience, significantly, it was not his mother or aunt, whom he recalled as "good church people," who drew him to the congregation; they continued to attend traditional institutional churches, which he saw during that time as ineffective as he moved about "negotiating the reality of the streets." Faced with gang conflict and the violent coercion he experienced to "body" other Black people, he required another kind of protective community, that of the "fraternity," to feel integrated into the set-apart. He exchanged one mode of homosocial connection for another.

At the outset, it was Smith's charisma that drew him out of the city's "uniform gang culture," defined in part by the preponderance of what he considered a "hoodlum, gangster, tough guy persona." Smith's stern and serious demeanor remained resonant with and challenged the model of bravado he witnessed in his affiliation with the congregations of the street. According to Rivers, Smith provided a transformative example: "He was a very solid individual, remarkably serious, and he provided additional structure and discipline." Although Rivers understood Smith's efforts to draw him into the "black church" as "the most transformative experience" of his life because it "pulled [him] gravitationally into another world," it is the particular body of the congregation as a fraternity that kept him.

The church was primarily working class and contained different values from those of his mother's middle-class Chicago church where he had attended services as a youth. As in many recorded migrant recollections in previous decades, the lasting reformulation of community and connection provided by lateral reformulations in this example through brotherhood proved to be the substance of his long-term connection to the figure of religious authority. The congregation, and particularly what Rivers described as the "fraternity" he found among the other teenage boys and young men among the congregants, provided the most compelling alternative to the Somerville Gang. Indeed, the fraternity served as the inverse of the gang in Rivers's experience and memory. As he noted, the Pentecostal congregation he joined had "hundreds of young people and lots of young men, all of whom look like *regular brothers*, but they were Christians." Here I emphasize "regular brothers" because of the ways this formation of social life and existence inverts but parallels the recollection of the gang as a congregation of the street. Here, the defining feature of the set-apart, its ethical and moral contours, are not attended by a corresponding physical distinction but rather an affinity through the familiarity and similarity of forms, the parallels between these modes of congregation rather than their radical departure in appearance and demeanor. Despite their shared grammar of masculine presence, the gang and the set-apart mirrored logics. For him, their juxtaposition, despite looking like "regular brothers," "made a world of difference because it gave [him] a sense of fraternity and a fraternity" defined by a "value system" with which he could identify, despite his rearing in his mother's more traditional institutional church.[51]

As Rivers's narrative underscores, within the context of segregated neighborhoods, the underground, and the set-apart, taken together as dark agoras, remained competing worlds whose overlap and disjuncture provided the keys to a continuum of spatial experience and the resulting alternative modes of placemaking, cartographic insurgency, worldmaking, and politics emerging from working-class Black migrant communities in Philadelphia. Despite the narratological importance of distancing himself from the underground through the set-apart, Rivers did not move away from gang worlds; rather, his earliest participation in ministry connected him directly back to the underground, this time through a relation of proselytization. As he remembered in the 1970s, he "got engaged in doing anti-violence, gang organizing out of the black church." Critically for Rivers, this experience with the Pentecostal Church movement, the strict pastor of which "drew" him in from the street, and his early ministry through the church's gang outreach shaped his politicization. For him, churches like the one headed by Smith were "functionally black nationalist institutions. They were run by black people. They were supported by black people. They were owned by black people and they were for black people." This model contrasted with what he considered the tradition represented by what he humorously called the "grandchildren of Saul Alinsky," who, he held, ignored "a black tradition in organizing that preceded" it. As he noted, churches (and by extension other non-Christian institutions) represented a unique organizing tradition. As he understood it, the Black organizing tradition that had built "sixty-five thousand black churches" were capable and "didn't need Alinsky to lecture black people about organizing themselves" or "about organizing or raising money, or building institutions, or organizing when they want to organize."[52]

* * *

In this chapter, I have identified a spatial axis extending between dark agoras, from congregations of the underground associated with the illicit and the congregations of the set-apart—here the often heterodox religious communities taking the storefront as their proliferating spatial form. For the Great Migration generations, the intensity of these encounters was amplified by the plot and the rural as an ongoing grammar of transformation and transcendence. Encounter, avowal, and disavowal across this fundamental axis in Black spatial experience continued to shape practices of place and grammars of collectivity as Black working-class Philadelphians continued to rewrite the city from below.

Before returning to these formations through Father Divine's Peace Mission movement in chapter 4, I use chapter 3 to engage the ways dominant urbanists viewed the spatial aspects of Black social life how, through their Progressive and post-Progressive legacy, they thought about the city and collapsed these formations, especially those associated with the street and "the slum" with sinister forms of darkness, relegating them to the social-spatial margins as antithetical to meaningful urban futures and to death.

3

Darkness as Blackness and Death

The Rise of Dominant Urbanism

In 1942, Philadelphia's Cooperating Council of Agencies Serving Negro Youth published what they termed "a statement on juvenile delinquency among Negroes in Philadelphia" titled "What Makes Johnnie Bad?" Chaired by Fern M. Colborn and with a steering committee comprising representatives from various agencies across the city charged with serving Black youth, including principals and settlement house workers, the brochure was an attempt to state the "facts and an attempt to interpret them" regarding what these agencies viewed as a mounting social problem: "A rising delinquency rate in 1941 over 1940 indicates that the problem involved in these facts makes attention more imperative than ever in the face of a grave world crisis." The council connected the production of disproportionate rates of Black "juvenile delinquents" to the social, ecological, and economic issues promoted by segregation. Since the Armstrong Association, Philadelphia's branch of the Urban League, was a primary initiator of the council, the pamphlet's critical interpretation of the increasing crime rate was centered for the council in inequality in the arena of labor. "Not only are jobs for Negroes relatively few, but also wages are low," the council posited. This in turn led to the production of related, if not directly causal, problems associated with increased delinquency, including the "cramped quarters" in which the majority of the city's Black children lived, increased rates of preventable and treatable diseases, the lack of Black teachers and other professionals serving Black children, and the absence of "Class A playgrounds" in Black neighborhoods. The council concluded that the "solutions" for these mounting issues manifested in growing "delinquency" were better jobs, housing, schools, and recreational facilities for these communities.[1]

"What Makes Johnnie Bad?" made the case that the issues of social breakdown, gaps in the reconstitution of normal social-spatial relations, could be garnered through the integration of Black communities into the infrastructures of standard living, including modern housing, recreation facilities, schools, and jobs. The council, attempting to dislodge the naturalization of links between Black youth and criminality, or the common sentiment that "Negroes are inherently criminal or Negroes just don't know any better," noted that their findings were "not [to] be regarded as a criticism of one group of our citizens, but on the contrary as an appeal to the feeling of common responsibility of all citizens toward the facts." "This report," the council emphasized, "imposes upon all who have the welfare of their community at heart the obligation—not only as Philadelphians but as Americans—to see that the conditions which have so largely contributed to child delinquency be remedied." This appeal to the common citizenship of the wider majoritarian body politic by agencies and committees working in the name of Black communities reinforced the interpretation of ideal white citizen as achieving his mission through and against its ability to engage in ameliorative or eliminative action on and against the "delinquents" and with them their forms of assembly associated in the urban context with a force capable of devolving the city.

Despite its critical sociological approach, the council reinforced a common framework that cast Black southern migrants as disruptive outsiders, ill-prepared for life in the industrial metropolis by their origins in slavery and the South. In a section titled "Cultural Background," the council noted that "the great majority of Philadelphia Negroes have migrated to the city from Southern rural areas." According to the council, "the low educational and cultural standards of Southern Negro communities are too well known to warrant detailed description here; suffice to say that few of the Negro mothers and fathers who have come to live in Philadelphia were prepared, either through education or experience, to take up life in a big city such as this." Moreover, the council concluded, "it is fair to assume that if the parents have one set of standards acquired in a Southern rural environment, and the children acquire another set in a Northern urban environment (such standards being acquired largely outside the home), some cultural conflict, with resulting disturbance, is almost bound to ensue." Although the council exhibited its own class and regional antagonisms in this assessments of maladjustment, they also inadvertently highlighted the active work of Black spatial and social imaginaries translated across generations of Black migrant communities that challenged order in the city. The dissonance provided in Black cartographies of the city underwrote the kinetics of Black spatial politics.

This chapter begins to contextualize the emergence of discourses marking Black socialities associated with the problematic reproduction within the metropolis of rurality and the South—here as distinct but often conflated relations to region and geography—as criminal and retrograde within the emergent hegemony of planning and state intervention that defined the context of the council's analysis of the delinquent as an ameliorable condition or, conversely, as a future economic and social drain. Appreciating the outlook of reformers and planners as a macabre science of death, sensually charged and voyeuristic as de Certeau calls for, is critically important for thinking about the ways that Black communities figured into the portfolios of established real estate interests, the Planning Commission, social reformers, and networks of housing advocates—the key local architects of the post–World War II cityscape. Black communities served as the dark mass, writing the city in social-spatial grammars unintelligible to reformers as anything other than the derelict, the vicious, and the already dying or dead. Indeed, anti-Blackness was essential to the nascent discipline and power knowledge of planning; by the early 1940s, the state had sanctioned and financed assessment of urban land for its various economic and social properties, the strategic reformulation of infrastructures to enhance profitability and growth and extend them into perpetuity. Within the cartographic imaginaries of dominant urbanism that consolidated in local networks and ascended to full political expression in the 1950s and 1960s with the backing of federal and state financing, Blackness came to serve as part of the grammar of urban statecraft and placemaking as a set of spaces and social relations defining the limit in Keynesian-Fordist citizenship and demarking territory beyond the parameters of self-governance in need of dissolution, containment, or the intervention of citizenly sovereignty.

Prior to the rise of the New Deal state, local politics in Philadelphia were controlled by the post–Civil War Republican machine, which was defined by graft and corruption. The landscape, in turn, was defined by growing territories of crumbling housing in the urban core as urban and suburban density spread farther outward from downtown, galvanized by post-1880s regional rail construction. In this context, during the early 1940s, men like chief city planner Edmund Bacon and influential architects such as Oscar Stonorov and Louis Kahn gained political ascendancy in Philadelphia. Their ascendancy was the intellectual culmination of the city's six-decade tradition of housing reform and poverty work, as well as the international modernist tradition seeking to reform Philadelphia's decrepit housing tracts and order what were viewed at its chaotic combined uses. Together, architects, planners, and lawmakers sought to transform urban governance from the previous laissez-faire approach to an active planning state. In this period, their efforts gained the support of federal power and finances with the postwar transformation in urban political economy and governance.[2] Newly endowed with unprecedented technocratic power, these men began to implement a vision of the city's future wherein social, economic, and geographic stability could be achieved through growth—the perpetual extension of markets in housing and commodities—which they sought to insure through the imposition of *standard living* (a play on *standard of living* and *standardized living* employed to suggest specific metrics of the Keynesian-Fordist biopolitical-necropolitical order).[3] They reasoned that through the careful calculations of urban planning, as opposed to the speculative development characterizing Philadelphia's historical trajectory, they could permanently resolve capitalism's consistent problems with overproduction, redundancy, and poverty.[4]

Between the 1920s and the 1940s, the Philadelphia Housing Association served as a key organization in the rise of urban planning in Philadelphia because of its efforts first in relation to advocacy for private homeownership and later its embrace of public power in the remaking of urban housing. Throughout the 1930s, the Philadelphia Housing Association sought to replace the poorly designed bandbox and alley court with the reformulated individual home built by independent, for-profit contractors and situated in a plant with space for orderly and productive leisure. The intent of these reimagined spaces was the reorganization of working-class social life, particularly among Black migrants from the interwar period forward, in the normative family and home.[5] The model Kelly homes, for example, were circulated by the Housing Association as ideals for midrange buyers, and as the interior suggests, the living room and other semi-public spaces were supposed to subsume social life to the interior of the home rather than in the street. As well, these semi-public sections of the Kelly homes were distinguished from the private sanctuary of the family, which was located in their individual bedrooms on the second floor. The Housing Association embraced this model of housing because not only would working-class Philadelphians be provided with housing that would not fall in on them or burn with them inside but also because the spatial design of the houses would help fix boundaries between public and private within and at the border of the home itself. In contrast to the unplanned and overcrowded homes that endangered youths, the association advocated for interiors that were well-enough apportioned to produce what they considered proper familial and social life. The sleek modern bathroom and the well-appointed kitchen visually contrasted and opposed the dirty and dilapidated privy and the outdoor standpipes that came to signify slum neighborhoods with concentrated Black populations.

Essential in shaping the Kelly homes and other model designs was an archive the association collected of what they considered counter-normal, insurgent, and criminal forms of life. Because of their origins in the city's nineteenth-century charitable organizations, reformers working before the advent of the federal city sought support from the city's wealthy for their work in slums by invoking danger and pity. They cast bad housing as the generator of antisocial forms that "should scare anyone," and by visually capturing the innocent lives of children among squalor, they tried to create pity for residents. By 1940, the slum, although understood as an economic phenomenon in its causes, had also come to describe a totalizing picture of segments of urban life that included poor housing *and* ill-formed working-class social institutions.[6] As director of the Philadelphia Housing Association Bernard Newman lamented in the 1932 report of the organization, "Philadelphia has held back on city planning and zoning, denying the proper development of the city," sitting "supinely while large central areas have gone stale, first as blighted districts and then by deterioration into slums" where "certain racial groups have been centralized, allowing the properties to become wholly unsatisfactory for *normal* life."[7] Here, Newman inscribed the slum as having inherently deleterious effects on the possibilities for normal social function. Moreover, the cessation of normal and functional social life threatened the city's social stability. According to Newman, this process by which blighted communities were transfigured into the totalizing slum through the city's neglect created "racial problems and . . . racial clashes, which have often forced other families to give up their homes and seek new neighborhoods."[8] For Newman, the problem of the slum threatened the entirety of the urban future, since he deemed it unlikely that "there will be enough safe and hygienic family accommodations to meet public needs," given the lack of planning, the racial violence produced through the slum, and the Depression era cessation of new construction.[9]

Central to Newman's notion of "normal" life was an interpretation of normative gender and sexual roles that in his view were threatened by certain kinds of slum housing. According to him, certain styles of bandbox or subdivided row house and apartment living of the city's slums threatened the reproduction of normal life, defined by labor, cleanliness, and proper social-spatialization. Newman moved beyond just the visual signifiers of slum life and invoked "the flare of the radios, the neighbors 'making whoopee,' which in the reverberating echoes of the walled-in courts" were "the despair of the tired and sleepy."[10] Newman invoked uncontained sexuality echoing off walls and the rowdiness of music to index the demoralizing effects of the types of accommodation that made these communities dangerous. Generated out of the sensuality of the poor and indexed through the promiscuous sounds in the cramped arrangement of the apartment were the looming threats of social disorder in dominant urbanists' visions of planning and futurity.

Even in the absence of explicit references to sex and sexuality, the Philadelphia Housing Association consolidated a visual vocabulary of the dangers of slums that took as its primary subject the "privy" and other intimate spaces held as threatening social and biological contagion. The organization collected and circulated innumerable images of dilapidated outhouses that while absenting people, nevertheless signified on the potentially dangerous intimacies of a communal toilet. The privy as a symbol of the decrepit urban core was also a racialized symbol of primitiveness that, as increasing portions of the white population made their way to the city's northeast section and the suburbs, came to signify Black neighborhoods. As the images from the organization's yearly report illustrate, the privy stood alongside vandalism in a diagnosis of the breakdown induced by improper housing. The Housing

Association projected privys alongside images labeled for their dangers to youth and their contribution to overall malaise.[11] In the 1941 educational film *A Place to Live*, the Philadelphia Housing Association advocated for housing reform and marshaled the dirty, disorganized, and discomforting dinner table of the protagonist family in opposition to the modern, clean, organized, and comfortable one that the reformers juxtaposed at the end to make explicit their goal of a reordered sociality.[12]

Critically, as the Great Migration shifted the city's racial demographics, reformers associated slums with racial difference. Within evolving discussions about how to prevent the further erosion of the urban core and to ameliorate destructive racial tensions, reformers, planners, architects, and other dominant urban futurists with the means to partially execute their visions traded in racialized descriptions of darkness that served as a primary part of the cognitive mapping of space.

Although the Philadelphia Housing Association and Newman initially rejected public housing solutions, they supported the city's first public housing project, the Carl Mackley houses, as exemplary, and they promoted and circulated other candidates for models in the "interlude between the laissez-faire Reconstruction Finance Corporation (RFC) of the Hoover Administration and the activist Housing Act of 1937."[13] Although the administration of the Mackley Houses and other housing projects that were proposed from Philadelphia challenged the association's earlier respect for private ownership, Newman and the organization promoted them because they adhered to their ideals of social life reconfigured through spatial design.[14] The Mackley houses excluded Black workers as a function of their exclusion from the union; however, they also illustrated how normative and compulsory forms of social life extending from the nuclear family were infused into the nascent federal city's landscape. The later development of public housing for Black communities under the conditions of segregation would mirror this ideal as reformers and the Housing Authority refitted blighted areas with concentrated public housing.

Based on the federal legislation and the Pennsylvania Housing Law passed by the state legislature on May 28, 1937, engineer W. W. Jeanes conducted a sociological investigation, employing students at Bryn Mawr College. Directed by Jeanes, the students contacted 1,400 of the

9,000 members of the hosiery worker's union in Philadelphia to garner a firmer sense of their housing conditions. They found that on the whole, the garment workers lived in substandard housing that was crowded and that in some cases lacked sanitation. The Mackley architect, Oscar Stonorov, designed the housing complex around a notion of domesticity, whose central feature was the "worker's wife" who "typically would spend more time at home, and presumably would attend to children for part of the day."[15] The homes were designed to insure the normative development of future workers and housewives.

If the organizational design of Philadelphia's first public housing project was configured to create the basis for a specific vision of social cohesion, it also insisted on a social-geographic conformity. This is evidenced by residents who were removed, as Jean Coman described in a 1936 survey of the complex. According to Coman, between 1933 and 1936, eighty-one families had moved, fourteen of whom were considered by other residents as "undesirable" or who found the accommodations unfitting. Even among those who remained, the assistant manager had to make daily contacts and routine inspections to ensure that "every household had a thorough cleaning."[16] Researchers, architects, and housing advocates viewed public housing as the incubator of able-bodied, social—as opposed to the marked anti-sociality of the delinquent—urban futures. They invested in forms of surveillance that accounted for the embodied intimacy of cleanliness and social reproduction, and through design, they instituted visions of citizenship that while mostly affirmative to white workers and their families surveilled them and delimited a subset as simply "undesirable."

Built into the designs of the first and best-designed public housing in Philadelphia were restrictive and normative notions of who could belong to whom and how. Stonorov's premise was an overall enhancement of workers' lives in ways that might ultimately enhance profitable industrial production and reproduction. Thus, even among those whom Bauman distinguishes as the communitarians, the vision was toward the telos of ever growing industrial productivity dependent on a normative social-geographic arrangement to ensure the vital site of the home for reproduction and consumption.[17] As Philadelphia's only public housing erected prior to the 1937 Wagner-Steagall Act, Stonorov's design still incorporated normative strictures around social-spatial belonging and delimited a horizon for development in the parlance of capitalist futurity. As public housing expanded, it would come to be more restricted and restrictive because of false austerity imposed by the Byrd Amendment.[18]

Despite the possibilities engendered within early Public Works Administration–backed housing in the window between the National Industrial Recovery Act of 1933 and the 1936 Walsh-Healey Public Contracts Act, federal housing policy redoubled in enforcing the ideals of "market regulation." The 1937 Wagner-Steagall legislation officially linked slum clearance and public housing construction. Despite the relative ambitiousness of the 1949 Housing Act legislation, after the Housing Act of 1954, the federal government supported commercial redevelopment instead of public housing as the answer to central-city decline, ensuring the use of public housing in fixing the uneven geography of the city.

Thus, as Black communities gained access to "modern housing," public housing incorporated into its underfunded structure a vision of social belonging tethered to the horizon of gendered racial capitalist production and reproduction. Housing reformer discourses culminating in the 1930s and 1940s with the city's first public housing available to Black people trafficked in a "variant of sentimentalist polemic . . . that— even as it aims to trigger the empathetic response with . . . repeated invocations of suffering . . . frames blackness as the object of white liberal agency, an object to be heard, and ultimately saved."[19] Public housing's growing advocates viewed the "Black family" as always in need of repair on the basis of normative modes of placemaking and belonging, drawing on a larger sociological imaginary that interpreted Black social formations through histories of slavery and linking them to discredited forms of collectivity and gathering associated with the moral, economic, and social degradation of cities into the future.

The Housing Association kicked into overdrive to press for the inclusion of more Black people in the city's limited public housing accommodations. As the Housing Association noted, the 1930s was a critical juncture for the city and the question of its future. It had made clear that the city's core would likely continue to lose population, even despite what appeared on the horizon as a boost due to looming war preparation. According to their calculations, the "movement from the center to the outskirts of the city" conjoined with the "progressive decrease in the average family size" to blunt the rate of the city's population growth. While the city's central district contained 42 percent of the total population of the metropolitan area in 1900, the core had a decrease by 6.9 percent between 1930 and 1940. According to the association, this exodus was driven primarily by "the search for more spacious and quiet surroundings," which in part defined the association's notions of normative social life.[20]

Although they were charting the large-scale economic and social transformation of the core, they did not indict this as the process by which those left behind, particularly Black migrants, would become desperate. Their solution was simply "more family accommodations" "of a smaller size."[21] As the metropolitan vision of the earlier elite planners gave way to the federalization of the city, the state helped to reinforce the hierarchical organization of price along a core stock to suburban continuum. By 1940, a full one-third of public housing residents were Black, and core neighborhoods increasingly became sites associated with migrant Black communities as more projects transitioned demographically and as the state used them to reinforce the racial organization of the nascent region. Despite the conjunction of *Shelley v. Kramer* and the 1949 Housing Act, which opened the construction of more than a half-million units, the federal government remanded much of the efforts to local control and ensured that the vision of hierarchy and racial exclusion would be reinforced and exacerbated. According to housing historian Arnold Hirsch, the two-tier system constituted by the Federal Housing Authority, the Home Owners' Loan Corporation, the Home Loan Bank Board, and the Federal National Mortgage Association reinforced the bifurcation of value in the housing stock of the metropolitan district. On the one hand, they "revolutionized homeownership in the US. In contrast, a truncated housing program constituted the lower tier and produced" the underfunded public housing projects.[22]

Between the last years of the 1930s through 1942, an ascendant class of urban planners rose to prominence and political power in Philadelphia, as well as in most other US cities.[23] Younger and more vivacious than their politically elected counterparts on Philadelphia's conservative city council and in the mayor's office, these "young Turks" set about to "fix" their city. Walter Phillips, who would later serve as the director of the Philadelphia Public Housing Authority, first organized the Philadelphia

Committee on City Policy in an effort to reform the city charter in order to provide municipal power for urban planning. Although the committee's attempts to reform the charter crashed on the shoals of the city's machine politics in 1939, it redoubled in its resolve to improve Philadelphia and began advocating for the revitalization and recapitalization of the City Planning Commission. By 1940, the Committee on City Policy had merged with other organizations to form the Joint Committee on City Planning. The Joint Committee galvanized more than 150 citywide organizations, as well as leading businessmen like Edward Hopkins, to pressure Republican mayor Bernard Samuel in 1942 to adopt an ordinance revitalizing the Philadelphia City Planning Commission. Subsequently, the renewed City Planning Commission, which had fallen into disuse following its 1915 founding, included nine mayor-appointed committee members and a city-supported technical staff that could carry out the research program generated by the appointees.[24]

Across their specific backgrounds, ranging from newly minted architects to time-vetted housing reformers, men like Phillips, housing reformer Bernard J. Newman, future chief city planner Edmund Bacon, Bauhaus-trained architect Oscar Stonorov, and jurist Abraham Freedman shared a technocratic vision of municipal statecraft.[25] Through their varied expertise, they sought to manage the city as a vast network of interconnected infrastructures and buildings to be surveyed, enhanced, redesigned, and perfected. Through technical knowledge matched with increasing commitments of municipal, state, and federal power, they sought to excise and replace what they understood as debilitative infrastructures, particularly ill-formed and ill-placed housing, from the cityscape while also preserving and remodeling the "historically significant" structures they deemed worthy of preservation.[26] These efforts were rewarded, especially in the aftermath of Pennsylvania's national-precedent-setting 1945 Urban Redevelopment Law and the federal 1949 and 1954 housing legislation.[27] These statutes garnered for local planner's new sources of fund allocation and explicitly sanctioned the Planning Commission and the Redevelopment Authority with the power of eminent domain.

Philadelphia planners' emphasis on housing, both in terms of unit design and layout within the wider urban terrain, reveals that at the heart of their vision for the amelioration and improvement of the city's physical plant was a vision for managing the social order through its physical features. Dominant urban futurists in Philadelphia and beyond gained political leverage through their consistent descriptions of what they viewed as the city's "slums." They marked these segments of the cityscape as eminent sources of an impending social and economic catastrophe and as totalizing and debilitative spaces that threatened not only proximate communities but the city as a whole.

This mode of engaging urban social forms through the description of the "slum" was an effect of the technical developments and the nascent techniques for surveilling and intervening on the lives of poor people consolidated during the Progressive Era between the 1880s and the 1930s and across the political spectrum from eugenicists to what might be described as anti-racists.[28] Specifically, developments in statistics, photography, and sociological methods of investigation for viewing a neighborhood and its residents made it possible for Philadelphia's dominant urban futurists to describe ever more specific segments of the population, its health, and its living environment.[29] In their dissection and diagnosis of the slum and slum life, they departed from an earlier vision of the problems of urban decay as matters of individual dwelling units, as crystalized in the first tenement reform movement in 1860s New York City.[30]

Countering the Social Darwinist tendency that was also the legacy of Progressive intellectualism, and which reinforced the laissez-faire approach to urban development that reigned through the 1930s in Philadelphia, dominant urban futurists rejected a notion that slums were natural or given social effects of biological inequality.[31] Rather, they posited them as economic problems that resulted from uncoordinated individual decisions about how and where to build. In January 29, 1940, Edmund Bacon, Philadelphia native and future chief of the city's planning commission, composed an essay, "Lower City Taxes?," from his station as Flint, Michigan's, chief planner.[32] Bacon, whose challenges to the recalcitrant political structure of Flint led him to lose his job, which eventually precipitated in his assumption of the role as chief planner of Philadelphia, used the essay to advocate strong municipal planning over the lackadaisical approach that dominated before the advent of the postwar period. For Bacon, the reduction in municipal taxes was not a viable solution for balancing what he termed the "total municipal economy."[33] Rather, Bacon posited that at the root of the problem was the fundamental issue of a city's physical layout. If, he reasoned, "the total assessed valuation is constantly reducing" because of the city's deteriorating infrastructure, municipal tax reduction would be insufficient to balance a city's budget.

Embedded within Bacon's vision for a balanced political economy for a metropolitan area was advocacy for urban planning. Bacon was among a new class of technocratic urban futurists who viewed the rational planning of experts as central to the future functionality and market viability of US cities. According to Bacon, the primary problem facing Flint, other medium-sized cities, and even larger ones was unplanned development whereby, according to his figures, Flint's developers brought onto the market an excess of 78 percent of new lots for construction in what had previously been farmland.

For Bacon, this overburdened municipal services: "This would have little bearing on the tax problem were all these lots concentrated in one place, therefore demanding no city services, and consequently being no drain on the city treasury. . . . The city is left with the responsibility of providing services throughout the entire area. In many subdivisions, the garbage collector must pass several vacant lots for each house served." Bacon went on to predict that "within the next twenty or thirty years [Flint] will face a depopulation amounting to a disaster. There simply won't be enough people left within the city limits to support the vast complex of city services which are already geared to an area sufficient for twice the present population."[34] Bacon next proposed a plan whereby the city would consolidate the redundant parcels of land, concentrate and rationalize new development, and surgically excise "blighted" structures that threatened future returns on investment from the city.[35]

According to Bacon, slums resulted primarily from the "unbridled liberty for private enterprise" that was "not so much the fault of any individual or concern, as the cumulative effect of the unorganized activities of a series of concerns and persons over a period of time." Despite Bacon's infrastructural analysis of the causes of blight, he also understood blighted spaces as areas where "the houses were shacks anyway" with the "ability to stamp the entire land resources . . . with the character of a deteriorated neighborhood." Blight—the dark and corrosive effects of unchecked private enterprise—also produced people and communities that, as Bacon signified through his naming of their living structures as "shacks," were also redundant and deleterious to the wider city. Bacon, like his contemporaries, took as commonsense that "if the neighborhood around a house deteriorates, the value of the house is gone whatever its structural soundness." He advocated the restoration of value to individual lots through the reassembly "of the ownership of the entire neighborhood" and the clearing "away of the factors causing blight." Here, the structures in which poor and marginal communities resided were viewed through economic calculation as simply "six substandard houses, which violate the State Health Laws anyway."[36]

Alongside the excision of blighted structures that he and most urbanists viewed as drains, Bacon saw his work as redesigning street layout, replotting individual lots, planting trees, and building playgrounds to attract "private builders on condition that it be developed along the lines of sound neighborhood planning principles." Here we get a view of Bacon's self-imagined elevated role within city governance beyond political contest and unfolding in the realm of expert spatial knowledge and economy in the service of futurism based primarily on a vision of perpetuating capitalist markets. Later, Bacon would write that "only the planner, through his background, is capable of mastering the total concept of the human, of the building, and of the neighborhood itself. It is only as the planner is able to clarify his concepts and to hold a key and central role to the entire development that this sort of attack on urban blight in American cities will take place."[37] Bacon's vision of municipal government was of a body designed to act "as a clearing house, undertaking a receivership of the abandoned and deteriorated parcels, and through the exercise of its coordinating authority [to correct] the mistakes . . . resulting from uncoordinated individual efforts in the past." Bacon wanted to return the land to private enterprise and the wider land market "cleared of past mistakes and clean and fresh for new development."[38]

Bacon's notion of blight demonstrates a key grammatical structuring within the thought of mid-twentieth-century planners in general and specifically Philadelphia's future chief planner. The description of the slum by dominant urban futurists sought to name and mark for amelioration and rehabilitation or removal the set of social-spatial relations that gave rise to what were considered social and physical forms that needed to be removed to maintain urban life in total. They employed architectural design to effect and enhance "the average man" redefined in this period in relation to the metrics of reproducing industrial extraction. As I develop further, this vision for transforming the conditions of the slum to protect urban society—understood as middle class and white—marked other forms of social-spatial life as a kind of antisocial sociality. Within this paradigm, Blackness was marked, through its association with blight, as the territory and the ways of life to be changed to ensure the biopolitical arrangement of the city, its infrastructures, and its future.

Within architectural designs, plans for redevelopment, and implemented developments, urban futurists sought to contain the darkness of blight and the slum. For dominant twentieth- century urban futurists like Bacon, blight at once signaled a relation of financial redundancy and glut, a critical space of social rupture, and a racial signifier threatening moral citizenship. For Bacon, blight was "the economic problem of the decline of property values as affecting the municipal economy, and the social problem of the decline of citizen morale."³⁹ As he wrote further, "The physical decline has resulted in a general breakdown of neighborhood morale. Residents who have seen the neighborhood deteriorate about them have become discouraged and embittered. They think of themselves as 'forgotten man,' think city hall isn't interested in their problem, and, as a result have not put forth even a reasonable effort to keep their individual property in shape."⁴⁰

Embedded within Bacon's intellectual thought and advocacy for planning were normative notions of citizenship that built on the earlier visual vocabulary of the slum articulated most by the Philadelphia Housing Association, of which he was briefly the director before becoming the city's chief planner. Bacon viewed the desire to maintain a particular visual aesthetic in housing property as natural and suggested that the city's haphazard relationship with planning was draining the city's citizenry and threatening its civil institutions. Bacon wrote that in

any neighborhood the vital force of regeneration is still alive. In almost any neighborhood in Philadelphia it is a shock, as one wanders about decaying sections, suddenly to come upon three or four houses, a half a block or a whole street where each property owner has kept his home in fine condition, all of the houses painted, new fronts, and sometimes even a whole street with the same colored awnings. In the midst of all this decline there still exists vitality to improve. These cells have within them the latent capacity to replace themselves and to restore themselves.[41]

Here, the metaphor of cellular regeneration through a reference to the human body signified on the intimacies that were also a primary concern of dominant urban futurists. Bacon argued that "only through tramping the streets, through laborious field observation . . . and extended conversation with the people" living in a slum could the processes of blighting be halted and the city protected against its further incursion on healthy and vibrant communities. Bacon advocated the surgical removal of blighted structures and the preservation of what he considered generative communal institutions undergirding normative civil society. He described the issues of blight and the slum as "a very complicated physical intermixture of the good and the bad which the planner needed to understand in order to remove only the bad in so far as this is possible."[42] Bacon never explicitly clarified his interpretations of that which was good and deserved preservation and that which was bad and needed to be excised.

Yet it is clear that for the most part, he advocated for the preservation of normative institutions like institutional churches and not the forms of sociality that remained opaque to him as an outsider. As he wrote, "Within any neighborhood, there is a series of institutions which tie people together and which are tied to the ground" that form "a structure of institutions which has vitality" and that planners should give "new strength and validity both through the processes of planning, and through the character of the physical plan itself."[43]

In 1944, architects Oscar Stonorov and Louis Kahn published *You and Your Neighborhood: A Primer for Neighborhood Planning* with the financial support of the Revere Brass and Copper company. The primer is a remarkable testament to the efforts of planners to shape a vision for urban citizenship and governance. Stonorov and Kahn envisioned a novel mode of citizenly responsibility that drew on earlier Progressive intellectual thought, architectural theory, and social reformism but that also signaled the consolidation of a novel affective structure reinforcing state power in the context of post–New Deal Keynesian urban governance. Stonorov and Kahn hailed citizens as people dutifully concerned and engaging in action to ensure the "the continuing value and future" of their neighborhoods. As opposed to viewing citizens as "mere residents"—that is, people holding physical space but not enhancing their homes, blocks, neighborhoods, communities, and the larger cities—Stonorov and Kahn called on them to "assume responsibility for [the neighborhood's] defense from decay." To prevent "the good parts" of the neighborhood from being "contaminated by the bad," Stonorov and Kahn's primer took up a pedagogy of citizenship whereby they walked residents through the processes of forming a community planning committee, assessing the conditions of their neighborhood, and galvanizing behind municipal planning commissions and politicians to achieve the task of "saving" the city from blight. The primer included sample materials that residents turned activated citizens could take up in the quest to enhance their neighborhood, community, and city.[44]

Essential to the vision of urban citizenship that Stonorov and Kahn promoted in the primer was the cartographic relief provided by the dark spaces of the slum. Before moving into their discussion about how to build and plan a functional community to achieve "standard" and "stable" living, Stonorov and Kahn distinguished the audience of the primer as the people living in "neighborhoods that are ALIVE" rather than those simply inhabiting "neighborhoods that are DEAD." For Stonorov and Kahn, these "DEAD" areas were parts of the city where "decay has gone too far." Although Philadelphia is never mentioned by the primer's authors, the image accompanying the description of "DEAD" neighborhoods is a sketch that depicts three faceless children standing beside an antiquated gas lamp in "an alley court," a dense form of housing reviled by reformers and planners and characteristic of Philadelphia's core neighborhoods in many instances through the 1960s. Although Stonorov and Kahn never use explicit racial signifiers in their primer, the overall descriptive thrust, as well as the development through images, projects normal citizenship against the backdrop of slum life that in their home city of Philadelphia became racialized with the mass movement of Black migrants from the American South and the Caribbean between the 1910s and 1945.

Without naming the dead zone as Black, Stonorov and Kahn express racial Blackness as part of a spatial idiom and grammar of *dark-*

ness whereby life, "standard living," and a stable and productive future came into sharp relief over and against darkness and Blackness. In their cartographic imaginary, the dark slum is marked as a space of exception that ensures the sovereignty of the Keynesian citizen. Operating within a vision for citizenship linked intimately with business, the slums for Stonorov and Kahn were too decrepit, too far gone to be saved by "private enterprise." Rather, the slums were "blemish[es]" that required "public responsibility" and "cooperation" from federal, state, and municipal authorities for their full "extinction." For Stonorov and Kahn, the darkened slum represented the ultimate proving ground for the Keynesian citizen as it tested the limits of the urban "public," which in the primer is constituted partly though the democratized power to eradicate the threats posed by dark slums to normal life and standard living.

In a 1949 talk delivered to the National Planning Conference, Bacon described the ways that he came to view the need for rehabilitation along with removal. He embraced both as primary tools of the planner. According to Bacon, his realization of the need to rehabilitate vaunted social institutions came as he walked "through a fairly dull two-story brick row house section of Philadelphia [and] came upon a baroque church which [he] entered." He was "suddenly plunged into the shadowy interior with its rising spatial vaults." According to Bacon, upon leaving the church, he "saw the old street with new eyes." For Bacon, the church "infuse[d] the entire area with a different kind of feeling than it otherwise would have." Bacon therefore understood preservation of the communal institutions reinforcing normative social worlds like churches as contributing social value to the landscape. This vision of what was valuable and should be rehabilitated and that which was perilous to the overall fabric of the community reflected one another. Rather than destroying the entirety of a neighborhood, Bacon advocated the remaking of the blighted housing infrastructures and the preservation of vaunted and valued social institutions like churches.[45]

In 1947, the newly revamped Philadelphia Planning Commission hosted an exhibition designed by Oscar Stonorov and Edmund Bacon along with help from Stonorov's business partner, Louis I. Kahn. Stonorov and Bacon designed the exhibition to demonstrate the civic, moral, and economic merits of urban planning, design, and rehabilitation. The two-floor display was housed at Gimbel's Department Store, and saw some 380,000 Philadelphians during its two-month course. Eliciting some of the energy of New York's 1939 World's Fair while also cautioning against its wild speculation about the possibilities for the modern American landscape, Stonorov and Bacon designed displays combining photography, film, a diorama, scaled models of the city re-made, and a full-sized replica of a South Philadelphia street corner to illustrate "what is wrong with Philadelphia, and what, specifically, can be done about it."[46]

Visitors entered the exhibition through a "Time-Space Machine" through which they were transported to various eras of the city's geo-graphic development. Projecting the city's landscape up through the year 1982, the centerpiece of the exhibit was an elaborate scaled model of a reconstructed downtown. As visitors moved closer to the model, they could see the city as it was currently in 1947. Next, paired with a voice-over, each section of the model flipped and was lighted to illustrate the various transformative redevelopment projects if the proposed changes were executed for the thirty years following the exhibit. In addition to the redevelopment of "slum" and blighted communities, the display also advocated a plan to bring on the fifteen thousand acres of undeveloped land in the city. These new designs in what remained relatively rural sections of Philadelphia would encourage suburban-like or garden-city-style development that would avoid future slums.[47]

Following the scaled downtown model, attendees of the 1947 exhibi-tion were transported to South Philadelphia, introduced first by a full-size replica of a street corner that was "complete even to a messy garbage can," re-creating "the atmosphere of drabness and monotony which blights many of Philadelphia's residential areas more than actual dis-repair."[48] The plans witnessed by the spectators for South Philadelphia included a playground, the removal of trolley lines from most residential streets and their concentration on thoroughfares, the demolition of an unused factory, the destruction of dilapidated housing, the construc-tion of a new shopping center, the creation of a nursery school, and the building of new apartments and row houses, all to "add convenience and pleasure to the entire neighborhood." The emphasis on order to add con-venience and pleasure sought to reinforce normative visions of repro-ductive futurity crystalized most pointedly in the redesigned housing infrastructure, the nursery school, and the playgrounds. The political leverage for planning as it ascended to the halls of power depended on an understanding that these efforts would insure children as further workers, housewives, and consumers.

In many ways a publicly sponsored advertisement for urban planning, the 1947 exhibition displayed key aspects of the vision of Philadelphia's nascent governmental elite. Central to this vision was an at times contradictory political stance that on the one hand embraced robust forms of state intervention in matters of housing and the wider human landscape, and on the other hand that encouraged a regime of personal property and responsibility in matters of housing. In their formulations about the place of planning in the postwar period, mid-twentieth-century urban planners in Philadelphia and other American cities drew on local histories of paternalistic charitable organization, the activism and paternalism of the earlier Garden City and Bauhaus movements, and the peculiar American variant of individualist and familialist ideology attendant to the sanctity of private property.[49] While their proposed edits to downtown advocated and eventually affected state intervention through eminent domain, the full-sized replica of a South Philadelphia street corner was designed to show individuals and families how they could enhance their private yards and street fronts to protect against the corrosive advance of blight. In the replica of the "typical row house," the designers created a replica of a back yard designed "to show owners how to improve their own property."[50] The display illustrated how with a budget of $75, homeowners could transfigure their "former dismal city yard" into a "handsome patio." Here, the planners conflated aesthetics with structure and structural soundness, further reinforcing notions of normative (white) middle-class citizenship against the backdrop of blight and the slums. They reinforced visions of collectivity derived through ownership and responsibility that marked other modes of living in the city as averse to collective health and stability and therefore as outside the purview of proper urban subjectivity and citizenship.

The mode of redevelopment and rehabilitation that the commission embraced was in part designed to attract favor from real estate interests and conservative segments of the public because they were not the more drastic changes implied in the development of "one-class housing projects." The strategies for improvement for the commission ran the gamut between individual homeowner improvements and small public edits on the worst effects of economic abandonment termed in the contemporary parlance as blight. This combination was strategic in that it sought to allay fears of a massive state redevelopment project by making it at once familiar, practical, and tangible.[51]

To convince the public of the merits of planning and to justify its funding, the six-year public improvement program section of the exhibit was divided into four sections—South, Central, West Philadelphia, and Germantown—so that "spectators can get a close view, locating their neighborhood and their own home. Thus, improvement gains a personal meaning which could not be conveyed by an abstract listing of projects." The practical plan outlined in the exhibit for the years 1947–52 included efforts at abating river pollution and the extension of sewer and wa-terlines, the development of the city's airport in the southwest section, replacement of elevated tracks in center city, construction of Penrose Ave. Bridge and approaches, the increased facilities and parks for rec-reation, swimming, and play, an extension of the Market Street subway, new health centers, schools, and other institutions, incinerator facilities for efficient refuse disposal, the completion of an additional pier at the South Wharves, new highways and street paving, and finally new police and fire stations.[52]

This is a vision for advancing the state through the efforts to repur-pose and reattune matters of infrastructure as the fundamental un-derlying relations enacted, rehearsed, facilitated, and disavowed by brick-and-mortar connections. Also, as part of the subtle imperative of bringing the population to view planning as a mere extension of their private activities to create a better living environment, the display also included a section designed by the city's school children. Imbedded here was a kind of pedagogy by which the council and the Board of Educa-tion saw an opportunity to "teach children how to integrate themselves into society."[53] The pedagogy here was in part about creating long-term support for redevelopment through an implied interest in the futurity of the normative (white) child. This went along with a program instituted through an experiment in 1945 in South Philadelphia's Third Ward to create a neighborhood committee for which "housewives" studied local transportation, lighting, and other features of the community to suggest improvements to the Planning Commission, which served as the basis for urban renewal in South Philadelphia. As Bacon later remarked, the

1947 display prepared a generation of voting citizens to embrace urban planning in the 1960s and 1970s.[54]

If Black communities garnered access to public housing that removed them from what were described as poorly organized and often dilapidated row houses, there were also assumptions inscribed in these practices in Philadelphia to reinforce normative inclusion as the horizon for Black migrant integration. Such assumptions ignored or reinforced the racial organization of the capitalist economy of space and reinforced the local connection between citizenship and sanitization, which would become increasingly violent, since within this notion of the planning state were forms of collectivity tied to individual nuclear families and normalizing institutions that were antagonistic to Black presence and the supposed anarchism of Black assemblies and living. Through public housing, reformers and the state sought to "invest" Black communities in good citizenship through a reinforcement of the normative lines of social-spatial life. The projects could reclaim motley migrant communities from their potential to regress into divergent and thus pathological forms of collectivity.

In a 1944 report of the Crime Prevention Association of Philadelphia on "Negro Delinquency," the organization suggested that housing might fix within the city's rapidly growing Black population a sense of values that would inoculate them against criminality:

> Sociologists and psychologists have for years condemned the manner in which we permit a broad segment of our population to live. We have condemned many of our citizens to live in crowded, undesirable neighborhoods, in shameful slums. One of the greatest factors in preventing delinquency is a good home. A good home means not only an understanding father and mother but also decent living conditions. The Negro has been hemmed in by the most undesirable living conditions. Added to all these factors is the hopelessness of the situation. To what can Negro youth look forward? Are there plans being made now for slum clearance, for adequate housing? Are we removing from his life economic discrimination and social segregation? The Negro has just cause for believing that his acceptance economically these last few years is only due to the war effort, and that he will be the first to feel the effects of the cessation of our war activity . . . There is nothing in the future to warrant a conclusion that

the extent of it [discrimination and segregation] is a passing phase of war activity. Thousands of Negroes will be forced to make a readjustment to their employment. Such an adjustment, unless there has been adequate provision, will involve many maladjustments, and maladjustments only too often mean crime. Thousands of Negro youths who are in the service of their country will returned to the community. . . . Does anyone think that they will be content to go back to the same environment and work under the same conditions which formerly existed? Unless we plan for them, too, we shall have a situation that is going to result in an increase in delinquency and crime. . . . Only by recognizing the factors that give rise to crime and setting about immediately remove them, is there any hope.[55]

In 1950, the Philadelphia Housing Authority produced a report chiefly to describe the financial and overall unit development it had engaged in between 1943 and 1950. As they outlined, between 1937 and 1950, the Public Housing Authority came to control 9,572 homes at a value of $71,444,809, with annual rentals of more than $4 million. However, the monetary value that the authors of the report assigned was subsidiary to the larger social values they hoped to impart through the units that replaced the dilapidated and crowded housing that had once inhabited most of the areas where the Public Housing Authority completed most of its projects. Particularly as they summarized their work in the opening pages, the report was to be "more than a report of financial stewardship and business management. It is a document of human values high-lighted by grown self-respect, increased opportunities, and better citizenship. It is a story of children given decent surroundings and brighter hopes."[56]

The notion that renewed housing could not only fix real estate prices in areas designated by the Philadelphia Planning Commission as blighted but also offer "brighter hopes" illustrates the depth to which the housing fix and real estate value should be investigated as not simply rational market-oriented concerns but rather as a numerical stand-in for the aspirations and values embedded in an able, heteronormative, reproductive future. According to the report's authors:

Much of the construction in this "City of Homes" is permanent . . . designed to provide the proper environment for families to prosper and raise children. Some of the facilities will have to be replaced in time. And the need for more dwelling units is still acute. It is the opportunity, and, at the same time, the responsibility of all of us to provide needed housing. The construction of adequate living units will put dignity and self-respect within the reach of those in the low income groups . . . will lay the foundation for the individual to better serve himself and his community.[57]

These units were intended to impart on individual families self-respect and acceptable forms of community orientation, which must be understood as based singularly on a patriarchal ideal, despite the fact that the families accepted in these units did not have men at the head of the household and were thus interpreted by the reformers as families in need of repair.

As the images from the report show, the internal features of the units were intended, even in the absence of the patriarchal head of the family, the father, to invite and foster visions for productive lives centered in the very same model. In one shot of the "modern kitchen" designed "to make housework easier," a single mother and her three children sit around a square table eating. Seated at the center of the frame is a male infant in a highchair who eats and who is bracketed on both sides by a washing machine and a modern gas stove. The two daughters appear diminutive and shrunken in the frame compared with their baby brother, who is at the center of the frame and who is the stand-in for his absented father. The visual narrative here suggests not only that the housing fix would stabilize the primary value form pertinent to the governing interests of the city—real estate—but also that the hypostasized form—price—embedded presumptions about normative social values.

Additionally, the "community buildings" were also to serve as "the center of all activity in all projects." Overall, this spatial-social rearrangement would provide children with "an atmosphere of neighborly good fellowship" in which to grow up in, thereby securing the future through the strategic rearrangement of the borders and boundaries at its smallest scales.

According to the housing authority authors:

The family is the root of society—the child is the flower. For this reason the Philadelphia Housing Authority has maintained that clean, sun-lighted housing featuring attractive surroundings and plenty of open space should be made available to everyone, regardless of income. In virtually every section of the city a large number of residents of dismal slums and overcrowded tenements have been placed in cheerful, clean, new developments where the word 'home' takes on new meaning. Provisions have been provided for playgrounds and group sports areas and, in addition, the need for recreational facilities for the aged has not been overlooked. Blighted lives have been brightened by surroundings where the will to improve oneself is producing results.[58]

What this extended passage makes clear is that the primary foils to these productive lives with futures, inculcated by the rearrangement of the basic units of social life, the family, and the community, were the vicious lives associated with nonnormative and nonproductive futures in the slum or blighted area which, in increasingly charged ways in this period, were associated with Black migrants. The spatial arrangement of the projects was to reorient their residents to what were viewed by middle-class reformers as acceptable social existences. The invocation of community centers in all projects serving all social needs was a direct negation of the propensity of the inhabitants of the city's blighted neighborhoods, given the absence of built-in facilities for public recreation, especially in the city's oldest sections, to congregate and create social life outside the home and in acceptable public spaces.

The violence of this paradigm of normative social-geographic relations was reinforced as sanitization in this period came to be formalized through the clearance or removal of blight. Even local reform organizations that had practiced a relative conservatism around the question of the state's involvement in real estate invested in eminent domain—the state-sanctioned power to take possession of and reconfigure a territory. Eminent domain allowed the sovereign power of the state to blossom as it is predicated on the removal and cessation of particular lifeways in the name of progress. Eminent domain is the death of a particular arrangement in order to insure a new one. Earlier theorists of the state, jurisprudence, and territoriality had essentially argued that sovereign states had original and absolute ownership, prior to possession by citizens, and that individual possession derived from grants from the state and was held subject to an implied reservation that the state might resume its ownership.[59]

Eminent domain, which ushered in a great deal of rhetorical, epistemic, and physical violence signified in "slum removal," linked expanding access to the benefits of citizenship with the logics of sanitization and removal—the practices that reformers had begun outlining in the 1920s as a prescription for Black migrants to be included in the wider administration of benefits of the state through the strategic reformulation of their biological and social connections. Local reformers of the Philadelphia Housing Association wrote in their 1935 circular that it had "nationally recognized by all parties that some form of exercise of the public power of eminent domain is necessary for the successful execution of rehabilitation. This is implied in the now accepted premise that rehabilitation must be done on the contiguous properties to protect values and to permit efficient, large scale management, an element in its success." Moreover, the Housing Association implored "the people of Philadelphia . . . to establish a program of rehabilitation" by which "they should first recognize that the public powers of eminent domain are involved, and therefore there must be some public agency to administer the powers in the public interest."[60]

In their support for a designated Black housing project, the James Weldon Johnson Homes, the ever conscientious reformers could not recall for their readership that the James Weldon Johnson homes had displaced more Black residents than it housed; and yet they congratulated the homes through a cost-benefit analysis that defined the cost of displacement against the gains in public health and safety: "Only the 54 units added in 1943 to the James Weldon Johnson Homes and a part of the 2,230 temporary units are open to Negroes. The number of newly converted dwellings made available to Negroes is not exactly known, but is probably more than offset by displacements resulting from demolitions and from combinations for reasons of public health and safety." Here, the violence of eminent domain was unleashed through an erasure and unaccountability for the number of Black lives adversely affected by the removal of "blighted" communities and justified through the logic of enhanced safety. Razing communities created deep and lasting trauma in the dense affective social worlds of what outsiders register as "Negro slums," with their own visions of social-spatial identity and futurity.

Richard Allen Homes, the first public housing project in Philadelphia to be associated explicitly with clearance of "slum," was built in 1942. The area of eight blocks between Fairmount Avenue, Poplar Street, and Ninth and Twelfth Streets was occupied by 593 buildings and replaced by 1,324 dwellings in 58 separate buildings, and although the garden-style development had been designed to improve the lives of the neighborhood's Black residents, it helped to further concentrate impoverished Black people into a necrotic geography that 1937 Home Owners' Loan Corporation maps had already designated as uninsurable.

In support of eminent domain, the Housing Association recommended a recapitalization of the City Planning Commission, which would become the city's primary agency dedicated to transforming the city's landscape along with the Public Housing Authority in the decades that followed. As the authors of the 1940 report lamented, "The City Planning Commission, the logical body to undertake the is function [coordinating efforts], has been without funds from some years and has become entirely inactive."[61] The commission, which had been an outgrowth of a 1941 National Conference on Planning held in the city, had briefly worked under Mayor Lumberton to amass technical knowledge to best administer the city, building on the by then redundant Tri-State Regional Planning Federation, which folded in the same year.

Subsequently, the City Planning Commission was granted such power, and between the 1940s and 1950s, it began to plot the redevelopment of the city using the power of eminent domain, which in the long term further exacerbated the concentration of Black communities in the city's districts with the highest risk. Building on the local desire to reorder the central city, which I have charted as beginning in the vision of elite planners in the 1920s, and with federal power and money filling its sails, the City Planning Commission, via its "Quality Housing Survey," outlined the districts that were in need of radical revision beginning in 1949 and the subsequent plans, between 1950 and 1960, for redevelopment of various areas. These plans were again envisioned ultimately through a concern for price stability rather than the well-being of residents; and yet they mobilized the notion that space could be used to reform slum dwellers into normative citizens.

The redevelopment of Society Hill, considered among the Philadelphia Planning Commission's most successful ventures, highlights the class and racial orientation of the vision of planning that Bacon and others articulated. The district, which had been a fashionable area in the nineteenth century, by the 1930s had rescinded into what planners described simply as a slum. As Bacon described in a later oral history, the area before its redevelopment had "no life there" and was "an amorphous mess."[62] Between the 1890s and 1930, Society Hill had shifted from being a primarily residential neighborhood to an area that also contained light industry and the city's primary market-distribution center. Its colonial and nineteenth-century housing stock had deteriorated, and many of the housing units had been converted for other uses or subdivided into small apartments. Modern aesthetic features had been added, including stucco and PermaStone that covered flemish bond bricks and other features that Bacon and the Planning Commission wanted to recover through preservation. As part of the wider Washington Square East Redevelopment area, Society Hill was also important for its proximity to a number of symbolic and historic buildings, including Independence Hall and the buildings that once housed the First and Second Banks of the United States. These historic buildings had been previously remade through the efforts of Edwin O. Lewis, the judge who had created the Independence Hall Association. In his introduction to a March 1967 pamphlet describing Society Hill's redevelopment, Bacon wrote that "the purpose of the city's efforts to restore Society Hill was to assure preservation of some of the nation's priceless historic treasures" by creating "an environment that would inspire families to move back into these old houses and restore them by their own efforts."[63] Unlike earlier efforts to simply ameliorate the conditions of housing for the poor, the Society Hill redevelopment project, pioneered by Bacon, explicitly sought to displace poor Black residents to make the district "fashionable" again so that middle-class and upper-class white residents would be attracted back to the area. This, in Bacon's estimation, was a rational economic decision, because only wealthy homeowners could afford to engage in the necessary work of restoring their houses to colonial styles. The redevelopment of Society Hill explicitly placed within the domain of planning the displacement of what were viewed as non-generative social forms, inviting normative white families of means to inhabit redesigned spaces.

By the mid-1950s, local cultural producers bought into these remapped visions of the city and conjoined them with America's place in a singular "global" world.[64] This constituted a definition of health and life tethered to the emerging geography of American production and consumption, against the stark relief of *other* places and times.[65] In 1955, for example, cinematographer Ralph Lopatin, writer and narrator Dick McCutchen, and producer and director Cal Jones of WPTZ shot a business propaganda film about Philadelphia they called "Miracle on the Delaware." The film served as an extended commercial that cast the television station as a progenitor of a newly emergent way of life. The film showcased the city as a jewel of industrial productivity and modern living. Framed as a conversation between McCutchen and a newborn, an able-bodied white boy who the audience is to presume is crying about the threat of a communist future, the film opens with a question that the montage and the overlaid voice seek to answer through the entirety of the nine-minute clip: "What comprises this greater Philadelphia area?" The answers to this question quell the crying infant, assuring his healthy and "secure future" in the productivity, efficiency, and modernity of "the American lifestyle." The infant is secure because he lives in a place defined by material abundance and a socio-spatial arrangement conducive to the dictates of health and ability that had emerged by the mid-1950s.

The filmmakers offset the secure future of health, vitality, and quietude that the white infant will inherit as his provenance in the productive, distributive, and consumptive superiority of American capitalism above other worlds that remain largely at the edges of the film. Of course, this film, like so many other cultural artifacts of the 1950s, is directly inflected in pitched ideological battle with Soviet propaganda about the capacity of one way of life to outperform the other. Not surprisingly, the narrator implies that workers who live in territories under Soviet influence do not enjoy the same standard of living as the newborn.

This is, however, not the central metaphor that contrasts with the life of the infant. It is a more proximate other that proves essential to the definition of his life and future as healthy in the neat parcel of suburban space where he lives. Although the filmmakers frame the announced WPTZ region around the largest potential market—Philadelphia— images of the weathered city itself are limited. In contrast with the full pans of Levittown, images of the vernacular architectural edits on Philadelphia's classic row houses are noticeably absent, with the exception of the final sweeping scene of antennas that reinforces the television station's projection of a region around its capacity to reach homes by analog signal. The longest scene that the filmmakers present of the city is what McCutchen refers to as the "wild, weird, and beautiful spectacle" of the Mummer's Day parade, South Philadelphia's New Year's festival. Residents of the city whirl about in elaborate red-face and black-face minstrel costumes while a Black mother and her children cheer them from their perch on the sidewalk.[66] The bodies of the woman and her children among those playfully and performatively crossing the racialized boundaries between bodies visually reproduce and ideologically support a border/limit within the larger-scale geography of the WPTZ region. The media station reinforced the dominant monetary evaluation of value in postwar American space because this arrangement aligned with the potential regional ad market.[67] Racial and class differences are here interpenetrated and presented as self-evident in the spectacle of Blackness as outside the boundaries of the metropolitan region at the same time that they are geographically and metaphorically central. The overdetermined Black city geographically underwrites the healthy and vital white suburb.[68]

4

The Peace Mission Movement and Black Queer Urbanism in Philadelphia

Pearly Manager embodied the United States' enduring plantation relations. A fifty-five-year-old man from the South living with his unnamed wife in Philadelphia, Pearly Manager had lost an eye and most of his teeth and was suffering some combination of emphysema and congestive heart failure when Arthur Huff Fauset interviewed him as part of his research for *Black Gods of the Metropolis* in the early 1940s.[1] In the world the Managers inhabited, straddling the South and Up South, a regime of debilitation meted out in the rhythms of intergenerational hunger, ramshackle housing, labor insecurity, and quotidian violence reigned over Black life.[2] Debilitation is distinctive from disability, naming an active process of "endemic" bodily harm and unmaking that is reserved for subsets of the population marked as outside the bounds of

Figure 4.1. Holy Communion Table, Divine Lorraine Hotel, Philadelphia

the social-spatial continuity of race and nation. Debility and debilitation account for "expected impairments," those routinized and managed as part of the operation of the biopolitical-necropolitical state nexus, the function within capitalism of racialized disposability, disproportionate exposure, and premature death.[3] Working-class Black migrants from the South like Pearly inhabited Philadelphia's crumbling core housing, whose designation as "dead" by city planners, architects, and politicians served only to entrench its slow deterioration and the ensuing racial antagonism and aggravated intracommunal tensions.

Maiming and debilitation were part of the effects of the heated and dense worlds that segregation built. Yet in straddling two worlds—in the spatial sense of mobility between but most significantly in their epistemological sense of a shared migrant consciousness enacted in and through the processes of movement, stasis, confinement, and plotting— ordinary Black people like the Managers attempted to transfigure and to partially realize enduring small- and large-scale edits on Philadelphia's landscape. Pearly, rather than accepting passively a fate of violent conditioning, took his life into his own hands. As he recalled, he "drank and smoked to his heart's content." This outlook, this attempt to seize a highly situated form of bodily autonomy—one that we might register as futile or self-destructive—was tied, however, to a larger outlook, a vision of personal liberation embracing the territory of the illicit and the shadowy gatherings of the underground and threatening to corrupt the orderly geographies proposed by dominant urban futurists. In addition to smoking and drinking at his own pace, Pearly generated a large amount of money "doing quite well as a bootlegger" in the 1920s and 1930s, distilling and distributing illegal alcohol for profit. Pearly's disregard for the law and his pleasure in doing what he wanted with his body indexed the creed of werk—an alternative vision of labor, productivity, and profitability outside the rubrics prescribed within normative growth schema. While often still privileging personal or familial gain over other modes of collectivity and politics, werk rearranges, in time, space, and priority, leisure, productive labor, and social reproduction. Early in life, Pearly found in the underground a sense of mobility, autonomy, and possibility that were generally closed to working-class Black southern migrants in so-called legitimate businesses and institutions in the South and in Philadelphia.

Later in life, pacified by the sudden onset of a likely mortal condition and forced to give up his life as a bootlegger, Manager heard with fresh ears his wife's calls for him to change his life. One day, at the "precise time his wife heard that Father Divine would be in Philadelphia having meetings" he was "struck" by the name of Father Divine. His wife inquired, "There is one tonight. When do you think you will go?," to which he responded, "I'm going this very night." They attended the meeting at 1207 South Forty-Sixth Street near Cedar Park, a row house converted to a worship space by the Peace Mission in the upper part of Southwest Philadelphia.

Despite Fauset's engagement with Pearly, it was his unnamed wife whose prior knowledge of and encounters with the Peace Mission illuminated the path toward this congregation and away from sickness and death. It was she who "heard" Divine would be in town—indexing a network of geographic and social knowledge unrecoverable because of Fauset's primary engagement with Pearly. This was unlikely a directly pedestrian encounter given the narrative of traversal Pearly recalled to heighten that the Peace Mission brought them into a new neighborhood with which they were previously unfamiliar. The unnamed wife possessed a map of the city; Fauset's ethnographic notes index a relation to space likely generated in intersubjective consciousness deriving collective meaning from encounter, exchange, and meaning-making around place.

Facing down death, Pearly was eager to discover the healing power of Divine. On their way, he walked a block ahead of his wife, driven by anxiety and anticipation. Just as they boarded the trolley heading toward the Peace Mission's church, Pearly recalled uttering a quiet prayer to himself, asking, "God, please prove to me that Father Divine is God by directing me right to that meeting." Alerted by the conductor for their stop at Forty-Sixth and Woodlawn Avenue, they made their way nervously to the meeting. They were not only uneasy about the future of Pearly's health but also worried that they were in the wrong place. As they approached, they remained skeptical about the likelihood that Father Divine's meetings would be held in such "a fine neighborhood" near the University of the Sciences. Finally locating the address and noting their impression as they approached the distinguished looking "big house," the Managers stepped out on faith, turning the knob and trusting that if it was indeed the place they sought, the congregation Manager felt he needed so desperately, the door would open without a key.[4]

As the door opened, "Peace!" rang out from a voice from upstairs, some unseen person hailing them into the new order with the most common greeting of Divine's followers. Although Pearly Manager and his wife came to see Father Divine, he was not there. Yet his believers continued with the worship service. During the service, Pearly locked eyes with an image of Divine. As he later recalled, all the pain left his body, and his nasal passage opened so that he could take what felt like his first full breaths since the iron knot began forming in his stomach. Although Pearly attributed his healing to his viewing of Father Divine's photograph, this object, like other sacred representations, acquired its power only through the significations, symbols, and ceremony of the ordinary people forming the body of the Peace Mission movement. The congregation, defined by healing and peace and formally by belief in Divine's divinity, created transfigurative energy, and in the name and absence of Father Divine the man, they cultivated a world within a world, one promising a defense against and a future outside of the enduring debilitating and death-dealing relations of slavery and its afterlives in the claustrophobic world segregated neighborhoods.

This is not to sanitize the encounter of perhaps troublesome enactment of the "charismatic scenario" reinforcing masculine authority along familiar lines of patriarchal authority attributed to the Father. It is to note the forms of spatial knowing—the unnamed wife's unrecoverable but acknowledged encounters with the Peace Mission and her desire to join prior to her husband's desire; the couple's movement across unchartered urban neighborhoods and the heightened experience of segregation punctuating the discovery of the service in a different neighborhood; the disembodied voice of a congregant calling out Peace; and the experiences with the ecstatic congregation singing and praying in Divine's absence—that ground this experience of Black metaphysics. Divine and his image serve as vehicles of bodily and spiritual transformation among the many, his power a composite of their desires for healing and peace and the power effect of his strategic performance and negotiation of these desires to generate mass appeal.[5]

Like many of the others who crossed from the world into the spaces of the Peace Mission and similar organizations, the Managers, especially

Pearly, were transformed spiritually through their shift from one form of disreputable congregation, that of the street and the underground, to another one equally marked—that of the so-called cult. While Judith Weisenfeld has raised generative challenges to this characterization of the cult, what is of great interest to me given the central focus of this book is the rogue urban phenomenology enacted in the consciously embodied transit across the threshold between the underground and the spaces of a community of worshippers set apart by their commitment to peace and abundance, as well as the dissonance enacted in the futures proposed by these congregants as well as the knowledge of where to find it which was according to Pearly the possession of his unnamed wife. The combined physical and metaphysical experience of traversal and transit between diametrically opposed worlds enacted through various folds of practical and experience-derived interpretations of space underwrote transformations in personal and collective identity and generated alternative futurescapes prickly and discordant with the rubrics of standard living.

The Managers were transformed in this passage from the world of hustlers and bootleggers to their new space among the flock of the set-apart. They became devotees of Divine, renouncing their sexual relationship, indeed their marriage in its old form for the new commitment of siblings under their Father. They began to "treat each other as brother and sister" and although they continued to cohabitate and sleep in the same bed for a time, they did not touch one another in the carnal sense. Eventually, according to Pearly, a ridge formed deep in the center of the bed, causing his wife to find a new place to rest in the housing they shared now as brother and sister rather than husband and wife. The Managers went so far as to abdicate responsibility for his children, likely above the age of sixteen—the age through which Divine required followers to care for any progeny they had before joining his flock. Pearly reported that he and his wife had children but that he was "not concerned about them, because 'each tub must stand on its own bottom.'"[6]

This reconceived matrimonial home in which the Managers, as followers of Divine, lived as brother and sister and Pearly's concession of his children's spiritual future possess critical elements of Black queer urbanism. Given the centrality of the home—that freighted construct held to reproduce normal social and economic life within the architectural and planning discourses consolidating in 1940s Philadelphia—the Managers' decisions to dislocate from this model is notable. Recall from the previous chapter how reformers, planners, architects, politicians, and others who invested in the city as a growth machine fashioned the home as a primary site in the architectures of neighborhoods, cities, and regions. They used housing and its design, up and out from the intimate spaces of bedrooms, to theorize the reproduction of properly gendered subjects tamed in their hetero-monogamous affiliations and developing along a normative trajectory from childhood to future breadwinners and housewives out across generations into the unending horizon of theoretically stable capitalist relations.

In this context, the Managers' decision to live as siblings rather than as husband and wife, their embrace of asexuality, their dissolution of what the predominant societies, Black and white, considered an indissoluble bond—that of parent and child—and their channeling of these energies into spiritual healing and ecstatic worship signaled a powerful edit on the horizon of the city. In moving from one set of dark agoras, those of the underground, to the set-apart spaces of Black esoteric religiosity, the Managers, like many others, plotted a vision for the world outside compulsory reproductive futurity: they reorganized life along lateral connections in the present and engaged in heavenly peace on earth, defined by the melting of hierarchy, conflict, and most of all, a satiating abundance. Pearly Manager's and his wife-turned-sister's commitments to a future of peace and healing in the name, if not the physical presence, of Divine subverted their other connections to the social world, making them agents of an alternative temporality and spatial ordering, that of the set-apart kingdom on earth—a figuration set beside, up against, and on top of the world and often in heated tension with the underground and the agents of order seeking to contain or displace all forms marked as insurgent Black life from the city.[7]

In this chapter, I historicize the efforts of Father Divine's Peace Mission movement and examine the group's fashioning of insurgent modes of social belonging wherein they defied customary and de jure segregation and violence and began to articulate a new vision of the future based in peace. I take together their heterodox visions of futurity and their odd spatial and temporal logics as a quintessential form of Black queer urbanism—again, various projects interrupting critical aspects of the dominant urbanist growth paradigm that emerged to reinforce gendered racial capitalism after the Great Depression. Adherents of the mission sought to remake property as a collective asset, disarticulating it from blood and familial transmission. They embarked on a program of collective purchasing across nascent metropolitan-scapes within deteriorating spaces in the urban core as well as surreptitiously in exclusive neighborhoods like the one that disoriented the Managers. The flock rehabilitated and reorganized the real estate they acquired for alternatively imagined use that was responsive and adapted to their cosmological and social outlooks, and through this process, they articulated reciprocal relationships between individual, community, and property under a novel paradigm of stewardship.

The cultural subtext of the aesthetic and social outlook characterizing much of the Peace Mission's theology represented an extension and transformation of the outlook born of the plot in the context of plantation and post-plantation Black life (chapter 1). The Peace Mission extended and formalized the outlook of the plot partially by enacting the cosmic break of heaven on earth millenarianisms articulated in the varying spaces of Black ecstatic religiosity under slavery and in its aftermath. It also drew directly on the grammar of feasting in its enactments of earthly satiation through the rituals and ceremony of the daily "Holy Communion" feasts held at each outpost of heaven on earth as well as banquets and feasts in their new ritual calendar. The highly stylized and ritualized communion table evidences what Imani Perry underscores in the context of the "Black National Anthem" as part of the tradition of Black formalism to emphasize the ritual worlds created by Black communities to sustain grace and resilience in the face of degrading and dehumanizing in justice.[8] The abundance that defined the shared dining tables of the flock drew its symbolic cogence directly from photographs and descriptions of the "Promised Land," a series of collectively owned and operated farms north of New York City that resonated with the migrant generations' outlook straddling two worlds.

* * *

In the period between the 1920s and 1960s, the Peace Mission, an organization of devotees of the esoteric teachings of Reverend Major M. J. Divine, or Father Divine, transformed various edifices in emergent metropolitan districts in the United States, including New York, New-ark, Philadelphia, Baltimore, San Francisco, and Los Angeles. The Peace Mission bought and remade twelve or more major properties between 1939 and 1952 in the Philadelphia region, transforming through their labor what were dilapidated, damaged, and abandoned properties. The men who adhered to Divine's teachings used their skills as carpenters and masons to create what observers repeatedly described as distin-guished spaces. At the same time, the Peace Mission bought properties in exclusive sections of these metropolitan regions, opening what had once been exclusive and segregated hotels and other spaces into ones accessible to working-class Black beachgoers, vacationers, and worship-ers; recall here the Managers' disorientation—their expectation that even God in the body of a Black man would be unlikely to have a church in such a "big house" in a small neighborhood containing few if any other Black homes or institutions.

Most of the Peace Mission's expansion in Philadelphia occurred after 1940, in an era during which the organization's dedicated membership began to decline in the broader movement. The height of the Peace Mission was during the Depression in Harlem, when the lavish spaces and banquets of the congregants competed with a number of other reli-gious and political movements, including the Garvey movement, Daddy Grace's House of Prayers, and famously, Reverend Lightfoot Solomon Michaux. Father Divine's movement, beginning in Georgia in the 1920s, appealed with food and fellowship directly to poor Black people facing hunger and economic destitution. At its peak in the mid-1930s while centered in Harlem, Divine's followers likely exceeded fifty thousand, and the Peace Mission's real estate holdings reached millions of dollars in value, with over 150 missions nationwide.[9] Despite a decline in mem-bership, the Peace Mission amassed and retained $885,000 in taxable assets by 1957.[10] In Philadelphia, adherents of the Peace Mission bought and transformed a network of churches and training schools in North, South, and West Philadelphia, the Divine Lorraine Hotel at Broad and Fairmont, the Divine Tracy Hotel near the University of Pennsylvania, twelve gender-specific live-in spaces, and various small businesses orga-nized cooperatively. They used these spaces to articulate alternative for-mulations of belonging, community, and collectivity outlined through the teachings of their Father. The flocked used these spaces to embody and practice the peaceful heaven on earth they believed Divine was calling forth.

In December 1943, the Unity Mission, Inc., purchased property owned by the Pennsylvania Railroad that had been used primarily as a YMCA at Forty-First Street and Westminster Avenue in West Philadelphia. The property was in a dilapidated state and had been "badly vandalized." Although the property was apparently in disrepair, the newly formed Unity Mission Church, Home and Training School, incorporated to inhabit and make use of the space under the auspices of the Peace Mission, employed a group of its members, trained in various trades, to restore the building. The community in which the building stood had in an earlier era been a relatively prosperous working-class ethnic white community. By the middle of the 1940s, however, it had been taken up primarily by recent Black migrants from the South. As Marcus Hunter illustrates, West Philadelphia and North Philadelphia were appropriated by what he calls Black citymakers, who extended new communities rather than simply being displaced.[11]

On March 20, 1945, Celestine Fulchon, a resident, teacher, and activist in the West Philadelphia community surrounding the Unity Mission Church at Forty-First Street and Westminster Avenue, attended the weekly Righteous Government Banquet to honor Divine and the Peace Mission for their efforts in restoring a key resource in what the city had come to see as simply a deteriorating neighborhood and community. Fulchon noted that she had "worked in this community for twenty years," during which time, residents repeatedly "told them down at the city hall, that in this community we need a building like this for all Americans." Prior to the efforts of the Peace Mission's cadre of men who restored the building, as Fulchon explained, the community's twenty thousand school-aged children had no "place between the Schuylkill River and Forty-Seventh Street and the railroad and Market Street to play and exercise themselves." Further, she had helped to organize "several thousand names while this building stood idle" which the community presented to the chairman of the city's Finance Committee, but all to no avail. Further, as she noted, the district had been noted as having the highest level of juvenile crime, and yet the city told the community members who approached them about remaking the old YMCA that it could not be reconditioned for use.[12]

Despite the efforts of Black citymakers to actively remake the city, Philadelphia through the early 1940s remained politically recalcitrant.[13] Then, with the rise of planning in the 1940s, Black spatial and urban thought remained largely demoted outlooks, marked as idiosyncrasies that were expected to disappear with the clearing of the slum and the rehabilitation of Black life through the imposition of the home and the extended spaces of the neighborhood, which were theorized to create a stable future population.

The Peace Mission had restored the building to full use and opened it to people irrespective of their racial identities, substituting community institutions in the wake of public abandonment and after a line of political mobilization directed at the city failed to produce results. At the edge of disinvestment, a border region erected in the city where social malaise and economic hardship created a necrotic zone, an area that police and planners viewed through its rate of delinquency, the Peace Mission revitalized a structure and appropriated the edifice as an alternative infrastructure of community, one capable of serving "all Americans." While in our modern post–Black Power political context and in the era of Black Lives Matter, the concern for including "all Americans" may sound naïvely integrationist, in the context of 1940s Philadelphia, before even the sanction of the 1954 charter for formal equality, this remained an explosive position associated with subversion and perversion. Philadelphia, especially in the neighborhood where the Peace Mission restored an abandoned YMCA, was riven in this period by racist exclusion and violence against Black people as white residents claimed collective ownership over homes and public space.

The Peace Mission used collective ownership and collective labor to create novel spaces that were shocking in their disregard for racial mores and that refused to concede Black abjection and austerity in the built environment at a time when the majority of Black communities across the nation were confined to poor housing. On August 8, 1944, for example, Peaceful Nimrod wrote to Divine about the July 30 opening of a new Mission in Oakland, California. After thanking Divine for the "blessing you gave to Oakland," Nimrod wrote, "Father Dear Lord the entire building has been redeemed inside and out and made beautifully clean in every corner and so artistic."[14] An unaddressed letter from an adherent based in Richmond, California, wrote on August 23, 1944, and confirmed the splendor of the new mission.[15] And, on August 9, 1944, Wonderful Sincere Grace wrote "thanking for the mission was rescued it looks so nice and you are certainly sending the people in to eat."[16] Similar to South, North, and West Philadelphia, between 1940 and 1950, as Oakland's Black population quintupled, the percentage of the city's black residents in West Oakland moved from 60 percent of the total to 80 percent.[17] The mission's local adherents in the San Francisco Bay Area, whom Nimrod called Father Divine's "unified children," rehabilitated a property in this section of deindustrializing cityscape defined by concentrated Black residency.

On February 15 and 16, 1947, the Peace Mission held a series of services and banquets to show to the wider world their work to transform spaces across Philadelphia into heavens on earth. At three o'clock in the afternoon on the fifteenth, the organization held a banquet and "Dedicatory Services" at the Unity Mission Church, Home and Training School, a large and handsome two-story stone gothic-style institutional church directly adjoining a major railroad thruway in West Philadelphia. At nine o'clock on the same evening, the Peace Mission hosted an opening and dedication service and a "Holy Communion Dedicatory Service" at a newly opened mission that was housed in a four-story neoclassical mansion transformed into Unity Mission Church, Home and Training School, and Bible Institute at 1530 North Sixteenth Street in North Central Philadelphia. On the following morning between 10 a.m. and 10 p.m., the Nazareth Mission Church and Training School at 1600–1614 Oxford Street (which no longer remains) opened its doors for "Inspection" so that all could bear witness to the splendid remaking of these properties through the dedication and labor of the people who dedicated themselves to a life of service in the Peace Mission.[18]

The Peace Mission mobilized the often surreptitious purchasing of collective property fronting its white membership as those engaged in the transaction and threatening racial and class exclusion after purchasing mansions, hotels, and other exclusively white and elite spaces to extend heaven on earth. In addition to these smaller properties, Peace Mission members also collectively transformed large luxury properties. To purchase the Divine Lorraine Hotel at the intersection of Broad Street and Fairmount Avenue in North Philadelphia, four hundred devotees of the Peace Mission pledged and put forward $1,000 each. Through this collective venture, they raised the requisite $400,000 to purchase the building that had previously served as a racially exclusive property just north of the city's central business district, first as a residential building after it opened in the 1880s and then as a hotel before the group's purchase. The Divine Lorraine and the Divine Tracey near the University of Pennsylvania accommodated ordinary people irrespective of race or class within the comforts of a luxurious interior as long as they did not defy the organization's prohibition against men and women sharing a room and bed. Although devotees renamed the hotel to suggest ownership by Divine, Divine technically held no deeds to these hotels or to any other property. These properties remained collectively owned by the four hundred original pledgers and the trusteeship of the Peace Mission through the early 2000s.[19]

In New Jersey, the Peace Mission used this collective ownership model to acquire luxurious properties, facing down explicitly racist violence as well as state action, both of which sought to uphold racially and class segregated leisure on the Jersey Coast. In the course of 1942, following the collective purchase of the exclusive six-dollar-per-night, six-story Brigantine Hotel, a controversy erupted. At the time, the Brigantine was the largest structure on the island near Atlantic City, and several of Divine's white followers had contributed collectively to the movement by paying the hotel's back taxes. White islanders and Black and white hotel owners were terrified of the possibilities for raucous interracial intercourse promised by the Divinites and the two-dollar-per-week rates. After a storm in March of the same year wiped out a portion of the boardwalk leading up to a pavilion affiliated with the grand hotel, the city attempted to simply abandon it. Divinites, of course, responded in and through the conviction that if Father Divine wanted a boardwalk, he would simply build his own.[20] In a follow-up by the state to discontinue the collective ownership by Father Divine's followers in 1943, the city attempted to reassess the property value and raise the taxes some 1,000 percent.[21] Only after the adherents of the Peace Mission resorted to public protests did the city relax the dramatic hike. In March 1944, the Ku Klux Klan burned a cross on the lawn of the thirty-room mansion previously known as the Grove Estate of Riverton, New Jersey. This was also not limited to New Jersey, and indeed, the Krum Elbow scandal, when Divinites purchased an estate directly across from the Hudson River from President Franklin Delano Roosevelt, was inflamed by the fact that the Peace Mission sought to integrate exclusive properties. In 1947, when Divine's followers sought to repurpose Hammond Morgan's twenty-seven room mansion in Los Altos, California, into another West Coast Heaven, the Los Altos Businessmen's Association galvanized enough support that the owner sold the property to someone else for less than the Peace Mission adherents offered.[22]

As the case of the Divine Lorraine Hotel demonstrates, the Peace Mission's expressed commitment to the economic independence of its members structured the ways that the organization procured these properties. First, to become a true follower of the Peace Mission, adherents had to settle any former debts and begin "paying as one goes." Next, followers were required to provide for any children younger than sixteen years of age. Finally, members were expected to refrain from using money in any sort of "gambling, smoking, drinking, drugs, unevangelical entertainment," stock or bond purchases, insurance coverage, or the hoarding of money. Freeing oneself from what Divine prohibited as the misuse of money, associated with greed and life in the darkness of the underground, the world of drinking, drugs, smoking, gambling and *the unevangeligcal*, would allow members to remain independent and perhaps, if they desired, to contribute to the Mission Cooperative System, through which the Peace Mission collectively pooled resources for the purchase of more properties in the 1950s. Prior to the full articulation of the Mission Cooperative System, Divine maintained consistently that the money flowing through the Peace Mission's coffers were not given by parishioners without the return of some tangible service or merchandise. And indeed, gifting was officially forbidden within the organization. As Divine pronounced it in a June 1935 message delivered specifically to the *Baltimore Afro-American*, "In reference to any person in connection with MY organization giving ME money without receiving something tangible for same, as merchandise in our stores, food in our restaurants, dresses in our dress shops or factories, or some tangible practical service given them is absolutely unfounded."[23]

The 1936 Righteous Government Platform of the Peace Mission, which developed out of the convention held in Harlem January 10–12, 1936, rhetorically anchored these properties to an entire economic system of production, distribution, and consumption orchestrated under the "Divine" Plan that would, according to Divine, replace strife with peace. Divine was fundamentally opposed to the New Deal, Franklin Delano Roosevelt's expansion of federal programming under the principles of economist John Keynes emphasizing the stabilization of capitalism through investments in demand through basic guarantees for the (white) working class. Divine argued that the New Deal would create a form of dependency that would be dangerous in the long run to (Black) working-class communities. Divine's plan called for protections and guarantees from physicians and the state-required insurance, "Equal Opportunity"—including the punishment of exclusionary labor unions, full employment through a reactivation of industrial production in spite of the Depression, a disbanding of all legal and extralegal impediments inscribed through "race," and fairness in all economic transactions. The plan, in short, sought to break with state dependency and lower prices and to make everyone prosperous.[24]

Under this alternative constitution, the Peace Mission's notion of property as a collective resource was reciprocal with its grand mission of spreading earthly peace. The accretion of the missions and heavens, would help the joyful cries of the followers to echo peace and to transform the atmosphere and thus the ways that humans related. As a publication by Mother Divine noted, this collective use of money for the purchasing of properties would be used for "the advancement of FATHER DIVINE'S Work and Mission, thereby putting the money to exchange for the common good of humanity."[25] As the second Mother Divine had to spell out in her 1982 defense of the work and the teachings, "A group of followers holds title to the property with the right of survivorship, but if and when it is sold, as many properties have been, the living owners share equally the amount received from the sale. Father and Mother Divine own no properties or securities of any kind." "The followers," she went on, "pay real estate and other taxes as levied . . . . The owners have not sought tax exemption on privately owned properties," and "properties owned by the Churches and operated solely in the service of the Church and the community are tax exempt."[26]

The understanding that Divine did not own property was contested throughout his life, and he was often labeled a charlatan. A May 1965 *Ebony* magazine exposé authored by Ruth Boas, a thirty-year member of the Peace Mission, reported that in fact, Divine accepted all the incomes from his "fully consecrated" members. Thus, while he might not officially own anything, she charged that he made millions of dollars from those who worked to contribute their full incomes to the Peace Mission over decades of their lives.[27] Indeed, the earlier scholarly literature on the Peace Mission emphasized that Divine was simply duping his followers and engorging his coffers with their often hard won finances. As late as 1982, scholar of Black religion and intellectual history William Jeremiah Moses described Divine as on par with the other "opportunistic, egoistic charlatans, who elevated themselves for purposes of self-aggrandizement."[28] Indeed, the earliest body of works about the Peace Mission and Divine described him as some combination of sensational cult leader and charismatic charlatan.[29] Engendered in the power to ascribe Divine with divinity was actually the ascription of value to productive and reproductive labor remade for communal spaces that held the capacity to feed and house a blend of ordinary people. The magic or the miracle, then, was an effect of the reengineered communal relations grounded in the infrastructures of heaven on earth, the labor of the dedicated women and men who sought stable housing of the missions, the conflict-free world of peace under Divine's reign, and the abundant food of the communion table. Centered in Philadelphia and surrounding communities but extending across the United States, the Peace Mission collectively purchased and remade both deteriorating and exclusive properties to reenvision the basis for community through collective stewardship and cooperative economics rather than individual or corporate profit. The Peace Mission remade property into a collective asset and employed the labor of dedicated adherents of Father Divine's esoteric teachings to transform the various structures, in various states of soundness, across Philadelphia's Black communities, in exclusive luxury destinations on the Jersey Coast, and out to Oakland and beyond. The Peace Mission appropriated and reimagined the uses of various kinds of structures ranging from segregated hotels to former institutional church buildings with white congregations, row houses, and dilapidated YMCA buildings as part of the architecture of heaven on earth. In the next section, I examine the spiritual nature of these efforts at re-creating the architectures of heaven on earth.

Spiritual Appropriation and the Remaking of Human Relations

The Peace Mission re-created spaces to bring about earthly transformation. As folklorist Leonard Norman Primiano posits, "Especially significant about the Peace Mission's expression of perfection is that they did not seek perfection by building environments of their own creation, but instead, in the words of Father Divine, they sought to '[bring] perfection' to structures already constructed. The movement created a unique religious vernacular architecture not by architectural design, but by a spiritualized appropriation of existing spaces."[30] This spiritualized appropriation laid the foundations for transformative relationships and the reengineering of the basic infrastructure of human sociality. The repair and rehabilitation of the building was not simply a matter of repairing the neighborhood but served the Peace Mission's wider mission of transformative community, a process that moved out from the city block to the wider universe. At the consecration of the new Unity Mission Church on December 20, 1944, a year after it was purchased, Divine delivered a sermon that demonstrated how this type of work to reclaim neighborhood spaces would shake the foundations of the unjust world that the disrepair signaled. Divine preached:

> I am changing not only the tides of governmental affairs, but changing the hearts and minds and characteristics and the dispositions of the children of men, bringing them into subjection to a supernatural presence that cometh not with observation! By this we shall have a Righteous Government and every adverse and undesirable system of men shall eventually be completely wiped out! I do not come representing races, creeds, nor colors, for every such expression of divisibility will eventually bring you misery, disappointment and failure. But as you hear ME say my composition and my inspiration in the actuated words of expression, "UNITY MISSION" this church in its name is bearing witness of itself in its characteristics, in disposition, in the very actuated words of expression. In this HOLY COMMUNION HALL where we are standing and sitting we expressing the MISSION'S name characteristically! Aren't you glad![31]

Divine argued that the Unity Mission Church "actuated words of expression because we mean to live our constitution and we also mean to live our religion, for they are synonymous in a Democracy like this one, where the very GOD of PEACE can and will and actually has sanctified you wholly!" Divine's pronouncements for the future enact a metaphysical crisis. They suggest the clearing of the world of any system threatening to ensnare people based on race or any other identifier attributed by society. Heaven on earth, although defined by a future horizon of peace, promises to "wipe out" any form of government mandating segregation and violence.

Although Divine credited himself with the miraculous collectivity of the Peace Mission, it is the communion table and the communion hall that he identifies as the site of the new world his adherents were practicing outside the evil of Jim Crow segregation. The central motif of the new theology was the communion table, which recenters the role of the First Mother Divine in the production of the miracles. Beginning in the organization's first spiritual center in Sayville, New York, in the 1920s and 1930s, she coordinated efforts to feed the parishioners, likely as important in amassing the early flock of believers as the preached sermons Divine offered. Communion banquets were codified in Article IV of the church constitution. The constitution drew on the Christian practice of Communion and extended it beyond its spiritual function as the means by which Christians symbolically demonstrate their faith in the resurrecting power of Jesus. For the members of the Peace Mission, the communion services were to occur daily "after the manner of the Lord's Supper" but also in recognition of the "practicality of our spiritual devotion and service to GOD and unto man." Like those of Paul's appointed deacons in the early church, the "Communion services were a happy and joyous event, more as a love feast or fraternal meal, rejoicing in the Presence of the Lord." Thus, Unity Mission resolved to hold daily meals "as practical service for the sustenance of our bodies and for the benefit of our souls, for our spiritual advancement and moral improvement," vowing to "put off the old man with the Adamic state of consciousness, and arise daily and walk in the newness of life."[32] In line with their commitment to the practical and spiritually transformational work of the Communion table, the Unity Mission stipulated that there was to be no compensation for the meals of the communion and that it was rather a "free gift to those who are worthy of receiving it, but let a man examine himself and see that none eat of it unworthily." Furthermore, the Peace Mission invited outsiders, "especially visitors of other Faiths and Denominations," to "participate in the Communion services if they wish to do so and if they are worthy." This, of course, opened the door on the daily communion feasts for people without the means to otherwise provide themselves with sustenance, in matters both of the body and of the spirit and soul.[33]

Here, Black women's creative and reproductive labor created the primary architecture organization—their work to prepare large quantities of food underwriting the communion table across the missions, sometimes in Father Divine's presence but more often than not in his physical absence. It is important to emphasize the creativity in this work. The communion table and the more elaborate banquet and anniversary feasts were not simple meals or flavor combinations; they were elaborate and labor-intensive productions that drew on the rich tapestry of Black women's knowledge of recipes and food to draw in the masses. As extant menus from banquets in Philadelphia demonstrate, the communion table was defined by abundance, the inverse of want. The most elaborate feasts included the service of multiple "salads"—"Asparagus Supreme; Ribbon Mold; Shrimp Grapefruit Spring Salad; Relish Plate; Lettuce Tomato Avocado"—diverse vegetable dishes—"Polynesian Rice; Confetti Shoe Peg Gorn; Crinckle Carrot Stiks; French Green Bean Almondine; Spinach Ring-Creamed Mushrooms; Cheese Breaded Cauliflower; Minted Peace; [and] Pickled Beets"—various breads—"Plain White Bread; Cracked Wheat; Pumpernickle; Jewish Rye; Raisin; Hollywood; Assorted Muffins; and Petite Fours" served with "Fancy Butter, Orange Marmalade; and Home Frozen Peaches"—as well as various meat dishes and accompaniment—"Cold Beef Tongue; Roasted Filet Mignon; Rack O' Lamb; Glazed Cornish Hens; Crab Cakes—Tartar Sauce; Roast Turkey; Stuffing; Cranberry Sauce; Gravy."[34]

In a sermon delivered on November 13, 1951, in Philadelphia titled "Kingdom of God Is Not Meat and Drink but Righteousness," Father Divine acknowledged, refuted, and then returned to an acknowledgment of the central symbolic power of the communion table in the group's meteoric rise and its steady if declining significance in terms of adherents by the 1950s. Divine acknowledged "in modesty" the "second to none" banquets and the "superlative" food that constituted the "material food" provided by the Peace Mission. However, he disavowed the elaborate feasts as the basis for the Peace Mission's power, attributing the material abundance of the elaborate communion banquet not to the women who created them but rather to consciousness of him as a materialization of God and underscoring his power as a spiritual presence of abundance preceding the feast. This symbolic sleight of hand enacts and recreates the grooves of the "charismatic scenario" truncating the sensorial and material experience of abundance through a remaking of the sumptuary order circuiting the various affective threads associated with commensality through the patriarchal figure utilizing these energies for the growth of the church. In the resolution of the sermon, however, Divine asks those in attendance to take their seats at the table as the Rosebud Choir sings "You Are Wonderful" in harmony over the clanking plates of food being passed and served. Divine refutes the symbolic and material significance of the labor of women in the Peace Mission embodied in the food and yet relies on it within the schema of the Peace Mission. The ritual around the communion table would also outlast Divine's physical life, continuing to anchor the schedule and calendar of elderly members into the 2010s.[35]

Black women, along with some white women, created this aesthetic of abundance at the communion meals, often in Father Divine's absence. At the invitations to the dedication of openings in West and North Philadelphia February 1947 mentioned above show, communions were the essential enactments of heaven on earth, the key means of reclaiming otherwise racially segregated spaces defined by dilapidation or exclusion, in opening a new mission and spreading heaven on earth. Father Divine blessed these meals, but he did not prepare them. Beginning in Georgia and later in Baltimore, Sayville, Harlem, Philadelphia, and beyond, Black women disciples prepared feasts to draw people into the folds of the flock, including the First Mother Divine, who fed the growing body that grew in the early Sayville mission. In this work, these women engaged in important if underappreciated intellectual work by theorizing new methods of collectivity and social reproduction that drew the plot into the communion table.

In its swirling smells and elaborate tastes, the sample menu above from one feast nearly a decade after Divine's earthly death invokes abundance, here a signifier not only of plenty but of a cartographic and social-spatial imaginary recalling variegated landscapes and waterscapes of the South and drawing forward the symbolic and material power of the plot. Hinted at in the accompaniment of "home frozen peaches," in this vast menu is the reality that these Black migrant women forward the sweetness of a land of peace immanently forthcoming that recalled the plot and the South. More directly, the communion table drew its symbolic coherence from the Peace Mission's efforts in the 1930s and 1940s to erect the "Promised Land." A series of outposts north of New York City, the Promised Land consisted of a number of cooperative farms operated and owned collectively by the Peace Mission in Westchester and Ulster Counties in New York. Many of the primary laborers were southern migrants who brought their knowledge of plant life to bear in producing the miracle of abundance. They planted vegetables and grain, raised chickens and various species of hens, pastured sheep, held hogs, and raised cattle for milk and meat. They created collective ownership, making all who worked in the name of Divine stewards. This is a critical reenactment of and extension of the plot as a robust imaginary seeking to transform the world. The cooperative farms of the Promised Land assured collective work and collective reaping, reestablishing use value and collectivity around the earth and in the symbiotic world of plant, animal, and human-animal life as a way out from the enduring violence of want and pressingly for Black adherents under Jim Crow's metabolic warfare. As I developed in the opening chapter, hunger and feasting formed the quotidian and embodied form of racial violence between slavery and Jim Crow and across southern and northern locations. Divine's unnamed secretaries strategically invoked the plot as well to appeal to the primarily Black public constituted around the New Day. They used images of Divine feeding farm animals including foul and lambs, standing next to bulls, and sitting on a white horse to invoke the powerful symbolism of the plot, a modality of power and social cohesion wherein Black communities could derive a wealth of food through small-scale subsistence, an intimacy with the dirt and with nonhuman animal life through animal husbandry. The imagery of the plot and its material and sensual abundance around the shared communion table extended the historical plot as a roving collective imaginary, adapting in its outlook and prospects to the context of the industrial metropolis, with its equally dangerous ecologies imprinted by plantation relations. A cognate of what Clyde Woods terms the blues epistemology, the plot as a mobile social outlook underwrote various Black gnostic outlooks wherein adherents embraced mystical leaders and in their presence and absence called for a radical remaking of the social-spatial-ecological relations that relegated Black life to living-in-death.

Photographs of the Promised Land gave coherence to the communion table, grounding abundance in an agrarian landscape echoing partially realized independent Black landholding in the South that began evaporating with the permanent agricultural price declines of the 1920s and the subsequent consolidation of agribusiness. Taken together, the menus and the reformulations of commensality they helped engender depended for their full power on the images of the god brought to earth—Divine feeds the lambs, stands by a bull, feeds the foul, and sits astride a white horse facing the camera head on. The plot underwrote new formulations for the reordering of social order, through the strange and new worlds of the new Black gods in the city. The invocation of the rural landscape for city dwellers, as well as the aesthetic and taste of over-abundance, drew on the imaginary of Black rurality for its proposals for a new order of being and power. The communion table gained its coherence in the symbolic world of Black migrants wherein the plot continued to supply the predominant metaphors of power, possibility, and transformation, a vernacular expressions recalling the plot echoing in and through Black urban modernity and the discordant autonomy of the cult.

In the name of a radically new societal order defined by peace, everlasting life on earth, and an end to strife and want, Black women collectivized their labor and resources along with others to draw in the flock. They subtly remade social order outside the dominant ordering of the sensorium around visuality, privileging observation, categorization, and segregation, through the guttural registers of mastication and swallowing, collectivities of bread-sharers. Eating food touched symbolically by God, adherents sought full satiation: spiritual transformation in and through bodily sustenance, ultimately the labor of women disciples. Thus, as much as the Peace Mission and other such groups represented unprecedented formulations for reordering the city and in practically transforming their earthly connections from racialized, classed, and gendered social hierarchy adherents embraced a form of abundance and fullness that drew on Black migrant vernacular expressions of the enduring plot as a challenge to dominion and mastery. Often expressed to describe a relationship with matters of spiritual wholeness and material well-being in their services, both words were made meaningful, in part because they invoked the fundamental metaphors of communion, the literal and symbolic sharing of food with God-come-to-earth. The pointed symbols of abundance in the live chickens of the plot and the roasted chicken passing through God's hands, as well as the symbols of mobility in a powerful wedding with the symbols of the historic plot, through the horse, closed the symbolic circuitry of Black metaphysical rebellion wherein they absconded the restrictions of poverty and property imposed through segregation and all of the world as it was, its conflicts of race, creed, religious doctrine, and domestic discord, its economic hardship and physical wearing of the body—for heaven on earth, defined by plenty of shared food passed through the hands of the savior returned. Despite the critical differences in the cosmological outlook that Mrs. W outlined (chapter 2), we see the shared enactment of Black metaphysical rebellion in quiet and confrontational enactments of violence on the social, spatial, and symbolic orders relegating Black life to death and violent dependency.

Abundance and fullness are an edit on the ceremonies built directly around the institutional Christian rites of the Eucharist. To take in the body of Christ is to constitute and regularly affirm Christian identity as "the body of Christ." The replay of the Last Supper, wherein Divine symbolically shared the food among his believers, was a particularly pointed symbol given the context of his ministry from the 1920s through the 1960s, a period defined by lynching. Divine's plan for righteous government, first drafted in 1936, included a forceful demand for the end to lynching. As Jill Watts insightfully recovers, lynching served as a central metaphor for the world of strife and violence that race and war built. In addition to protesting traditional lynchings, Divine and his believers defined the act capaciously as any public attack from white neighbors and legislators. In his earliest years ministering in Georgia and later in Sayville, Long Island, Divine deployed the language of lynching to castigate efforts of his detractors who took collective actions to remove him and his followers. Moreover, Divine's earliest devotees believed that their messenger had escaped a number of white lynch mobs, attributing scars on the back of his neck to the nooses they believed he had evaded. The

Peace Mission's symbolic transformation of the Eucharist inverted the depraved violence of white mobs killing and making souvenirs of Black bodies, and by the 1930s in Harlem, Divine was understood to be the earthly embodiment of God returned.[36]

The adherents of the Peace Mission, even in the absence of Divine himself, continually remade possibilities for the world around the communion table, Black and white women and men embracing, chatting, and eating. Indeed, around the question of commensality, the Peace Mission sought to make an enduring edit on the undergirding human infrastructure of the emergent urban-suburban-rural landscape, one that organized different relations for the whole of society. As anthropologists recognize, commensality is a deep well of cultural memory that critically shapes the ways that various human groups organize in space and time. Ingestion is a critical and ritualized practice that varies widely across space and time and bears collective social memory.[37] The Peace Mission created a distinctly queer sense of hearth and home around the extended banquet table. They did not shirk from the notion that all people needed appropriate housing and other facilities to reproduce social life but rather opened these to a form of collectivity that defied the boundaries prescribed by reformers. In turn, they created not an exclusive preserve of nuclear family life in the home but a space for all who might enter.

Black Queer Urbanisms and the Peace Mission Movement

Out from the communion table, adherents of the Peace Mission articulated a vision of futurity out of order with and incomprehensible within mid-twentieth-century urban politics. Adherents, many of whom moved into missions, but also others who remained in their homes, absconded from social-sexual reproduction through marriage and monogamy. As part of the belief that they were no longer organized in the dominant social hierarchies of white and Black, rich and poor, educated and uneducated, Divinites built up and out from the communion table an alternative form of belonging, a novel form of "family" with all relations, including husband and wife and parent and child (past age sixteen), dissolving into "brother" and "sister." As Divine noted in correspondence with sister Dorothy Moore in 1948:

Truly when you belong to the family of GOD you are not a stranger but become one in that great number. It is such a marvelous thing to know that GOD is your FATHER and you never had another and further, to know that all who claim HIM as such are your brothers and sisters. In this knowledge you become to be universal in nature and cease to live in that limited concept of mentality but can revel into the glorious liberty of the sons of GOD.[38]

The re-territorialization of affective connections at the basis of socialized belonging, as part of the sisters and brothers of the flock, was indeed disruptive for many of the adherents of the Peace Mission and helped precipitate novel and lasting formulations of belonging. As scholar Jill Watts described, as early as 1913 and 1914, Divine found himself in trouble following a mission trip to the US South. After a few months in Valdosta, Georgia, he created a stir among women who had given up sex with their husbands when he pushed them to share equally in caring for the home; the Black men of the area him charged him with lunacy. As Watts explains regarding Divine's first efforts in New York:

> Within his Brooklyn colony, he reconstructed familial relationships and provided his followers with the ideal substitute family. Before joining his flock, many disciples had suffered through divorces, abuse, and homes wrecked by social and economic hardships. The Brooklyn colony was a happy alternative, a financially sound and stable family guided by a stern but loving father and a compassionate and dependable mother. As children, the followers relinquished a certain degree of control over their lives but gained security and tranquility.[39]

In 1933, nearly a decade into their marriage, Lillian Roberts decided to leave her husband, Charles, a tailor in Baltimore, and pursue a life, along with her children Elliot, Abner, and Enos, in New York with the Peace Mission. She had joined the Peace Mission in 1932, no doubt in response to the growing efficacy attributed to Divine following the publicity of his miraculous abilities in the early 1930s. Although Charles Roberts had desired to prevent Lillian from taking their three sons with her to join the "cult," he was unsuccessful. However, after a month or so in New York, Lillian contacted Charles to let him know of the children's whereabouts. Charles retrieved not only the three boys but Lillian as well. Immediately, however, Lillian refused to continue conjugal relations with her husband, moved into a separate room, and eventually left completely to live with another woman who was also an adherent of the Peace Mission. Vernon Caldaira, also of Baltimore, testified in court that Lillian had told him that her devotion to Divine would not permit her to continue marital relations and that she would instead need to reincorporate her relationship with her husband as one organized horizontally along the lines of "sister" and "brother." Caldaira quoted Lillian as having told him that she got "everything she wanted for Father Divine in natural desire."[40]

In September 1934, Jean Goldsmith filed for a full divorce in a Los Angeles court. Her husband, a chiropractor, had "abandoned" her and their young child, hitchhiking to New York City to join the proximate orbit of the Peace Mission around Divine. According to Goldsmith she had attended a meeting of the local mission in Los Angeles, to the great excitement of her husband. However, after he grabbed her in glee, another adherent warned him not to kiss her. According to Goldsmith, from that point forward, her husband had stopped kissing her and engaging in the conjugal aspects of their marriage.[41] In July 1935, Samuel Green Jr., a post office clerk, forced his estranged wife, Madeline Green, to appear before New York judge Samuel D. Levy. The court had subpoenaed Madeline several times to face the court for having "abandoned" her husband and seven children. As reported in the Baltimore *Afro-American*, Madeline had chosen to leave her children and husband for a life in the Peace Mission movement and in the tread of Father Divine. Although she had attempted to convert her children to Divine's teachings, against the "prayers they learned at the Bethel AME Church," her husband's refusal to transition into a life as prescribed by Divine eventually led her to take flight to the mission house located at 21 West 117th Street in Harlem, New York. As Madeline recounted, "I had been attending the meetings of Father Divine and learning more and more each day about his teachings. I desired to live like that—to live a life of sacrifice. Everything else must fade before sacrifice. Nothing else matters. I couldn't live with my husband; that would be living in the flesh and living in the flesh is sin."[42] In the end, the Samuel Green decided to give his children to the Children's Society for the Prevention of Cruelty to Children.[43] In November 1949, Judge Heran E. Hillenbach granted a divorce because of abandonment to Mary L. Queenan of Orange, New Jersey. She and her husband, whom she had married in 1917 and with whom she had raised three children, had "abandoned" her in order to become an adherent of the Peace Mission. According to Queenan, her husband, John, had also given his lifesavings and insurance to support the mission cooperative.[44] In February 1934, Theodore Jones of Clifton Place in Brooklyn appeared before the Kings County Supreme Court concerning his wife, Fannie's, refusal to live in marital relations and her "cooling" in sexual intimacy.[45]

Faith in Father Divine became a way for ordinary people to challenge the strictures and social codes expressed through patriarchal power, trading one form of direct and violent patriarchy for a more abstract vision of fatherhood that undermined familial and other kinds of social relations. Here I follow Ula Taylor's methodological sensibility about the complex decisions Black women engaged in as they embraced, in Taylor's framing, the promise of patriarchy.[46] The Peace Mission allowed new formulations of kin and belonging, animating Black women's challenges to patriarchal authority and violence even in the name of the formal institution. Although some left to live close to the flock, others remained in their communities, leaving family and others but not leaving the places in which their former families resided. With indeterminable and uncertain consequences, the women in particular claimed sisterhood and nonauthoritative relationships with their new "brothers," defying husbands and fathers to live among the Father's flock. Miss Mary Justice of Bishopsville, South Carolina, described violent encounters with her biological father, who protested her disaffection with his authority and devotion to Father Divine. After thanking Father Divine, she went on to divulge "some of [her] problems." Justice recounted leaving her family's home at the age of eighteen in 1938 and joining "a Brother and Sister in your mind and spirit" who introduced her to Father Divine and his teachings. She credited Divine with giving her a "new mind" and for healing her. In contrast, she recounted that beginning in 1939, her biological or "so-called Father" came to her demanding that she see her biological parents and to honor them as such. She went on to describe that her interactions with her biological father grew worse with time, leading to his threat to "fix" her if she did not "honor him and call him father like the other children do." Justice continued to deny her bio-logical kin, instead clinging desperately to the promise of the mission against the increasingly violent berating by her biological father to the odd familial arrangement she developed with her "Brother and Sister in your mind and spirit." Justice closed her letter commanding Divine, to whom she was devoted, to tell her what to do.[47] Justice held onto Father's divinity and his authority as part of a demand for reciprocity from God on earth.[48] She devoted herself, and she also demanded freedom, most pointedly from her biological father.

Absconding from biological family, friends, and anyone else not part of their new lives, many of those who joined the Peace Mission perma-nently severed their other social relations. A number of the spouses, sib-lings, and children whom people left behind to join Father Divine wrote to Divine to ask about their loved ones or in some cases to inquire about matters related to insurance policies held on a long-departed loved one presumed dead.[49] Here, the consequences of adherents' practices of changing their names as a reflection of their new identities, their new lives of holiness, and their set-apartness gained new force. Divinites, seeking to forever forget the lives behind them, lived, died, and were re-born in the presence of their earthly god as Wonderful Joy, Happy Sing, and other names exuberantly proclaiming their positive outlook and their contributions to the kingdom. Their family members and loved ones, knowing them only in their lives before Divine, could not trace them.

In late August 1948, Dorothy "Dot" Moore, a new Divinite, left follow-ing her first visit to the Philadelphia missions. Wonderful Joy—"Wonie" among the other Rosebuds—filled a lunch pail for their new sister in the faith with the elaborate victuals Dot had come to appreciate while living with them over the course of her short stay. Wonderful Joy wrote, "I just know you didn't eat all that food on the train. If you did, I expect to see a nice round butter-ball the next time you come. (if you come)."[50] Here, Wonie's inquiry about the state of the lunchbox indexed the voluptuous communion table, illustrating the enduring significance of abundance in drawing in and retaining the flock. Next, Wonie explicitly mobilized the longing that she and the other sister Rosebuds felt about Dot in order to entice Dot back at the next break in her studies. She asked, "How did you find college after your return? I can imagine how glad they were to see their favorite little bundle of charms. But remember how sad we were to see that little bundle leave. In fact, I betcha your little ears were burning like everything because Dorothy was the only subject while going home from the station, and 'We are Floating' was the only song on our minds."[51] Again, to draw Dot's heart and affections nigh, Wonie invoked the joyous sounds of the renowned Rosebud choir of which she was a part. Here she sought explicitly to redirect any of the attachments and affiliations that Dot experienced at college among the nonfaithful, whom she also described as "usually proud and arrogant," back through a rather circuitous economy of feeling to Divine himself.

After engaging in the retrospective, Wonie turned her attention to the future, again to elicit the joyful moments of sociality that she and the others created in the name of Divine and in order to draw Dot back. She wrote, "Well, Dotty, this weekend we will be going to Pine Brook for Labor Day and I will remember you as I sit down to eat. I say when I sit down to eat because I'm thinking of all that food you had on the train and how you must have tried very hard to digest it. At least that's the way it is when I see a lot of food before me to eat." Again here, Wonie invoked the "abundance of the fullness" of the communion table to draw Dot's sentiments more fully into the orbit of the Rosebud sociality and to Divine himself: "I know you will make the best of it and if Father is still deep in your memories, I know everything will be Wonderful, Wonderful, Wonderful!"[52]

In closing this first in a series of correspondence, filled mostly with these sorts of enticements, Wonie asked for "a picture of you [which] will be just the thing for me to keep on my dresser so that you'll also be remembered by the rest." Although the expressed goal of joining the Rosebuds was a proximity to Father's divinity, this desire for a photograph, a visual cue for remembering that one can hold, touch, and feel, suggests that the bonds were also about the homosocial relationships fostered among sisters or brothers, the queer affective bonds kindled and maintained between members. In a September 18, 1948, letter, Wonie thanked Dot for the photograph and promised to send her own: "I will send you mine as soon as I can take a presentable one. Right now I don't own any, but will try to get some very soon. I showed yours to all the Buds and they seem to like it very much." Again, the affective economy around the touching gesture of sending the photograph suggests that once Divine and his visions for utopian peace are blurred, a vision of small-scale re-formulations of belonging becomes visible, one based in the outlook of the plot and its attendant aesthetics of satiation and abundance.

Divine, although the central animating figure for the whole social world that adherents constructed, was not always at the center, further suggesting the alternative reading of these letters I am posing. In the same September 18 letter, for example, Wonie wrote that Dotty should expect to hear from the other Rosebuds, and in the postscript, Wonie promised that she would give Dotty's regards to Father in her next interview. Here, Wonie's primary concern was her and Dotty's connection, then the other Rosebuds with whom Dotty had interacted during her trip, and finally, and seemingly as an afterthought, Divine himself. A letter that Divine wrote to Dotty supports my emphasis on the affective economy between adherents and suggests that there was always more happening between adherents for which Divine might account. After noting that his efforts to arrange various believers traveling to engage his presence had delayed his response to Dotty, Divine noted that "Mother and the staff have mentioned you on several occasions and I AM sure that they would be glad for ME to say 'Peace' for them as I don't believe they carry on much correspondence."[53]

Wonie noted her surprise at receiving a letter so quickly from Dottie on September 24, 1948, after she had written that she did not require a return letter for the ones she sent. She then proceeded to document the various trips that she and the other Rosebuds had been on between New York, New Jersey, and their home base at the mission in Philadelphia. Again, it is clear that Wonie intended to index the vibrant social world that she and the other sisters practiced in order to draw Dottie back into the fold. On Saturday and Sunday, the Rosebuds attended the annual church meeting at Pine Brook, New Jersey, where they "went swimming and had a gay time." Next, after rehearsing the rather mundane details of her daily work at a Peace Mission–affiliated soda counter in North Philadelphia, Wonie, noted "Oh, gee, I guess I think I'm talking face to face because usually that's when I always forget to stop." After signing "Yours, Wonie," she again noted in a postscript that she would transmit Dot's love for Divine directly to him.[54]

The Peace Mission's destabilizations of affiliation, its reassembling of the biological and conjugal kinship bonds in the name of siblings, as well as the bonds to the underground life of bootlegging, represented an alternative horizon of urban futurity, one in which ordinary people embraced (at least publicly) radical asexuality and the dissolution of nuclear intimacy (and its attendant violence) and exchanged the rubrics prescribed by urban reformers, planners, and politicians for generative urban futurity, for one of abundance, dedication, and collectivity, drawing on, extending, and radically reformulating the vision of the plot. Specifically, the adherents of the Peace Mission rejected the conjugal-nuclear home organized in support of breadwinner-ism and embraced instead affiliations as sisters and brothers around the holy communion table. The Peace Mission recombined aspects and aesthetics of the plot in a novel social-spatial formulation under the rubrics of heaven on earth, queering and critiquing from a distinctive Black migrant vantage, the city as plantation by the replication, recombination, and transmutation of the plot in in the opaque world of dark agoras, here again, the set-apart spaces of Black filiation (even those including white members) outlining devastating metaphysical reorderings, sometimes in quiet reflections on, sometimes in rapturous prayers for the end and for a new world of abundance and earthly satiation in collectivity.

Healing and a Radical Edit on the Plot

Recusing themselves from the bonds of matrimonial expectation and sex, devotees of Divine joined one another as sisters and brothers, distilling sensual energy into consistent work, enraptured worship, abundant communion, and deeply felt intimacy organized spatially and socially beyond the bonds of nuclear family and the attendant model of social, economic, and geographic reproduction it anchored within orthodox urbanist thought. Peace Mission adherents cultivated a body of those embracing an esoteric and heterodox belief set that included racial integration, radical asexuality, and an ecstatic-miraculous healing tradition centered in the sensuousness of touch that I describe as "ecstatic consecration," wherein in the name of devotion to Divine, adherents created healing spaces defined by bodily transformation. Through touch—that is, in being touched by Divine's words or through being compelled by an extension of hapticity, emotion, and memory through correspondence with one another—devotees of Father Divine's Peace Mission created death-defying spaces in the city, believing collectively that they could ward off the vulnerability of debilitation and physical mortality and shield themselves from the scarcity to which they were condemned by reformers, dominant urbanists, politicians, landlords, and police, keep themselves from the want imposed on Blackness. This requires a method of archival analysis that takes seriously what presents an epistemological challenge as the unreal. What remained unreal for outsiders served as one of the primary bases on which many of the flock joined. Many adherents over the years attributed to Father Divine miraculous physical healing from a range of ailments, many of which were directly associated with the conditioning of Black life straddling the plantation and post-plantation worlds. Thus, a critical material and epistemological legacy of the plot manifested in the abundance of the communion table, the primary ritual of earthly deliverance manifesting the Peace Mission's spiritual work, drawing people into the fold of siblings in the flock.

The plot manifested in the ecstatic worship and miraculous healing, the institutionalization of the hush harbor, the longing for deliverance that was also part of the matrix of Black social reproduction in the context of the grinding relations of plantation and post-plantation life. As Pearly Manager suggested, the capacities attributed to Father Divine through embodied worship, even in his physical absence, were held by believers to have restorative power. The belief in miraculous healing drew believers together with their focus on the metropolis and the Promised Land, not for the promise of industrial labor but for the promise of healing from debilitation and even resurrection from death and an eternal earthly life. In a December 21, 1940, letter thanking Divine, Brother Ernest Leshley described his miraculous recovery from "this disease now forty years in this body." Plagued by filariasis, a condition now understood as a parasitic disease affecting the lymphatic system, the development of his permanently swollen legs below the knee would have made basic functions associated with walking difficult. Since Leshley wrote from Montreal, Canada, where the climate limits prevalence of the disease, it is likely that he was a Caribbean migrant, especially since filariasis is most often attributed to mosquito vectors that live primarily in tropical regions. Brother Ernest referred to Divine as "the Great Physician" and attributed to him his miraculous return to "normal legs." He asked that images documenting his miraculous recovery be "posted conspicuously at the Rockland Palace, New York City" so that the other faithful members of the flock could see the power of Divine to perform "a cure of this incurable disease of such long duration." Ernest also included the measurements of his legs and closed his letter with song lyrics that served as a reminder that "Everybody Ought to Know that God Is in the Land."

In their acknowledgment of Divine's capacities as their last resort, many of these letters present a tacit skepticism of Divine's capacity to heal. Other letters illustrate devoted patience to Father's time, and still others tacitly acknowledge the kinds of networks and support for the ailing provided by siblings in the faith. In an undated and unsigned note, a nameless believer pleaded with Divine to keep her well. She acknowledged that she prayed to him daily, and she asked that he "take all pains" from her body. Yet she was not yet healed, and her desire to be pain free remained unmet despite consistent prayer and faith. Nevertheless, she acknowledged the power and possibility of ecstatic consecration among the flock even in the absence of Father himself, writing that she was thankful for "what my sister has done for me."[55] Ecstatic consecration in this context included the partial realization and enactment of a world beyond the debilitation and death of Black people wherein ordinary migrants remade small-scale social and communal relations in the name of prosperity, peace, and care in and through the miraculous and the embodiment of the spirit and of otherworldliness in untamed worship.

In a letter from June 20, 1946, a believer wrote from Topeka, Kansas, thanking Father Divine by providing him tickets to reach him in Philadelphia. He acknowledged, though, that he remained too weak to travel. Likely suffering from congestive heart failure or perhaps a condition of the lungs, he could not "walk across the room without short stopping to rest." Refusing doctors, who remained ineffectual in their treatments, and eschewing the advice of the people in his community who thought him crazy for believing in the healing power of Father Divine, he promised to visit Divine using the tickets he had sent as soon as he recovered some of his energy and got a handle on his breathing difficulties.[56] An undated letter from Marta Wick described her desperation in turning to Father Divine, despite her nonadherence to the lifestyle he promoted, especially the renunciation of her husband and children, who were, in fact, at the center of her desperate written plea. She asked for help because her husband was paralyzed and her children had tuberculosis. Moreover, she could not secure sufficient work to care for them financially while also engaging in the labor to care for them in their ailments. She stated frankly to this earthly manifestation others held to be God on earth, "Life is so unbearable." When asked that Father Divine preserve her children, acknowledging "Winter is coming" and seeking his empathy and support for a warm home in which to spare her children from death from the deadly lung condition. Mrs. E. M. Terry, a woman with enough means to hire domestic help, told Divine that she had heard of his miraculous curing work through a domestic worker she had met who was a follower. The unnamed domestic laborer, who was a follower of Divine's transformative presence, made what she said about Divine believable. Eventually, she began to share the New Day with her employer, who herself began to believe in Father Divine's capacity to heal. Although Mrs. Terry's new domestic worker had made her feel better since she began working there and sharing Divine's message, Mrs. Terry acknowledged an enduring pain in her ankle that lasted more than three years. She asked Divine to heal it in order to further confirm his miraculous capacities.[57]

There is a form of critical diasporic consciousness animating Leshley's longing and desire for cure from the incurable, a conditioning of his birth in a plantation landscape enduringly defined by debilitation often brought on by unseen and unknown forces—in his case, as a child in a landscape where the land remained unfree and where monoculture and the ongoing dislocations of the plantation jeopardized all forms of Black life and collectivity through exposure. The adherents' preoccupation with the healing and miraculous recovery of the dispersed and far-flung members of the flock illustrated a central system of value, expressed within the so-called cult as a quintessentially migrant institution wherein those debilitated, disfigured, or otherwise adversely affected by uneven development and enduring accumulation through expropriation and violence were drawn together foremost through the affect of the miraculous, a return to some semblance of wholeness. Despite being unbelievable to many outsiders, these narratives are tacitly critical of a world in which across space, slow and eventful violence rendered Black flesh prone to violation.

Adherents also disbanded one of the critical aspects of the plot in its historical context in the South's plantation ecologies. Father Divine banned death in the constitution of the church and in his preaching. The notion that true believers were immune from death and the subsequent abandonment of funerary rites for dead adherents who severed ties with their spouses, children, and previous social connections enacted a seismic cultural rupture from a central aspect of the plot—the replication of Black vitality at the site of the body's interment. Many of the adherents in the 1930s and 1940s who died while living as part of the flock were abandoned to the city morgue and buried unceremoniously in potters' fields without physical marker or acknowledgment of location. This disjuncture is surprising but not unprecedented in the transmutation of cultural resources in the heat and freneticism of mass demographic dislocation.

As is well noted in the literature, the organization's orientation to death was mutable, adapting after the death of the first Mother Divine in the early 1940s to incorporate a form of reincarnation to justify the spiritual marriage between Father and the second Mother Divine, a white woman from Canada, and later with the earthly death of Divine himself, as members continued to practice the various rituals like the communion table well after 1965. Yet in the initial radical departure from the plot as a site of the body's interment and its attendant rituals, and finally, after the elaborate 1965 entombment of Divine himself and the regular processionals to honor his grave, we see this aspect of the historic plot as a point of transversal—of leaving behind and returning that generated ritual power and energy to sustain congregations and worlds set apart within the world of the segregated metropolis.

The enduring ritual life of the Peace Mission after Divine's 1965 death suggests the complex terrain of charisma and the "absentee patriarch." The Peace Mission, and later MOVE after 1985, continued in the aftermath of their founder's deaths, often through symbolic invocation of the absented father-founder. This relation further reveals the bottom-up expression of the charismatic scenario in all the historicity and complex social function Edwards assigns it. The devotion of Divinites continued after his death, underscoring both that his physical form had been imbued with resounding power to disband want and hunger for abundance, haunting death for present life, and the unromantic aspects of the plot's ongoing recombination, segmentation, and rearticulation characterized by its materialization of the gnostic leader.

5

Insurgent Black Social-Spatial Life and the Geography of the 1964 "Riot"

Just after 9:30 p.m. on a temperate, late August evening in 1964, two police officers, patrolling near the intersection of Twenty-Second Street and Columbia Avenue in North Philadelphia in response to a report of the street's being obstructed, found the street blocked by Odessa and Rush Bradford's car. The couple was embroiled in a heated domestic dispute. Despite officers' commands for the couple to move the car, Odessa refused to remove her foot from the brake, preventing her husband from driving the car away from the intersection. Her refusal in the face of police commands registered to the officers as obstinacy. While she sought to resolve the matter with her husband then and there, the officers viewed her as obstructing traffic. In response, the officers attempted to forcibly drag her from her car, to which she responded with resistance, "shouting and striking at the officers" and landing blows on their faces and bodies.

As the raucousness of the unfolding arrest attracted a crowd, at least one man, forty-one-year-old James Nettles, whom investigators later described as an intoxicated reveler in Columbia Avenue's tap rooms, the center of the city's Black underground, attempted to intervene and to block the police from arresting Bradford, arguing and fighting with the officers alongside her. As the police arrested Odessa and Rush and took them away in a police wagon, "the crowd thickened, and from the rooftops of several three-story houses nearby came a barrage of bricks and bottles" that destroyed the windshields of the police cars as well as those of nearly a dozen other cars parked near the intersection.[1]

Based on a tactical plan developed by Mayor James H. Tate's administration in the wake of a similar disturbance in 1963, the police attempted to use sheer numbers to intimidate residents and to clear the streets of North Philadelphia.[2] This strategy backfired. As more police descended on the area, more residents gathered, and more bottles and rocks crashed police helmets and cars. Among the crowd of increasingly angry North Philadelphia residents was a local "exhorter," Raymond Hall, a twenty-five-year-old "Negro known as an agitator in the area but with no identifiable political or organizational affiliation shouted out to passers-by at 23rd street and Columbia Avenue: 'a pregnant black woman's been beaten and shot to death by a white policeman.'" Subsequently, in the unusually thin and cool air of late summer Philadelphia, the report of Odessa's death spread rapidly, calling even more residents who formed an unsanctioned "multitude" from the neighborhood just west of Temple University chanting what police and others described as anti-white epithets.[3]

What would later prove to be an "unfounded" rumor initiated mass action galvanized by exhorters and revelers in the underground. As Stephen Best writes, "Rumors wither under measures of truth and falsity like flowers under hot water," and indeed, the quickly spreading message of the police's killing of a pregnant Black woman was hastily repudiated by officials.[4] Civil rights leader and local NAACP chapter president Cecil Moore successfully beseeched the city to free Odessa and preceded to ride around the affected riot area with her using a bullhorn to note that she was very much alive.[5] This had very little effect on the outcome of the riot; the rumor had allowed residents to vocalize and enact retribution against an order premised on exploitative confinement in a deindustrializing neighborhood characterized by white domination and the daily harassment by white shopkeepers, police, social workers, and city officials.

As folklorist Patricia Turner's classic *Heard It Through the Grapevine* demonstrates, rumor, myth, and other forms of information that are believed by dominant society to bear no meaningful impact on rational action circulate as forms of heterodox information that help working-class Black communities to derive meaning and coherence in a world defined by steep imbalances of power unfavorable to and conditioning Black people's experiences. Although these narratives are sometimes not verifiable, they do, as Turner underscores, diagnose the dynamics of power from the vantage of their circulators, despite having no legitimated source.[6] As Kwame Holmes has developed further in relation to Black queer urban histories, rumor and gossip are forms not often considered historically significant forms of information; and yet for those barred from the formal levers of institutional and intellectual power, these forms of information hold significant bearing and can help us historicize the social and political actions of those who usually appear in archives as the condemned or as victims.[7]

While Odessa's death was not, in fact, a reality, the idea that police killed a pregnant Black woman drew into public view the "private transcript" of the oppressed, particularly analyses about policing and violence that threatened vulnerable Black people leading to acts of "declared refusal to comply."[8] North Philadelphia's Black residents cast off their subdued or quiet despising of officers of the law and their adherence, despite the want that was so clearly evident around them, to capitalist demands for the respect of property, and enacted their alternative visions for other figurations of place where the law and its ordering of property were temporarily destroyed.

As subsequent accounts suggest, the crowd was driven further by religious-political dissidents and by a direct meeting of the underground and the set-apart. People like Hall moved from the edges of Black institutional and political life to the center in a moment of crisis, further incensing the crowd, demanding freedom and the destruction of the current order. In addition to Bradford, Nettles, and Hall, leader of the African-Asian Culture Center, Shaykh Muhammad Ali Hassan, known alternatively as Abyssinia Hayes, stood in front of the center shouting and engaging in what police understood as "obscene exhorting of the crowds" as he "jumped up and down, screaming curses interspersed with" the demand for freedom. Ali Hassan was further set apart by what officers considered his sartorial delinquency, his "white jodhpurs, a green and gold fez and a single dangling black earing"—the symbolic link between his exhortation and the dissident religious world of "a self-styled Muslim leader" according to police.[9]

In a dialectic of supposed loud unreason, impassioned exhorters with heterodox religious and political leanings demanded the end to Philadelphia's order, defined by deadening segregation and the expropriation of neighborhood enterprises by white businesses. Fueled by the heat of demonstration, taproom goers and others participating in North Philadelphia's semi-illicit nightlife, as well as the youth, who took to the roofs to pelt police with glass, commandeered the streets in the opening salvo of the days long revolt. Although the spirited space of discourse opened by the exhorters is not recoverable, what is clear is that it drove the sudden and incendiary political upheaval, articulating forward in a different context rebellion and the passing erection of the Black commons.

Through Odessa's resistance and refusal, she had inadvertently launched a mass rebellion in which hundreds or thousands of Black residents of North Philadelphia sought to uproot the most visible signs of white economic domination and policing. Residents taunted and injured police, and they seized goods from corner stores, bars, furniture stores, and clothing retailers. The sudden and fiery blending of otherwise incommensurate social spaces powerfully illustrates how the transposition and refraction of the plot through the spaces cultivated through dark agoras continued to underwrite the architectonics of Black life in the city. Although averse to one another in their quotidian functions beside one another, and often clamoring for territory and people and therefore often at odds, in August 1964, Philadelphia's self-regulated borders between dark agoras, as underground spaces and as set-apart geographies, gave way, creating the conditions for an urban riot as a momentary reordering of civil, social, economic, and political sovereignty effecting a breach of order and law, defined under normal circumstances by the state's exclusive hold on violence and the smooth operation of power on the part of property possession.

In the intervening days after Odessa was arrested, residents claimed alleys, stoops, corners, rooftops, and other spaces as extensions of their apartments and as the primary sites of their social existence, in need of defense against the "mushroom" of invading police.[10] In the juridical sense, most Black people in the "riot zone" had no right or claim to streets and alleys, as these were public space; less so given the preponderance of Black renters who could make no effective claim to legal ownership when police attempted to force them off their stoops or away from the corner. These assemblies and their claims to place illustrate the active and robust, if often less pronounced, counter-interpretation of urban order active among Black migrants and their cultural progeny in the city from within dark agoras. The right to the streets, even in areas that one did not own, was the territorial and cognitive extension and transposition of plotting into the city, the counter-force of the original plantation enclosure reverberating in the quotidian rewriting of the city from its edges through claims to space and through unsanctioned collectivity. Through those alternative spatial lexicons of Black social existence treading within the territory of the illegible, a novel form of temporary sovereignty emerged expressing a fleeting world of capital's disbandment and the appropriation of urban architectures and infrastructures for the full expression of Black social life. Ordinary residents took space and held it according to their own designs as opposed to the logics of flow, extraction, and legibility embedded by dominant urbanists in sidewalks, streets, row houses, and other spatial features prescribed to regulate urban sociality by taming desire, steadying market demands, and ensuring access by police.

During the initial disturbance, Black communities manipulated the spatial features of the slum, working an epistemology born of the intimacy and connection to spaces that outsiders viewed as totalizing in debilitation and death, to create fleeting possibilities for plotting and fugitivity, underscoring the continued significance of the cross-hatched and complex interweaving of the underground and the set-apart shaping Black politics. Residents negotiated the dynamics of ongoing spatial domination in the city through the strategic manipulation of darkness and hidden spaces, the shapeshifting locations of dark assemblies or dark agoras, to express the elementary means of everyday refusal and worldmaking in and through the matters of place, drawing on more quotidian formulations of use to defend their own claims to territoriality through the Black vernacular landscape that was the result of everyday cultivation of autonomous cities within the city.

Rejection of the police's enforcement of the mayor's orders for a curfew drew to flickering public light, if not full transparency, the vision of territoriality that Black communities extended in the context of the row-house city in the period before the demographic reversal of Black migration toward the South. Although policing functionaries countermobilized and weaponized the bird's-eye-view perspective of dominant urbanism with helicopters, the sudden use of these spaces to defend against the invading force of police indexes other spatial registers and alternative uses of urban geography that are not easily captured in the forms of surveillance, from the vantage of the beat patrolmen or the top-down vantage, suggesting the centrality of alternative imaginaries of geographic and infrastructural arrangement outlined in chapter 3. Glass bottles thrown from rooftops, for example, suggest sites of supra-domestic places of congregation not foremost organized contra the state and its functionaries embodied in the Philadelphia Police Department but rather preceding the riot in the quotidian expression of a social-spatial grammar literally on top of the geographies of standard living, the creation of livable space in the dire conditions of cramped housing and confinement.

I am indebted to the possibilities for understanding this as a feature of Black worlding or worldmaking through the children's and young adult literature that Black feminist urbanist June Jordan produced following her encounter with the "riot" that erupted in mid-July 1964 following police officer Thomas Gilligan's murder of a Black teenager, James Powell. Although in direct response to Powell's murder, the week of disorder drew into the open the community's rage against ongoing discrimination and violation at the hands of police, the arbiters of the violence that articulated the state's juridical order of inequality, injustice, and a lack of practical protection. In the midst of the crowds that formed on the second night of the rioting near the funeral home that received Powell's body, Jordan, a native and resident of Harlem and Brooklyn, bore witness to the ongoing relevance of insurgent mortuary practice in the reproduction of Black geographic life. Following the riot, Jordan embarked on a decade-long literary endeavor that she hoped would draw young Black people into an understanding of their power to shape the city through small edits on their own living spaces. Through her work, Jordan intended especially to convey the fully insurrectionary potential of Black youthful efforts to create collectivity through designs respecting, rather than seeking to displace, Black vernacular landscapes as the basis for urban futures.[11]

Understood through the rubric provided by Jordan's work, these are sites of possibility of self-creation and sociality that in the context of a cascade of collective rage become sites of an impromptu guerilla mobilization.[12] Rooftops and other spaces of assembly were literally on top of the geographies of standard living, creating tactical spatial possibility resonant with, if not coequal to, the ways that enslaved Black people mobilized unsanctioned assemblies and sometimes weaponized the interstitial spaces between plantations to reproduce insurgent forms of social life. People enlivened these spaces, along with stoops and other sites of insurgent Black social life, by stretching the state's account of the organization of urban space and its attempts to enclose, rationalize, and generate long-term stability through confinement or dislocation. Under pressure, these formulations of autonomous Black spatial and social existence returned to a resonant form, the feared object underwriting anti-Black repression that had originated with the planter state and survived its ruptures and permutations—the open rebellion against the police and the order of gendered racial capitalist relations they back through violent force. Black residents articulated spatial possibilities within sites that do not register in dominant urbanist thought and practice and that are fleetingly powerful against heavily armed riot police with their tactical formations.

A Note on Method

Before returning to a partial reconstruction of the riot's geographic profile refracted through the prism of the plot's rearticulation through translocation, it is important to critically examine the archival basis of this chapter. The riot's meaning is a function of the grid of intelligibility across time staked in and through the formation of the competing discourses seeking its containment and producing it as an episode with a discrete psychological, geographic, and social profile. Like other instances in which the "private transcript" of oppressed Black people pierces public order and hegemony, the urtext figured as the slave revolt, the riot is ultimately unknowable and persistently semi-opaque as an expression of Black migrant working-class futures for the city, due in part to the multiplicity of meanings for those engaged in the activity marked as rioting, but more significantly because of the competing fault lines of meaning and origin that emerged in its wake seeking to contain it.

While the discourses and archives housing the riot offer tantalizing glimpses into the world fleetingly erected, these discourses fail to reveal a comprehensive picture of the horizon visioned by "rioters" because the event is narrated in the archives of its repression and strategic reformulation in the service of some other force. Here, I draw particularly on the insight of historian Ranajit Guha's "The Prose of Counter-Insurgency," which addresses the pitfalls of the archives and the resulting historiography of peasant rebellions in the context of colonial India. According to Guha, the description of these rebellions from competing and complimentary modes of discursive inscription reflect their original repression. Furthermore, the "historiography has been content to deal with the peasant rebel merely as an empirical person or a member of a class, but not an entity whose will and reason constituted the praxis called rebellion."[13] As Huewayne Watson delineates through an engagement with the politics of naming the 1831 uprising in Jamaica, the terming of revolt, rebellion, and revolution delimit the contours of how we later interpret the efficacy of the enslaved for their own liberation.[14]

This contested inscription of the 1964 "riot" begins with the terminology used to describe it. According to the *Online Etymology Dictionary*, the word *riot* originates in twelfth-century French to describe a dispute, quarrel, argument, or domestic strife, as well as modes of living associated with debauchery or amorality.[15] These original uses are significant for the sedimented meaning of the word's deployment in response to what the state understood outside of the public's purview as part of a palpable threat, an emergency across Black urban neighborhoods coextensive with the revolutionary nationalisms that had embroiled the globe in the 1950s and 1960s.[16] The designation of riot helped to give a public presentation of the disturbance as a set of interlinking problems related to Black domestic instability and the excesses associated with drinking and the underground in continuum with Black heterodoxy and religious militancy. Although the state was obtuse in its investigations, the FBI suggesting that the Bradfords and others might be shock troops for some unannounced skirmish in the Cold War, these formulations embedded in the designation of the series of eruptions as riots provided a convenient ruse, which white liberals, Black and white journalists, and Black political leaders also backed in a strategic effort to deescalate the federal state and the broader white public's paranoia that the disruptions represented a wider conspiracy of Black religious-political subversion, particularly that of Black Muslim militancy (as evidenced in Ali Hassan's later castigation and trial). The grammar of riot, drawing on its original sedimented layers, draws out the ways that police interpreted the Bradfords' disturbance and the resulting actions that culminated in a period of sustained cessation of the city as the insurer and arbiter of capital, foremost through the prism of Black domestic disturbance, debauched living associated with the drinkers and revelers in the strip of taprooms that were held to be the primary infrastructure of the city's underground, and in the violent rhetoric of Black religious dissidents who were marked in the state's purview by madness.[17] This demarcation as riot helped to contain the extent of the violence and disorder and to make sense of the event as a problem of Black domesticity and the related problem of the urban neighborhood, isolating the disturbance from the wider uproar of anticolonial movements that were roiling the earth (although it was unable to deter the paranoid schema of the FBI, which saw behind every sentiment raised against the violence and death of segregation the specter of Soviet involvement and communist international subversion). Is there a space there, or a there there, within the geographic actions of the collective, that is irreducible to any other contemporary's program? What can the Black subaltern articulate through its spatial presence as its discursive modes are rendered incomprehensible, crude, and backward?

Serving as the principal archival collection are the police arrest records that seek to subdue through documentation of violations and neutralize the series of collective actions. This primary archive constitutes the bulk of information about the riot and has served as the basis of subsequent inscriptions by journalists, social reformers, politicians, and historians. Police records form an archive of violent containment with a characteristic colonialist vision of police versus a boisterous and uncontrolled mass. It is a detailed account of the police forcefully dispersing and arresting the crowds—as often as not ordinary people engaging in Black modes of collective living in the city—and enforcing the mayoral injunction against any form of outdoor activity in the "riot zone" as criminal. This archive is structured by euphemisms for brutal assault hidden in passive past tense constructions by state officers licensed by the mayor's injunction against purchasing or consuming alcohol, congregating outside, or leaving one's domicile after dark, no matter the reason. As Alexis Pauline Gumbs writes, "The passive voice is the language of the state. The status quo. The enforced state of being. It generates the mythology that violence of the state is inevitable."[18] These officers violently punished Black people for what they inscribed as loud insolence and banditry, writing it into the traceable archive in constructions that disappear the officers as agents of violent force.

This demarcation of the foregone cessation and containment of the riotousness through the phrase *was subdued* and the term *containment* in the primary archive also shaped temporal and spatial parameters of the riot as an event in subsidiary discourses created in its aftermath and seeking to establish the "truth" about the disturbance. The second major archive producing and partially containing, while also stretching and changing, the meaning of the riot are newspapers. As Brent Hayes Edwards underscores in his treatment of the 1964 riot in Harlem and discursive production, newspapers and journalists created the eventful nature of the riot within the temporal and corollary spatial ordering expressed through seriality. As Edward writes of disturbance, it was in part "produced by—a form that can only be termed serial." "The build-up, the increasing levels of panic, anger, and frustration," Edwards continues, "is intimately linked to the serial form of the newspaper and the particular effects it allows: the steady inflation of numbers, the accumulation of insinuation, the linking of categories (one disturbance to another)."[19] In its first report of the 1964 Philadelphia riot, the *New York Times'* coverage sought to inhere riotousness to a very specific segment of Philadelphia, a "teeming rectangle" known as "the Jungle" that was demographically dominated, according to journalists, by Black migrants who had come from the South after 1940.[20] In September and November, the Times had re-created the series of events through its coverage of the arrest and charging of individuals whom the Philadelphia Police Department accused of inciting the riot—including Florence Mobley—and most dramatically in their coverage of the trial of Abyssinia Hayes, Raymond Hall, and others whom the police eventually held responsible for inciting the violence and the looting and helping to solidify it as an event characterized by collective madness in and through Black religious heterodoxy—the out-there nature of the enduring Black set-apart worlds.[21]

Building on police and journalists' records and on subsequent interviews was a tertiary set of inscriptions that, while not literally archival, expanded the premises of the primary archival record of the riot as a spontaneous eruption defined by rumor, misunderstanding, and collective frenzy followed by distinct termination. Characteristic of this body of material documenting and seeking to render intelligible the procession of the 1964 revolt was Lenora E. Berson's published pamphlet, *Case Study of the Riot: The Philadelphia Story.*[22] Working on behalf of the American Jewish Committee, Berson used police records, interviews with police officers, journalists accounts, and a discussion of the economic, social, and political character of the neighborhood to establish a picture of what happened during the upheaval. Berson wrote foremost to understand why Black communities in particular had seemed to target Jewish-owned businesses in their "looting." Berson replays truisms about the nature of the transformation of the urban neighborhood through ethnic succession, which helps account for Black migrant's demographic preponderance and Jewish shopkeeper's disproportionate concentration.

While Berson details the mechanisms of Black Philadelphian's violent inclusion in the cityscape through dilapidated housing at exorbitant prices for mortgage or rental, usurious credit for clothing, food, and furniture stores, and violent policing without significant protection, Berson's conclusion about the resolution of the conditions reinforce the further deracination of Black migrant geographies, prescribing the eradication of the slum and the full integration of Black communities into the economic, social, and political normative relations of US society. This outlook embeds a blind spot in the liberal tertiary formulation of the riot that refuses to engage it as a plebiscite against the horizon of racial capitalist domination and colonial-style policing and isolation from the larger infrastructures of working-class Black political consciousness spanning neighborhoods, cities, and regions.

The formulation of the 1964 disturbance and other similar eruptions in Harlem and in other cities as riots—a term burdened by its association with domestic disturbance and unscrupulous living—placed the origins of these moments in the supposed mess of Black life. During her interview with the *Tribune*, Odessa Bradford denied this formulation, suggesting instead that the origins of the disturbance were to be found in the state's actions to treat her as outside the territory of the human. As she said explicitly, "If only the police had handled me like a human being none of this (rioting) would have happened." Denying the media access to the details of the tensions between her and her husband—"It was a quarrel between me and my husband. . . . I would really prefer not to tell you what the argument was about"—Bradford redirected the media's attention to police and their actions to violently handle her. Journalists at the *Tribune* capitalized on this to further diminish the significance of the disturbance's historical significance, strategically isolating it within the realm of Black domestic disturbance and violent police intervention. Generalizing calls alleged to have emerged at the scene of Bradford's violent arrest, the *Tribune* writer noted that onlookers who intervened called out to police that they would not manhandle or abuse a white woman like they did Bradford.[23]

Finally, there are also the strategic inscriptions by Black civil rights leaders that show up across these discourses and archives but that must be distinguished, given their strategically different relationship with working-class Black residents of North Central Philadelphia. While these visions are sometimes indistinct from those of white liberals mobilized in part by Berson, by centering a notion of spokesmanship on behalf of men like the local NAACP chapter president Cecil Moore (for whom Columbia Avenue was later renamed), they suggest a different relationship with insurrectionary activity. People like Moore saw themselves as representing and embodying the underlying will and desires of the rioters. These narrations simultaneously deploy and obscure the rioter for political and social leverage, not for the direct empowerment of working-class Black people but at least in part on behalf of them. Recall that it was Moore who called for the city's release of Odessa Bradford. Also, in response to the police's paranoia about the role of Black nationalists in fomenting the riot that reinforced the demarcation of the riot as a distinct and spontaneous event, Moore sought also to sanitize it of any potential larger movement or sentiment among residents that might be considered subversive. According to Berson, "Cecil Moore scoffed at any insinuation of premeditation. 'The rioting here,' he said on August 29, was 'a spontaneous thing It was due to a long history of police mistreatment.'" Moore's truncation isolates the unfolding of the riot from larger dynamics of political and economic analysis on the part of Black working-class people rendering it as a reaction to police brutality. As Matthew Countryman has identified, Moore's distillation of the riot into an isolated series of events defined by misinterpretation rather than premeditation furthered his own political agenda as the local NAACP leadership. Particularly, Moore's rehearsal of the riot as spontaneous reaction was part of his attempt to mark himself as enacting a distinct form of leadership outside of what he considered a conservative clergy and others who preferred reconciliation from the top down. As the rioters' public interlocutor, he hoped to parlay the power of the otherwise spontaneous expression to forward the full social and economic integration of Philadelphia.[24]

Sadie Tanner Alexander, another well-recognized Philadelphia-based civil rights leader, asked Mayor Tate to deputize "5000 responsible Negro leaders" "to support the police" in their efforts to reign in the rioters during the 1964 revolt. While this is a dangerous prospect, illustrating and demonstrating citizenship through a willingness to police and contain poor Black communities, it evidences a larger relation of mediation envisioned within mainstream Philadelphia civil rights theorizing, organizing, and action.[25] Alexander also diminishes the autonomy or consciousness of rioters. Alexander, who happened to be on the scenes of the 1964 riot in Philadelphia as well as the 1965 Watts Rebellion, conveys something that she heard among the rioters in Watts—"We won"—into a vision seeking integration, "prodding" rioters to understand what this meant to discover that the sum total of the action was state recognition:

> By reason of fortuitous occasion, I arrived in Los Angeles in the midst of the Watts riots. Through the courtesy of City and State officials I was permitted to drive through the streets and talk with some of the residents. Almost every person I interviewed conveyed the same thinking viz., "We Won!" It took deep prodding to ascertain what these people though they had won. Finally, I realized they meant that despite their continuous protests, for the first time they had won attention of the City, the state, the Federal Government and the nation to the shocking inequalities in education, employment, recreation, and housing to which they had so long been subjected.[26]

While at first, she had no idea what it meant that the rioters had won, it was ultimately the recognition by the US nation-state that they had achieved, according to Alexander. Here resides another convenient and strategic truncation capitalizing on the groundswell originating from the so-called slum-dwelling Black people to reinforce the role of the well-educated interlocutor between the masses of Black city dwellers and the city/nation around the needs for school desegregation—a slightly different but not radically alternative vision from that of deputized officers of the law. These formulations also fail to attend to the full ramifications of the claims to space and the practical end of Black austerity that the police archive catalogues. It predefines the riot in terms of American citizenship—a strategic and effective harnessing of this power generated from below but a distortive framework prematurely delimiting riotousness to a vision of US political-economic integration.

As Berson documented, rioters hurled rhetoric marking Moore and other Black leaders by way of their class station and orientation as these entities attempted to contain their actions on the bullhorn. Residents forcefully wrote back with the description of Moore as the "handkerchief head Uncle Tom," suggesting his class's representational politics as those subservient to the interests of whites. This forceful demarcation as retrograde the politics of civil rights as the domain of the educated interlocutor between the disaffected and the state suggests the bottom-up generation of the transformative power harnessed for a particular paradigm of social change by a charismatic leadership class but distinct from and preceding it the enduring political potential generated through worldcraft and reterritorialization in the face of dislocation, fallowing, and enclosure within dark agoras, the derided spaces of the underground and the set-apart in and through an enduring relation to one another. Again, as I developed in the preceding chapters through Erica Edwards, charisma is a complex power formulation. It derives from potential and in this case kinetics that precede and exceed its articulation, striking back against the charismatic figure himself, challenging the interlocutor's capacity to mediate on behalf of.

Somewhere outside of these acts of containment registering in the competing inscriptions is not the truth about the riot but rather an incomplete and flickering refraction of plotting's enduring materialization and power to effect visions of the urban future in the context of the beginnings of deindustrialization in Philadelphia. There is a horizon glimpsed in the gaps in these inscriptions of a temporary injunction against the state's prerogatives of violence, abstraction, and disposability. There are inscriptions of uncaptured Black life assaulting symbols of the domineering power enacted in urban segregation, throwing bottles and rocks from some unseen location at helmeted officers or their vehicles and breaking into and commandeering goods at stores in which they were usually forced into humble subservience to price gouging for critical lines of credit for food and other basic necessities.[27] My rewriting of the riot is a formulation of retrospective strategic essentialism, where I read the collective actions of the marked body of rioters as the glimpsing of a horizon beyond landscapes of property and exclusion and characterized increasingly in North Philadelphia after 1950s–1960s urban redevelopment into geographies of radical inequality, where difference could be walked, felt, and seen.

Although Bradford later gave an interview to the *Tribune* in which she was able to partially speak for herself and was pictured, the majority of those involved in the aftermath of her arrest were given no such opportunity. When she appeared there, it was to defiantly continue her denunciation of the police's violence, but it was also partially obscured by the use of dark sunglasses. In the remainder of the chapter, I use this embodied effort by Bradford to stand defiantly before the photographer while also shading herself from direct view to justify that darkening out of names to obscure the biographical information used within police records.

This act is critically different from redaction. Redaction is generally one of the state's primary tools to hold up a putative freedom of information while also obscuring its own subversion and violent repression. The darkening out helps to form a visual poetics in this chapter that some readers will find frustrating because of the inability to follow basic biographical information across incidences. The darkening out and obscuring, following the lead of Bradford in her appearance in the *Tribune*, draws out the defiant spatial acts that precipitated this archive of police records while parting with the fantasy of full knowability and intelligibility. This is not meant to render the rioters as pure action, either. Rather, it helps to paint a portrait of collective spatial dynamics of everyday resistance in a context of unilateral power heightened by the Cold War context of urban emergencies. I draw on Christina Sharpe's critical dyad of Black redaction and Black annotation as possibilities for generating histories toward otherwise horizons within archives of violent containment.[28] My hope is that the strategic obscuring will bring to the fore the everyday acts of spatial politics that constituted the disruption and its aftermath, beyond binaries of calculated premeditation and radical spontaneity that de-agentalize rioters by marking them as either the dupes of outsiders or as emotional miscreants led to violent action as a generic mob formation. Using this formulation of Sharpe's "Black redaction," and specifically embracing Bradford's presentation before journalists of direct defiance while maintaining a semblance of personal privacy, not allowing viewers to engage her eyes directly, facilitates fabulation around the spatial elements of this archive, bringing in fleeting view the geographies of quotidian existence as they morphed into geographies of resistance during the disturbance.

Reconstructing the Geography of the Riot: Black Re-Commoning

During the aftermath of the initial eruption, Black residents of North Philadelphia claimed a right to "standing and talking" in the street despite the limitations imposed by the mayor's curfew. In their rejection of the order to move from corners, stoops, and streets, they revealed an alternative (Black) map of the city wherein the rights of property remained communal and tied to inhabitance rather than to the titled designation of ownership in deeds and private space that serve as the interface between the state and racial capitalist markets in urban land.

At 12:10 a.m. on August 30, twenty-four-year-old ██████████ and twenty-six-year-old ██████████. were among a crowd of more than twenty people standing outside on the 2200 block of North Sixteenth street. When police demanded that the group disperse, they collectively refused. Officers then arrested ██████ and ████ in an attempt to coerce the remaining people to disperse. The arrest did not achieve the desired effect, and the crowd remained. Interviewed at the precinct, ██████ and ████ claimed that they had committed no wrongdoing. Despite the mayor's orders for a curfew and a ban on congregating in the streets in the blocks affected by the riot, the men claimed "that they were just standing talking."[29] Officers read the idiom of quotidian Black social life as insurgent, dangerous, and in need of clearing. Although officers were hostile, they were justified in viewing "just standing talking" as an insolvency, as a lack of desire to submit to the reassertion of law. Here, "just standing talking" signified a claim to sovereignty and autonomy, defiant in the temporary outlawing of Black social existence embodied in Tate's proclamation.

At just after 4:00 a.m. on August 30, police arrested ██████████, ██████████, ██████████, ██████████, and ██████████ at the corner of Nineteenth and Fountain Streets. The men were sitting on the steps of a row house when officers approached and demanded that they disperse. They would not get up, using their refusal to press back against the mayor's proclamation seeking to render their claims to communal life after nightfall illicit and automatically tied to the riot.[30]

At 9:35 p.m. on August 31, highway patrolmen George Gundy, John Herbert, and Joseph Beukers spotted a group of twenty or more Black people assembled near Marston and York Streets in Strawberry Mansion. The officers ordered those assembled to disperse, invoking Mayor James Tate's public edict calling for the arrest of all residents of Central North Philadelphia who decided to remain outdoors after curfew. While the majority of those assembled disbanded, ███████████ "refused to move" and was thus "put under arrest." Refusing to go without a struggle, ████████ then attempted to take patrolmen Herbert's night stick and break free. In retaliation, police violently subdued him, later writing in euphemized passive past tense that "sufficient force was used to keep the arrest." Caught in the wide dragnet of policing powers legitimated by Tate's attempts to enforce unlawful assembly laws in the wake of the public breach of law and order by ordinary North Philadelphia residents, ████████ statement at the time of his arrest underlines the dialectic between legality and order and Black fugitive geographies in their expression within the terrain of the city. When asked if he was "aware that he was not to be on the corner during the period of the recent riots," ████ ████ responded that "he was aware but he lived just nearby." His words illustrate the different territorial claims of residents of Strawberry Mansion over and against the state's claims to order and security. ████████ maintained a vision of communal property in the outdoors that Black communities held onto and enforced over and against their violent suppression by the state, driven in its imperative to protect the recognized property rights of storeowners and other property holders.[31]

Police officer Arnold Dehn arrested ███████████, a twenty-three-year-old resident of North Forty-Second Street, just after midnight on September 1. Accused of "loitering and acting in a disorderly manner . . . stopping automobiles on the highway," ████████ was arrested for violation of the mayor's curfew. While even a regular beat patrolman might not have viewed ████████ actions as dangerous, Dehn was a park patrol officer, unaccustomed to the daily social-spatial dynamics of North Philadelphia. In his statement to investigators, ████████ explained his stopping of passing cars as attempts to secure a lighter for his cigarette.

Dehn interpreted these actions as disruptive rather than communal, and in the expanded powers of the mayor's orders, arrested ▮▮▮▮▮. For ▮▮▮▮▮▮, this arrest was a violation of the collective ownership of the outdoors. When the interrogators asked ▮▮▮▮▮ about his failure to obey the mayor's proclamation, he denied the rights of the state to supersede the communal and collective rights of city residents, defiantly claiming his "right to be on the city streets" despite Tate's injunction of all outdoor activity in the area of containment.[32]

Claiming space on one's stoop or on the sidewalk or street adjoining a residence, which the police registered as refusing to obey the injunction against congregation, suggested another set of claims on urban landscape, ones not guaranteed by law but worked out in the quotidian appropriation of the stoop and other spaces beyond the row house or apartment as part of the functional geography of use and through that a claim to sovereignty in relation to that geography outside of the state's regulation through use. Given the ways that many of the residents rented their living spaces, these claims suggest competing visions of territoriality, control, and power in the urban landscape staged from those with little legal protection in a city that regularly experienced the collapse or ruin by fire of so many Black spaces. This claim of a relation to space in front of one's rented apartment in a subdivided row house in North Philly is not recognized by law. In the face of the law's enforcers, Black communities' use of the stoop and the sidewalk adjoining one's place of residence as part of the territory over which one argues for propriety heightened in significance in the legal climate of a mayoral order since this form of assembly registers only as obstinacy. The effort to extend claim to the dimensions of the geography of vitality in the stoop, on the sidewalk, and at the corner indexes an alternative system of value, an enduring complex and competing ethos of sovereignty, ownership, and connection through utility and possibility over the demands of extraction, profit, capitalist reproduction, and public "safety."[33]

Matters of intimate connection led some to defy the police-enforced curfew. For example, in spite of the curfew, at just after 10 p.m. on September 4, ▮▮▮▮▮▮ attempted to hail a taxi at the corner of Thirty-Third and Berks Street to visit his girlfriend across town. Suspicious because of an unidentified package he carried under his arm, officers John Marcus, James Tierney, and Charles Wszolek approached ▮▮▮▮▮

to inquire about where he was going and what he had in his hands. Annoyed by their questioning and the delay they imposed on his trip to meet his girlfriend, ▇▇▇ refused to answer their questions and according to the reporting officers "became loud and boisterous." He refused to answer any of their questions, and although they thwarted his plans with their arrest, he intended to evade the curfew to continue his own social life.[34] Black social life, even the mundane details of a lovers' late-night rendezvous, were tented with suspicion in the gaze of the police, who could see nothing in Black street life but the potential for further violation of order, breach of the peace, and potential theft.

Sometime after 11 p.m. on September 4, eighteen-year-old ▇▇▇ ▇▇▇▇, walking to meet his sister to escort her home, ran into some of his friends, among whom was twenty-year-old ▇▇▇▇▇▇▇. ▇▇▇▇▇▇ and ▇▇▇▇ stood together in a covered doorway talking when officers Reuben Jones and Milton Giddien approached them and shoved them against the wall. Although officers reported that the boys were "acting in a disorderly manner" before being approached, the corroborating accounts by Warner and Wellington demonstrate that they became rowdy in response to the policemen's physical aggression. Angered by the officer's use of the riot sanctions to enact an even greater level of violence than normal on Black people leading their everyday lives, ▇▇▇ yelled at the officers as they subdued him and his friend that he "whoop their ass . . . if they did not have a badge and gun."[35]

▇▇▇▇▇▇, twenty-one, of North Carlisle Street, threatened officers who arrested him, ▇▇▇▇▇▇, and ▇▇▇▇▇▇▇ for supposedly "acting in a loud and boisterous manner" just outside 1950 Marvine Street in North Philadelphia. When officer Richard Watson began to pat him down and asked if he had any concealed weapons on him, ▇▇▇ responded that "I don't have a gun or a knife." Looking defiantly at the officer, he continued, "But if I did, I would kill you."[36] ▇▇▇, like many others, espoused a tacit refusal of the mayor's proclamation. While others made explicit their collective right to remain outdoors despite the mayor's prohibition against congregating outside and the banning of alcohol in the neighborhoods surrounding Columbia Street, ▇▇▇ simply "could give no reason for being out other than he wanted to see his girl," according to the investigator's record. Likewise, ▇▇▇▇ ▇▇▇▇ and ▇▇▇▇▇▇, both arrested by the same officers as ▇▇▇

██, "could give no reason for being out," despite admitting to having "heard of the Mayor's Proclamation," tacitly acknowledging their claim on the spaces of corners and stoops despite the mayoral order to protect property as a set of material possessions and capital in land.[37]

Black youth demonstrated their contempt for the occupation by delighting in the jumpiness and nervousness of officers. Two juveniles, ███████████ and ███████████, manipulated officers' fears of the rebellion to derive a joke at their arresting officer's expense. In the middle of the afternoon on September 2, as they saw three officers patrolling the areas around Nineteenth and Sharswood Streets, they feigned distress and yelled out that around the corner, an officer was in trouble facing a crowd of rioters. Just as the officers began to sprint in the direction in which the youths pointed, the youths began to laugh, taking delight in their ability to make the officers run unnecessarily. The offices, of course, marked the two youths as having breached the peace and arrested them along with two adults who were also part of the group making fun of the officers.[38] ██████ and ██████ exposed the fragility of the officers' sense of peace and control despite the permissions granted by martial law to violently assert dominance over Black North Philadelphia. These boys, like many oppressed communities besieged by an occupying force, used the tactics of the weak, those exposing the uneasiness of the occupiers in the face of their superior fire power and reclamation of the sole uses of violence within the cordoned space of the riot zone.[39]

These claims to territoriality spilled into the renegotiation of property relations that governed Black residents' lives through hunger and want. Theft, and the circulation of contraband food, liquor, clothing, and other resources, show a glimpse of the intersection of the enforcement of violent lack through hunger and the injunction against these relations signified in the taking of food. In particular, I am interested in food for what it can say about both enduring hunger and the visions of collectivity through fugitive commensality. As police entered families' apartments and homes in the aftermath and found an excess of food, clothing, and furniture, they considered it contraband, either because they determined that the residents could not afford them or because they looked out of place in their current environment, too pristine to have been there before the beginning of "looting." Looting, despite violent inscriptions by the state, in this context names a means of expressing Black futurity from the vantage of the captive. It signifies the appropriation of the means of care in a neighborhood defined by urbicide, joblessness, and hunger to establish the means of a new urban horizon. As Rinaldo Walcott argues, "The purpose of looting is not stealing . . . as it is commonly understood . . . nor is it about reparations." Rather it draws on a legacy "like breaking tools and damaging buildings . . . during slavery" to send a clear message to those subjugating Black life and communities to the dictates of property.[40] According to Vicky Osterweil, mass public taking of mobile goods and the destruction of private property serve to redistribute material wealth and send a forceful collective message to police, property owners, and the arbiter of these relations, the state.[41]

People who were criminalized for procuring food, alcohol, weapons, and other items police determined did not belong to them or of which they were in illegal possession pushed back against the discourse of looting and theft with a discourse of discovery wherein they told police that they found things or were gifted things. This marks the fugitive possibilities in fungibility that C. Riley Snorton describes in another context, feigning ignorance or forging the names of some obscured entity collapsible into the otherwise indiscrete Black mass of North Philly's neighborhoods usually operative within police's beat patrol orientation to neighborhood geography. The idea that one had simply found or by happenstance come into the possession of items ranging from lima beans and beer to a loaded weapon from some absent individual, "Johnny," dead-ended the officers' investigations in murkiness and obscurity. It also redeployed the figuration of the generic juvenile delinquent we encountered in chapter 3. Fugitivity in Black fungibility facilitated a foreclosure of further interrogation even as it entangled the individual in charges associated with disorder.

While police viewed the veiled lies about where those caught had gotten items as mere ruses for theft, taken together, they demonstrate the cogency and coherency of the momentary rebellion against insurrectionary networks that provided them with the received stolen items. The stolen goods evoked a network of re-commoning—the redistribution of concentrated things withheld as property to advance the ends of Black social life in and through insurgency. As ████████, a twenty-eight year old living on North Eleventh Street walked past a taproom at Simmons Café, at 2165 North Twelfth Street near Susquehanna Avenue, he saw five other people exiting the bar with bottles of whiskey and gin. ▇▇ followed suit, helping himself to five full and half-used bottles from the bar's reserves. Police caught him as he exited carrying the liquor. Likewise, ▇▇▇▇▇▇▇, an eighteen-year-old, told police that he has seen unnamed people carrying liquor out of the location and decided to act. Rather than entering the bar, however, he maintained that "the bottles were on the ground outside of the bar" when he picked one up. The intentional obscuring of the other unnamable and unrecalled assailants, or "looters," and in ▇▇▇▇ case their effort to place bottles on the curb, use the haziness of individual identity in fungibility to dead-end investigation and to shelter a fugitive nerwork in what the police documents highlight as absurd claims.[42]

In some cases, the obscuring of Black networks of absconding with goods, an organized attack on property through re-commoning, took the form of flat refusal. When police arrived at the Place Pigalle Bar at 1527 West Columbia Street, they "observed a group of men run from the taproom" with beer. While the police could capture none of these men, who were successful in their escape, when they entered the bar, they found ▇▇▇▇▇▇ and ▇▇▇▇▇▇▇, both of North Philadelphia, "piling cases of beer on the bar" and assisting the fugitive network lifting alcohol against the city's prohibition of its sale and consumption across the neighborhood. During their interrogation of the two men arrested for burglarizing the Place Pigalle, the arresting officer asked the men why they were inside the taproom. According to the police record, both defendants responded, "What taproom?"[43] While the police record is unreliable, given its bureaucratic shorthand for Black inferiority in repression, this response reverberates the history of refusal, the radical interruption of further interrogation with the feigning of complete ignorance, even for something for which you have already been caught by the law.[44]

A juvenile at the time, ▇▇▇▇▇▇▇ had prior experience with law enforcement, as evidenced by three previous arrests. After visiting his sister on Diamond just west of Broad, he began walking home when he claimed to encounter "several boys trying to break into" the Clover Bar at the southwest corner of Twentieth and Montgomery Avenue. Maintaining no previous familiarity with the boys and denying that he was involved in the attempts to break into the bar, ▇▇▇▇ told police that he ran when the police arrived because "he did not want to become involved." The police, as in many other files, inscribed over this "seen by police" in a handwritten addendum, negating ▮▮▮▮ denial directly.[45] Read from the angle of fugitive fungibility, however, this shadowing with what officers understand as a mere ruse for culpability by someone they already considered delinquent because of an existent juvenile record refuses further interrogation and disavows any knowledge of the group of boys who scattered as he was caught.

The city's underground in the period of the riot was seen as being anchored in North Philadelphia's taprooms. These sites doubled as one of the most common sites of re-commoning, with police making dozens of arrests at these sites in the context of the mayoral prohibition against alcohol purchase or consumption within the designated residential community under siege by police. The mayor and officials seeking to "make sense" of the riot in its aftermath blamed the concentration of taprooms and the shadowy assemblies—the dark agoras—associated with the underground for which they served as an infrastructure for the disorder. In late November 1964, Mayor James H. Tate stated that police investigators "are convinced that the civil disorders in North Philadelphia were greatly intensified, if not actually caused, by the heavy concertation of taprooms, taverns, barrooms and similar establishments."[46] According to Berson, the area near Columbia and Ridge in North Philadelphia contained 255 taprooms at a ratio of one to 855 residents. This ratio exceeded the 1,500 residents per taproom that was recommended by state law, and according to the district attorney cited by Berson, these spaces generated a number of "run-ins with the police." According to the attorney general, the tap rooms along Columbia Avenue and on some of the corners along side streets in the neighborhood incubated "gambling, prostitution, sale of narcotics and other illegal drugs, assault and battery, larceny and rape."[47]

The taprooms also represented fundamental sites of the city's political reproduction. As Berson also noted, many of the same taprooms thought by Mayor Tate to have fueled the riot also funded the city's democratic political machine, sponsoring events that served as fundraisers for block captains and others at the base of the city party system. Taprooms signaled danger because of the role they played in fueling Black insurgency; yet they also served as the social-spatial fold where municipal power was imbricated with and regenerated itself through an enduring if often unacknowledged link to the underground. The state, as envisioned by reformers from the 1940s, manifested itself through the sanctioning of concentrated vice through the party structure and the ostensibly contradictory move to rearticulate state power by the marking the taproom and all it represented for negation and violence. And yet the taprooms sponsored calendars for the city's Democratic Party, purchasing ads from Democrat block captains. The "looting" of bars doubled as exposure of the edge of city politics and governance, an assault on where juridical order was made and unmade.

The theft of liquor underwrote the redeployment of the earlier formulations of illicit drinking culture among row houses in the neighborhood that interwar migrants recollected. On September 4, at 10:45 p.m., officers William Mc'Kelvy, Guy Katz, and Melvin Goldslum entered a row house on 2917 West Columbia. Although they did not report why or under what legal authority they entered the home, they arrested a group of seven middle-aged North Philadelphia residents on charges related to alcohol possession after finding them "sitting drinking" on the second floor of the building. Holding that she had purchased the liquor and beer that included whiskey, gin, and Ballantine and Schmidt's brands of beer for a Labor Day celebration, ▮▮▮▮▮▮ denied that she was selling the alcohol. Nevertheless, the police charged her not only with a breach of peace violation of the mayor's proclamation but also with illegal alcohol sales and a "disorderly house." Before, during, and after the riot, the progenitors of the Black informal economy or the underground, along with "radical exhorters" and other political dissidents, remained primary targets of police aggression, viewed by the state, politicians, and police as the primary drivers of the mayhem, easy scapegoats for the disregard of normative property relations exhibited in the riotousness.

The underground, as a form of congregation that shadowed normative expressions of social living in the city, continued endangering the visions of urban futurity that were rooted neatly in the confines of the home and extended spaces the ethos of the Black commons to the tight blocks of North Philly and other sections of the city. The underground, the shadowy and often opaque or hidden spaces of disreputable Black sociality and insurgent social life, provided a lifeline to many of the marginal residents of North Philly. ▮▮▮▮▮▮▮▮, a forty-one-year-old unemployed man living in the neighborhood, could not get stable work, but he was able to connect with "Slim," who tasked him with purchasing eight cases of beer and delivering them to an address. Police caught him in the act and arrested him for breaking the mayor's ban on alcohol consumption in the riotous sector of North Philadelphia. The underground exposed its most vulnerable participants to policing, so it is not some heroic space of purity wherein one might find uncomplicated subjects and power relations. Nevertheless, in the absence of remunerable work for a Black middle-aged man facing unemployment, the underground served as a point of access to the resources denied by the owners of capital. "Slim" and ▮▮▮▮ articulated a relationship of mutuality and possibility, hidden from and shadowing the normative relations of property and resources, a relationship that police, especially in the context of the riot, viewed as suspicious and punishable.[48]

Part of the transgressive spatial vocabulary of the riot was the disregard for property imagined by police and sometimes realized in the contraband that emerged. Police officers' policing of objects that they considered to be beyond the means of Black residents of North Philadelphia implied a familiarity of these agents of the state and the exclusion from American materialism imposed on and enforced through moralism only in the nation's slums while promoted as part of the normative functions of the white home in the reproduction of racial capitalism. Officers arrested ▮▮▮▮▮▮▮▮, a twenty-six-year-old resident of the neighborhood, on September 2 because he had a tape recorder in his possession. Officers approached him and questioned him because they acknowledged that a young Black man in the deindustrializing section of the city was unlikely to have access through normal means to such a luxury item. When they questioned him, ▮▮▮▮▮ retorted that he had not stolen the item but had found it on the sidewalk on Columbia Avenue.[49] Again, there is an impertinence in denial, in the feigning of ignorance. Denial continues to cloak the underground networks of Black insurgent social life within opacity, unintelligibility, and unknowability here strategically deployed to obscure.

Some among the crowds amassed stolen objects to create a shadow market. After receiving a report, police went to Fifteenth and Callowhill and found ▮▮▮▮▮▮▮ selling men's trousers out of the trunk of a car owned by ▮▮▮▮▮▮▮▮. Alongside what they considered contraband pants, police also found a crowbar, which in the report, alongside the men's clothes, buttressed the characterization of the men as involved in the reappropriation of commodities from stores along Columbia Avenue and adjoining areas. Later, when ████████ returned to his car from a nearby automotive parts store, police questioned both the men, who denied knowing one another prior to the police's inquiry. Their denial of even knowing one another dead-ended police questioning, even as it rendered them more suspicious in the eyes of their arrestors.[50] Police apprehended ████████████, a forty-three year old residing on North Fifteenth Street, carrying men and women's clothes. Although he could not produce any receipts for the items, he maintained that he had purchased them from the store. It is unclear whether he intended to sell the items or had procured them for himself and someone else he knew intimately. He was arrested and charged with receiving stolen goods.[51]

Stopped by police on North Berks Street for a traffic violation, twenty-three-year-old ████████ was found in possession of tools, several quarts of oil, a garden hose, and a baby's car seat that appeared to police as "new and unused." ██████ said that he had purchased the garden hose and the baby seat at a store on Tenth Street. He also admitted to buying the quarts of oil and tools from people residing in nearby housing projects, although he refused to name anyone.

The 1964 riot arrest record embodies the ongoing visceral dynamics of hunger—here the desire for food but also a desire against the horizon of never enough for basic material goods to incubate against exposure, and overall shaping insurgent Black social life. While under Father Divine's influence, Peace Mission adherents defied the racial and spatial organization of hunger by opening the communion table, "rioters" driven on by "exhorters" engaged in the illicit confiscation of food, the urban manifestation of fugitive commensality in a world that continued to be defined by intergenerational starvation. After 2 a.m. on August 30, a young Black teenager handed ████████ a cardboard box containing a small feast—two bags of frozen lima beans, a strip of spareribs, a pork shoulder, and three pounds of butter. Arrested for "breach of the peace," █████ was assumed to be a looter because of the large cache of food confiscated by officer Joseph Gleason. The next day, again around 2:00 a.m., police arrested forty-nine-year-old ████████ in the same vicinity carrying seven dozen eggs. He claimed to have purchased them in New

Jersey, but because he could produce no bill of sale, police charged him, too, with breaching the peace. The investigator, Harry Erickson, marked in pen an addendum to the report noting that Ben's Market, owned by Ben Naiburg at 1235 West Diamond Street, later reported the theft of forty dozen eggs. While it is not clear if the two ███████ were blood relatives or if they knew one another, the proximity of the addresses reported and their shared last name suggest the possibility of a collective founded in kinship but reinforced with food contraband.[52] The theft of food during the riot signifies a critical cultural continuity in crafting the Black commons that extended in time through a desire and aesthetic of abundance against lack into 1960s Philadelphia, as well as the ongoing role that state-backed collective starvation played in shaping everyday Black experience and resistance. By their assumption when they arrested people that only theft could provide such abundance, police acknowledged quotidian hunger.

What officers described as looted objects when they investigated Black people's interiors suggest the dialectic of violent want and the erection of the Black commons as a space of commandeering the means of captive maternal collectivity and futurity beyond a horizon of depravation. When officers entered twenty-two-year-old ███████ apartment, they found that she was in possession not only of lady's pocketbooks but also children's winter coats, children's easter hats, winter socks for youth, three children's winter snow suits, a girl's dress, a pair of child slacks, and women's underwear. Despite saying that she said she had found the materials discarded in front of her row house apartment, ██████ was arrested and charged with receiving stolen goods. Although she was caught, she employed the grammar of looting to literally insulate her small children from the cold and to engage in her own pleasure through fine underwear and purses. She also was committed to having the appropriate attire for church.

Following a lead, officers of the Major Theft Unit were issued a search warrant to enter a home near Nineteenth and Columbia Ave. Upon entering, they arrested thirteen year old ███████ for a cache of items that he admitted to "finding" on Columbia Avenue, according to police. Officers confiscated two end tables, boys shoes, a brown dress, a boy's gray sweater, boys pants, twelve fresh white T-shirts, a box of name-brand dishware, two serving trays, and a baby's bassinet. This list of items suggests the ways that the transposition and transformation of the Black commons in the urban context through re-commoning in the city during the riotous breach extended visions of captive maternal futurity against the terrain of austerity and violence. The serving trays and dishes and the baby bassinet signal forms of collectivity and futurity marked as contraband but nevertheless reappropriating the means of possibility in the shared meal, in the comfort of the young baby also residing in the residence.

The stakes of placing Black collectivity and futurity as a horizon of being and becoming over property given passage in the breach drew on the rubrics of plotting in the refractions of its translation and transposition and opened the road for the emergence of the era of radical Black Power in Philadelphia, which I take up in the subsequent and final chapter on the organization MOVE.

6

On the MOVE

Dark Agoras and a Black Phenomenology of the City after the Riot

The daily rhythms of post-riot North Philadelphia left an invisible but traumatic mark on Janine Phillips. A seventeen-year-old living near the corner of thirty-first and York Streets in the Strawberry Mansion neighborhood just west of the riot's epicenter, she suffered debilitating anxiety that by her late teenage years in the early 1970s manifested as an inability to breathe. "I couldn't eat, I couldn't breathe," she remembered. With time, Janine's physical and mental well-being deteriorated ,and she eventually "developed a condition where [her] throat would close up." Despite seeking the treatment of physicians, going from "doctor to doctor, hospital to hospital," she could find no relief.[1] As Celeste Henery argues beautifully and damningly in contextualizing Black women's collective inability to breathe, Black women's "bodies course with their exposure to hostile worlds" manifesting as truncated, subdued, and foreclosed breath."[2] Unlike Pearly Manager in the 1940s, whose physical debilitation—the result of straddling the South and Philadelphia and living in the underground—was outwardly visible, Janine's debilitation took the forms of less-tangible anxiousness that nevertheless resulted in a familiar refrain in Black life, "I can't/couldn't breathe." Janine, like members of the generation preceding hers, was debilitated through the routinized "expected impairments" associated with disposability that was exacerbated in the 1970s by deindustrialization and the rise of a fascist municipal regime under Frank Rizzo.[3]

Janine embodied the trauma and stress of a cityscape defined by a patchwork of deterioration and urban redevelopment, sequestration, and containment, bearing it as a constant sense of panic. Anxiety and the inability to breathe it produces is a common condition in postindustrial worlds left behind by organized capital, especially in the absence of collective formulas for abating the worst effects of market fluctuation and capital's geographic movement. This is particularly true in the worlds of imposed fiscal austerity that constitute the distinctively neoliberal response to economic transformation after the 1970s in the United States. In Philadelphia, the economic restructuring of the city precipitated for large swaths of North, West, and Southwest Philadelphia, "slow urbicide," a formulation "underscore[ing] the violence against the material conditions . . . of coexistence."[4]

A predominantly working-class Black community, Strawberry Mansion was defined beginning in the early 1970s by its economic dislocation. Rapid deindustrialization through plant closures and the attendant increase in under/unemployment rates drove the preponderance of violence and delimited residents' social and economic opportunities to the bottom rungs of the globalizing city. The effects of the city's broad economic decline in the area were exacerbated by the effects of the riot. White business owners and others permanently closed in the riot's wake, and the city's leadership was redefined by the law-and-order severity of Frank Rizzo, who rose from police commissioner in 1968–71 to mayor in 1972. These processes manifested as the physical deterioration of housing and public infrastructures and the intensive carceralization of certain neighborhoods that were defined by the imposition of surveillance, policing, and other modes associated with and connected to the expansion of jails and prisons. Those who could find work among Black working-class communities found marginal positions as late twentieth-century Philadelphia expanded reliance on hospital facilities, tourism, and other non-industrial labor markets that employed Black residents in the least lucrative care industry and service work. In this context, large segments of the population in North, West, and South Philadelphia experienced redundancy or permanent unemployment in the legal economy. Those who did find work often found jobs defined by the violence of poorly compensated, tedious, and repetitive work or undercompensated or uncompensated care and reproductive labor.

Like Pearly Manager, who drank and smoked at his leisure, Janine took her body into her own hands. She began to self-medicate, turning to body- and mind-altering substances to cope with being "sick all the time," to deal with her "whole system . . . breaking down." She began to combine alcohol and drugs, using the altered psychological and physiological statuses they provided to temporarily ease anxiety, then declared later that "I was a drug addict, alcoholic, whatever . . . anything I could do to calm my nerves ease that pressure." The use of mind- and body-altering substances, as Janine acknowledged, opened a channel away from anxiety, pain, and trauma and created a momentary salve in an otherwise unlivable world, connecting the ecstatic location of the historical underground to that of the late twentieth century. Despite this capacity for drugs to transubstantiate the dire reality of the ordinary, to transfigure the tedium of poverty and redundancy, however, Janine's use of substances to cope with the uncontrollable anxiety she experienced drove further insecurity and damaged her relationships with her children and her husband. "We argued every night; he drank every night; I took drugs every night, and we fought every night" she recalled. This discord left her despondent: "I felt hopeless . . . I was at the end of my rope."[5]

Then, on an afternoon in 1973 while walking in the city, Janine encountered a group of people whose message radically altered the course of her life. According to one of her first recorded recollections, the organization MOVE, led by John Africa, "was having a demonstration and I just happened to be passing by. I stopped to see what was going on, I listened to them speak and what really caught my attention was the strength, confidence, and assertiveness of the MOVE women." Although she later suggested that she had intended to attend the street rally, this earlier account of a chance encounter with the transformative message again underscores the significance of the phenomenological experience of the city's underwriting of discordant and heterodox Black urbanisms. Janine's initial attraction to the vocal and strident MOVE women was confirmed in the tranquility that washed over her after "seeing the people, seeing and feeling that peace" from the street demonstrators.[6]

Although the women who joined MOVE were by 1973 already known by police and by other activists and organizers for their use of profanity and for what many considered their brash political tone and their loud and public denouncement of all things associated with mainstream politics and culture—including other civil rights and Black Power organizing efforts—this vociferous street-demonstration style elicited a feeling of peace for Janine not unlike that which so infused the converts to earlier movements, including the Peace Mission. Alongside their more antagonistic denunciations of the federal government, the police, local politicians, markets, jails, prisons, zoos, and all other factors contributing to the destruction of human and nonhuman life on the planet, MOVE women also preached the possibilities of transformation back to a "natural state"—an inversion of the current order of separation and violence and the return to a state of harmony between people, the planet, and other nonhuman species. In particular, in their role as mothers and leaders in their own right, MOVE women asserted that they could help bring about a catastrophic revolution to the spatial, political, and economic ordering of the city. These women embraced a vision of urban futurity that not only parted with the imperatives of economic growth anchored in the social and economic reproduction of white nuclear families and homes but directly confronted this model and sought to uproot and displace it from the block. They rejected growth, seeking instead to decolonize the urban landscape starting up and out from the row house.

The MOVE women's rap helped Janine site her anxiety not as a personal flaw but rather in the "reform world system," which Janine specifically associated with her schooling at Dobbins Technical and Vocational School in North Philadelphia and that the members of the organization understood more broadly as the combined corruptive force of racial capitalist markets, bureaucratic institutions, the state, and all other functionaries radical or reactionary that reified these entities by not moving outside of the system to build a natural order. For Janine, this was a revelation. For Janine, like other members of MOVE, school had served as a site of violence, reproducing discipline and anxiety rather than preparing them for what they considered a meaningful existence.

MOVE captured the all-encompassing scope of their religion and philosophy in a single phrase identifying the object of their combat: "the world reform system." Their naming of this broad mission proclaimed their refusal to isolate a particular agency as the singular culprit for insecurity, death, and destruction, rather holding out its connections across the various functions of the state and markets. The group viewed policing, war, pollution, and sickness as the products of an interconnected set of institutions, ideologies, and practices that were animated primarily through channels of violence and death operating at the planetary scale.

MOVE's terminology remained capacious, drawing together under one name the various sources of violence shared between markets and state functions along a continuum from policing to development. As

Micol Seigel's work demonstrates through the formulation of "state-market" functions in relation to policing, the easy demarcation between functions of the state supporting market growth and the state's policing functions maintain no clear distinction, with actors and ideologies moving between these functions.[7] The containment of insurgent Black social life constituted a set of coterminous projects aimed at stabilizing urban political economy that planners enacted from the 1940s to the 1970s. MOVE's efforts at injunction against the ongoing articulation of the "world reform system" at the level of the home, the block, and the neighborhood registers these connections. Delineating not one central agency but an entire coordinated system meting disease and death in the name of life, their naming of the "world reform system" demanded attention on the sinews connecting projects to "reform" the cityscape, market imperatives centering growth, and collective debilitation and death.

Like the Managers before her, Janine's encounter with the women of MOVE and subsequent physical and mental transformation through the principles of John Africa drew her into a new existence. For her, the adoption of the principles or philosophy of life that were forwarded by the group transformed her sense of social well-being that before she had defined primarily by her capacity to mother her children: "After joining MOVE my children and I became very close, because of me incorporating the principles." Renouncing her previous indifference and avoidance of spending time with her child, a product of her substance use, her embrace of the teachings made her what she described as "a true mother." As she noted, for the first time, her child wanted to spend time with her. Because she left the street and the quests for drugs, she began to focus her attention intensely on her child until they were inseparable. This description of political transformation, foremost through the embrace of true motherhood, perhaps seems at odds with liberation in relation to Black women, ostensibly consigning them to confining traditional gender roles in relation to care and social reproduction. However, this claim in the name of true motherhood takes on alternative registers in relation to Black reproductive justice invoking the desire for the capacity to escape austerity and anxiety imposed limitations on social affiliation and familial connection in order that one might enact new worlds with those of one's own choosing and in this book's account of the consistent effort within the spaces of the set-apart for the cultivation of other worlds through the reimagining and redeployment of reproductive labor. As Ula Taylor develops in her treatment of the women who joined the Nation of Islam, women often adhered to what outsiders registered primarily as restrictive formulas for proper gender expression like the mother and wife roles, and they often did so for the promises afforded by patriarchal protection in a world defined by the consistent violation of Black girls and women, their economic, social, and sexual exploitation.[8] As well, Shamara Wyllie Alhassan's work to recover Rastafari women's worldmaking efforts in Jamaica underscores the importance of Black women's spiritual and placemaking practices to the early Rastafarian movement from the early twentieth century.[9]

Janine's embrace of true motherhood through her adherence to MOVE's doctrines was confirmed for her not in the baptism of the holy spirit but in the reciprocal affection demonstrated by her children. The shifting relationship between Janine and her children, their affection, their touch, their attention, and their desire to want to spend time with her, are what ultimately affirmed her transfiguration by the teachings. This focus is not to ignore the question of charisma and its role in reproducing the violent gendered and classed hierarchies of movements and other lines of flight. It is, however, as Ashley Farmer models through her work to bring together women working across various paradigms to transform Black Power politics, to take seriously the wide-ranging experiences and responses of Black women and their political outlooks to the corroding violence of the US urban contexts post-migration communities in the era of Black Power's emergence.[10] Moreover, it helps to explain Janine's and others' enduring commitments to these teachings and their transformative power in their personal, familial, communal, and political outlooks after being separated and isolated in prison, as well as after their founder, Vincent Leaphart was murdered by the Philadelphia Police Department's 1985 bombing of the group's home in the Cobbs Creek neighborhood of West Philadelphia. It was Janine's relationship with her children and her connection with them that was transformed by her adherence to John Africa's "Law of Life." It was her sustained commitment to that transformative experience, with its embrace sustaining her and nourishing her politics, that endured, despite the separation of a decades-long stint as a political prisoner and the loss of MOVE's leader after her arrest and conviction in 1978.

This chapter centers MOVE as a radically set-apart Black Power–era organization in the decade of its formation before the infamous May 13, 1985, bombing of the organization by the Philadelphia Police Department. While the group, until recently, fell outside the purview of Black Power politics for its prickliness and discordance, it has emerged in scholarship and public writing primarily in relation to the catastrophic violence of police antagonism.[11] While attending to the 1985 bombing and the series of events that it culminated is significant, this chapter builds on Richard Kent Evans's work to center the group's theology and to relocate MOVE within a broader trajectory of political and social formulation, especially regarding experiences of the city and placemaking that emerged from the longer history of post–Great Migration Philadelphia.[12] Viewing the group's formation through the formulation of urbanism enacted through passage between dark agoras and the dialectic formation of identity, belonging, and geography that articulated the underground and the set-apart, centers MOVE as the historical expression of an ongoing counter-movement against enclosure and displacement in the urban context rather than as an aberration defined through its relation to spectacular state violence.

MOVE's doctrines and narratives of radical transformation evidence the familiar refrain of prohibitions against modalities of living and being that have been associated with the underground and with its attendant states of degradation and impurity across the other chapters. MOVE, however, operating in the context of the shifting political and social terrain of the post-1964 era in Philadelphia, radicalized the set-apart formation, connecting it with an explicit lived practice of decolonization that seeks modes of life and living outside the ordinances imposed through sanitized citizenship and an alternative lifestyle. MOVE's geographic formation is at once unique and familiar. Like many set-apart groupings before them, they did not simply resign themselves to removal from the underground or the world of West Philadelphia's "the Village" but rather continued to interface with elements of the street and the underground, combining the "rap" and the form of vociferous renunciation associated with the 1964 riot to fish new members and to create a solid line between those who were adherents to the teachings of John Africa and those who continued to live a lifestyle that participated in the colonization of all forms of life and the earth's ecological processes.

Eddie Africa grew up on Kingsessing Avenue in the city's Southwest section. Eddie described his community as "a poor neighborhood" and "the ghetto," and indeed, in the 1970s, the once bustling industrial working-class community began to crumble as deindustrialization eroded the economic base of the region. Unlike other MOVE members, including their leader, Eddie had completed high school and "was getting ready to start college" before joining MOVE. He described aspirations to become a social worker but also admitted that school served as a ruse for thrill-seeking and fun rather than for serious academic study: "I was going to school because of all the parties, all the women." Eddie ultimately became disillusioned and "talking to teachers, they never interested me, so [he] dropped out." Following his defection from the trajectory of middle-class aspiration, Eddie began to live as a hustler, taking formal work in order to *werk* and tracing a rogue phenomenology of the city wherein the life of hustling traced a more fundamental expression of a Black anti-work ethos that later informed his decision to convert to the teachings of John Africa. Eddie described finding positions in businesses where he "would last six months." After gathering a sense of the rhythms and money of the business, however, he recalled, "I'd wind up trying to rob the place and get fired or just stealing." Eddie's appetite for theft and indulgence in a life of hustling was driven by the "certain things [he] wanted or thought [he wanted]: cars, clothes, the drugs." He described the illicit spaces of Southwest as spaces that influenced his use of drugs, indexing the wider social world of dark agoras. He later entered under the auspices of MOVE as its minister of education. According to Eddie, his friends drew him into drug use through the subtle replication of values conditioned through his capacity to "fit in." His use was further fueled, however, by escapism akin to the earlier modes of ecstatics described in previous chapters and here a discredited form of futurity defined by the extrication of one's consciousness from the present hell of confinement, surveillance, policing, and economic exploitation for even a few minutes of a high. "I was doing drugs then because I was frustrated and I just thought it was a way out," Eddie reflected. Escapism for Eddie, the illicit pleasure of doing what one is not supposed to, perhaps passing the time in a state of timeless floating for downers or psychedelic drugs or rapid uptick in one's rhythms for uppers, brought him into direct conflict with the police, which helped define his eventual transformation as part of MOVE.[13]

Eddie's testimony also detailed the proximity of religious purism around sex that reinforced formal matrimonial patriarchy in MOVE and the illicit sex mapping of Philadelphia's Black sexual communities. In addition to his drive for women before and during his marriage, Eddie also described his dabbling "in the life." Twice during his testimony regarding his life before joining MOVE, Eddie describes sexual contact with other men. He accredited his encounters with "a life style of homosexuality" to his parents, who "did what they were taught to do . . . [and that] wasn't right." He also described how the instability of his relationship with his wife because of their mutual infidelity and consistent separation and return over a ten-year period "was leading [him] towards homosexuals." Although following the doctrines of MOVE he renounced these encounters, they brought him near the unwieldy affects of the "Black ecstatic," which as Aliyyah Abdur-Rahman describes, represents an "alternate structure for the black queer beyond, one rooted not in the temporal logics of futurity but in the affective, embodied, and relational pleasures of the disastrous now."[14] According to Eddie, his encounters with the ecstatic through queer sex "perverted" his outlook and made it so that "anything was all right . . . anything was acceptable." Although Eddie and other MOVE members renounced these forms of sex under the teachings of John Africa, their proximity to them registers the complex cartographic imaginary traced between the underground to the radicalized set-apart, which was fraught with frenetic sensuality and untamed desire.

Like members of the Peace Mission and other esoteric movements of an earlier generation, MOVE's vision for large-scale social organization departed from the visions forwarded by dominant urban futurists that, again, is the basis of the definition of Black queer urbanism as a disruptive social-spatial force up and out from the plot, materializing changes small and large, fleeting and permanent, on the cityscape. MOVE adherents repurposed the nuclear family through its connection to the larger MOVE "family"—a meso-social formulation that for them superseded the extended connections of biological or blood relation and that was

defined by strict adherence to the teachings of their leader. As codified by the 1980s, these principles encompassed visions for familial, social, and ecological sanctity and rejected the mainstream associations of
progress, citizenship, and urban order and futurity:

> 1. 'education' is not education, but training to serve 'the system;' 2. 'Justice'
> is not justice, since many are prejudged and never receive fair treatment;
> 3. Canned and processed foods are carcinogenic. Therefore we eat raw,
> unprocessed foods; 4. We intend to keep our children from being con-
> taminated by the system; 5. We use profanity on purpose to show how
> people can be revolted by profane language but not by a profane soci-
> ety that does such violence to so many; 6. Animals should be treated as
> humans.[15]

To codify their new commitments and affiliation, adherents adopted
the surnames Africa. Despite the group's rejection of homosexuality,
they embraced an equally queer formulation of connection through adherence rather than blood that disrupted the vision for tamed intimacy
forwarded by dominant urban futurists under the rubrics of standard
living that promoted a binding connection between hearth/residence as
a private social space and neatly defined familial connection through
"blood." In their adoption of the surname Africa in particular, we
can also see hints of a version of what Alondra Nelson terms "root-
seeking"—a desire to anchor oneself in a context outside the racial violence of US communities—which she investigates as part of her work
on Black genetic ancestry testing.[16] The adoption of new surnames for
MOVE served as a primary signal of the new hierarchy they constructed
in their formation. They no longer sought legibility in relation to the
state or some outside entity of power; they were now part of an unmovable and resolved formulation of collectivity anchoring itself outside
of the domain of US sovereignty, even as they remained committed to
staying in Philadelphia. Critically, they embraced what Yannick Marshall elucidates as the political position of the Maroon—as those seeking neither recognition nor resolution with the settler-colonial state or
the city.[17]

MOVE, like the Peace Mission and other groups that were closed
to the outside world a generation before, reinforced certain patriar-

chal visions of social order in the service of a disruptive vision of non-normative futurity; in their case, a committed vision to devolve the territorial relations of dominant urbanism into what outsiders could only interpret as disorderly and unsanitary. Like their forebearers, they collectively purchased a building and reimagined it according to their theological and ideological specifications. Beginning in the 1970s, when the organization began seeking to amass more followers to their doctrines, MOVE built a "headquarters," which for them signified an outpost of the coming world remade in the teachings of their leader. In part driven by the escalation of the group's first standoff with police and the siege eventually declared by Rizzo and police, the organization transformed an ordinary row house into a rogue territory within the city, rendering it a space fleetingly ungoverned—outside the jurisdiction of city and US sovereignty and territoriality and offline from city gas infrastructures—a space wherein they could reproduce their own vision of autonomy, health, and well-being defined theoretically by social and ecological harmony and in a common refrain from previous chapters, peace.[18] This physical manifestation of the group's metaphysical rebellion is what drove the ire of neighbors and police. They were viewed early on, especially by white homeowners in Powelton Village, as a disparaging force; one University of Pennsylvania scientist describing the changes they enacted on the block as akin to transforming it into a "pigsty." MOVE terrorized the horizon erected by reformers in their vision of standard living and growth by invoking and embodying various tendencies of the plot—eventually as an armed Black subversive force disarranging urban order through the invocation of rural imaginaries associated in their paradigm with "the natural," which for outsiders also registered as the group's deterioration of their community into a "pigsty."

We can register within Janine's conversion narrative a de-spiritualization of certain lines of flight recuperating and replaying the plot in the post-1964 context of Black urban politics and culture in the wake of the rebellions. However, to treat MOVE as solely political and to ignore its theological basis is to ignore the metaphysical reordering that the organization sought in its renegotiation of the earthly terrain. By embracing and articulating new modes of connection with divinity and with place, MOVE engaged in a mode of stewardship whereby it embraced disruption to redefine and partially actualize mutuality as ways of resisting materialism, separation, enmity, violence, and war. Beginning as the Movement for Christian Life before becoming MOVE, the organization's members possessed an abiding faith in their leader as the true arbiter of divinity on earth and even in his absence, continuing after his 1985 death. They enacted his vision of earthly peace not as a passive relegation to silent prayer but rather as a vociferous demand to create a new sovereign order of being, belonging, and earthly reciprocity as the means of what in other contexts might be understood as the promise in insurgent Black theologies for condemnation of those dominating Black life and subsequent millennial peace.

MOVE's formula for an alternative lifestyle governed by the immediate decolonization of all life forms from the "reform system" in action competed with and directly confronted two other formations that shaped Powelton Village after the redevelopment projects associated with the University City redevelopment that were spearheaded by the University of Pennsylvania and Drexel University. On the one hand, the group confronted gangs and other groupings that they viewed as corrupting forces and, according to their self-produced history, dampened tensions between these groups and university students. Additionally, the group had confrontations with several neighbors who sought to create what we might view as the emerging sites associated with a nascent rubric governing city life—livability. For example, while neighbors, primarily homeowners, wanted to build a community garden, MOVE wanted to use the same space to exercise their dogs, whom they considered coequal life forms. MOVE confronted (white) livability head on, building tension between the group and neighbors. Neighbors accused MOVE of maintaining unsanitary living conditions and noted especially the potential for disease that such a lifestyle brought. MOVE countered these accusations, charging that the lifestyle of livability grafted onto the neighborhood by reformers and planners and backed by city power and universities' financial resources was the major force undermining all forms of life, human and nonhuman, at a global scale. On August 12, 1975, the *Tribune* published an article titled "Neighbors Claim They're Terrorized by MOVE Folk," asserting that the organization beat and abused their neighbors and turned the area around their home in Powelton Village into a "pigsty." "They're not the sweet little lambs they pretend to be," Phyllis Babcock told the *Tribune*. "This used to be a peaceful community where Black and whites respected each other's rights, but MOVE is terrorizing people and trying to destroy the community," she continued.[19]

According to another neighbor, theoretical physicist and University of Pennsylvania professor Gerald A. Goldin, members of the organization "physically broke into [his] house and screamed that they were going to kill [his] wife and children." This alleged violence and intimidation was in large measure a conflict over space and resources. As Goldin noted, tensions between him and the group grew as the organization attempted to force its way into a food co-op "to use [it] as a dog kennel," according to Goldin. When Goldin and others refused, the group allegedly turned to threats of violence. Moreover, according to the same article, "several residents" of the apartment building adjoining MOVE's headquarters moved, leaving the building completely vacant in response to MOVE's harboring of trash and refuse in their backyard. Neighbors then alleged that members of the organization began to squat in the vacated building illegally. Goldin concluded that positive coverage of the organization emphasizing its peaceful nature by the *Tribune* amounted to an "affront against every decent resident, Black and white in our neighborhood."[20]

In a direct refutation of these accusations, Louise Africa used her "On the MOVE" column at the *Tribune* to directly contest Goldin and the other neighbors' accounts of the organization. She acknowledged that part of the discrepancy was an epistemological problem attributable to their very different outlooks on the neighborhood, the city, and the urban future. "We told ya'll time and time again, that you don't know what you lookin' at, when you look at MOVE," she wrote. "If these people's eyes were seeing clearly, they'd be able to see," she continued. For her, as was true for the other members of the organization, Vincent Leaphart's teachings, his embodiment as John Africa, and the principles attributed to John Africa for a social existence in harmony with all living things provided the only prism through which to engage life. It led her and the others to understand their work and lifestyle as set-apart, against the backdrop of all other modalities of living that they associated with the debilitation and death of the system. Louise went on to denounce the allegations that they terrorized their neighbors. According to her, "These so called 'terrorized neighbors' come to us asking advice about child rearing, about diet for their children . . . seeking advice about how to properly care for their dogs, and they attend our study sessions as well." As further counterweight to the allegations of the group's brutality, the reality that they weren't "lambs," Louise recalled the efforts by several neighbors who, to aid Davita Africa during her forced eviction, went so far as to come forward as witnesses to the brutality that Davita and other MOVE members faced during their removal. Calling attention to the dynamic of contested terrain between various uses by white professionals and the organization, Louise intimated that other neighbors sided with MOVE against the food co-op. Further, Louise emphasized the ways that the group interacted in mutual and meaningful exchanges with the majority of their neighbors, who chatted with MOVE from "their porch during the summer" or who came "over to chat with MOVE members, while we wash[ed] cars." Louise also invoked the groups' collaborative efforts to celebrate one of the elders from the block, sixty-three-year old Pop Johnson, for whom, she maintained, the group threw a birthday party in 1974. Contradicting reports that they threatened the elderly, she noted that some of the elderly residents of the nearby nursing facility "ask[ed] MOVE members for money to buy cigarettes, coffee, an ice cream cone and we [gave] it to them."

Next, Louise countered the idea that the group physically attacked neighbors, arguing that they had made Powelton Village "safe for people to walk the streets." In noting the transformation of the neighborhood, she outlined the basic contours of how the group's set-apart vision manifested for them as a practical and theoretical remaking of the community outside the entanglements of the deadly world reform system. Rather than antagonizing the white residents, as Goldin and Babcock implicated, Louise held that the organization "made it safe for white college students to walk the streets," while at the same time, it also made it safe for "Blacks to walk the streets of Powelton by eliminating the threat of being harassed by these 'overzealous' cops." What outsiders identified as the group's terrorizing, Louise understood as its practical leverage: "Gang members are very careful about beating up a white, because they don't know whether or not that 'white' is a MOVE member, and they know what MOVE is about, so it is with cops who just want to 'stop' Blacks—they too are careful, because they don't know whether or not that 'Black' is a MOVE member—and they also know what MOVE is about—and what we ain't about."[21]

According to Louise, MOVE had established a new sense of territoriality and order grounded in the "writings of JOHN AFRICA" and banished other forms that had the potential of corrupting their ability to access spiritual enlightenment and bodily well-being, those associated with Powelton's designation in Philadelphia vernacular as the Village. This shortened designation employed by Louise suggests the ways that the mappings of this space within the matrix of the Black underground preceded the group's remaking of it as a territory governed by the teachings of John Africa. The inscription of the Village was a coproduction of Black vernacular description connoting the neighborhood as having a reputation and the inscription by the media and police as a site of the subversions associated with the underground. Despite efforts in the late 1950s for the transformation of Powelton Village through the rehabilitation of apartments by the Powelton neighbors and the recognition by the Pennsylvania State Chamber of Commerce for its "do-it-yourself" rehabilitation program, local redevelopment efforts on the part of white homeowners could not completely scrub the Village of its image as a seedy Black sector. MOVE wanted to reclaim it from the reality of vulnerability to bring the area in line with its vision of social-spatial-cosmological integrity through separation rather than integration into the global economy and the state.

Some among those who had once taken part in Powelton Village's gang warfare and who also took part in "'joint' parties, alcoholic orgies, and almost any other thing you can name" gained in the teachings of John Africa the means to self and communal world reform system. "THESE PEOPLE are now deeply rooted committee members of the MOVE Organization," Louise wrote.[22] Here in Louise's assessment, the organization got its primary political imperative, what she identified as "DIRECTION," as well as its political leverage vis-à-vis police, white neighbors with more social and economic power, and street gangs in the area's reformation from the Village to a territory governed by the group's esoteric teachings, its attendant life style, and its modes of placemaking in the neighborhood. Although MOVE members rejected their former affiliations with the underground, it was their experiences as urban subjects with varying affiliations with the underground that brought them to the teachings of John Africa. Recall from above how Janine Africa first saw the forceful women of MOVE, whose energy drew her into the

"rap." Although a more recent online profile suggests that she intention-
ally attended the rally, her earlier 1981 recollection suggests powerfully
that it was by chance encounter that she met those proselytizing the
teachings of John Africa. Janine's subtle edits here are attributable to the
fluctuating nature of memory. Especially for those committed unwaver-
ingly to what they believe not only as politics but also as religion, fluctuation around the initial encounter suggests an earnest attempt to make
sense of and situate spiritual and political transformation over time.

Like the Peace Mission movement and other heterodox religious organizations vilified as "cults" in previous decades, MOVE adherents traversed spaces of social and economic abandonment and bore firsthand
witness to the devastating effects of this on the physical and emotional
well-being of poor Black communities. During the trial of John Africa
in 1981 stemming from the 1978 police siege of the group that led to the
destruction of the group's compound and the death of a police officer,
Eddie Africa described a life of transformation and healing that freed
him from the clutches of an "unnatural" existence defined by physical
debilitation, psychic and spiritual hardship, social conflict, violence, and
illicit living associated with the lot of Black people under the "world reform system" for the "natural" living outlined by their leader. Eddie's testimony, like that of Janine, was not designed to make a reasonable case
for the innocence of the defendants, John Africa and Alphonso Robbins.

The 1981 trial followed Vincent Leapheart/John Africa's near two-
year evasion of law enforcement seeking to arrest him and Robbins for
the 1978 shooting of a police officer during MOVE's first standoff with
police at the Powelton Village headquarters. The same charges landed
the MOVE 9 in prison for thirty years. The MOVE 9 is a designation
that members, especially Pam Africa, drew attention to along with John
Africa's most well-known adherent, Mumia Abu Jamal, as the group's
political prisoners. MOVE members who testified did so largely to dis-
seminate their dissident vision for a social-ecological order. Rather than
seeking the kind of legibility usually associated with innocence, or reasonable doubt, in American jurisprudence, MOVE members embraced
their nonconformity and dissonance while in court, advocating vocifer-
ously for the retraction and devolution of the infrastructures of standard
living. Recall that standard living co-constructed a multi-disciplinary
metric and a program of urban life and futurity whereby reformers, re-

searchers, charitable organizations, and city officials defined Black life as death through competing discourses and practices oriented toward the city's long-term growth from the Progressive and post-Progressive eras.

The conversion narratives of Eddie and other MOVE members reveal the geographic and social proximity of the illicit spaces of the street, such as the corner and the drug den, and the compounds and other meeting spaces of organizations and religious groups considered heterodox, esoteric, and cultish to outsiders, reinforcing my analysis of the critical if under-studied seam in mid- and late twentieth-century Black urban life wherein the creation of value around life and living did not adhere to the edicts of gendered racial capitalist order. Rather, post-migration Black communities continued to express through conversion from the illicit to the often hyper-respectable, esoteric, and cultish spaces they cultivated a different axis of value organized around Black vitality rather than markets and recognizably stable social-geographic forms. MOVE's development in the course of the 1970s prompted by their growing conflict with the Philadelphia Police Department and other policing agencies of the state, such as the ATF, public health officials, and social workers, also powerfully illustrates the ways that the underground and the set-apart were drawn together by their geographic and political grammar. Though set-apart, under constraint and pressure from the state in the mid- and late 1970s, the organization converted to a spatial and social forms weaponized in the formulations usually associated with the underground. They fortified their Powelton Village house against police, staking a claim to spatial and political autonomy. Before that, however, MOVE invested its primary energies in the resolution of Black death through the destruction of the system they analyzed as meting out death across lifeforms by drawing people in through their "rap."

Eddie, like other members of MOVE, did not leave the illicit, fugitive geographies of the Black underground in an attempt to access the features of a normative bourgeois lifestyle of property, homeownership, and row-house domesticity. Rather, he left the life to join a form of Black gathering considered dangerous to urban social order in Philadelphia and maligned as a deviant formation defined by supposed cultishness. Eddie's trajectory, like that of other members of MOVE, illustrate the complex terrain created by dark agoras as the spaces of Black underground culture and dark agoras as the opaque sites cultivated through esotericism. Before joining MOVE, between it and the underground, he noted that he "was a Black Muslim" who "didn't like white people." The proximity—indeed, the circuitry—between the underground and various types of religio-political communities defined through heterodoxy generated a force that provided friction against, at a minimum, and often outright refusal of key aspects of the vision for the city's future outlined by planners, architects, public health officials, and the police.

Eddie's transit from the underground did not take him away from illicit dark agoras; it redefined his role within them, marking a radical point of departure for value and values in and through place afield of property and propriety in the normative senses outlined by dominant urban futurists. Working-class Black communities and the institutions that generations of southern migrants shaped served not merely as the placeholders of anti-value but as practitioners, theorists, and phenomenologists articulating, maintaining, and defending a set of values anathema to the stable production of racial capitalist relations and geographies whereby the spaces of Black gathering imbricate producing a different map of the city and thus often a radically different vision for the city's future. Eddie's testimony demonstrates the endurance of alternative axes and registers of spatial consciousness that continued to coevolve with the formation of the underground as other discredited formations of Black sociality and collectivity.

Eddie's mission as minister of education contrasted sharply with his life prior to joining MOVE. As he testified, he had two children prior to joining MOVE, "and they were doing as [he] taught them which was crazy. Just hanging on the street, no kind of exercise, whatsoever, just hanging around." For Eddie, this resulted in his eldest child's weakness; he noted that she "could hardly walk sometimes . . . she couldn't run unless she would fall." Additionally, in contrast to his mission under the direction of MOVE of preaching to the people he described as alcoholics and gang members, Eddie's life prior to the organization often crossed into the dark aspects of the Black underground, the space of illicit leisure that threatened to subsume the productive and (normative) reproductive capacities of bourgeois social order. In particular, Eddie described a penchant for stealing from the places where he worked. In his life before MOVE, Eddie subverted the workspace as a place of producing and accumulating capital, engaging in theft and pilfering rather than productive work in a continuum with the re-commoning brought into public during the earlier 1964 "riot." This brought him into direct conflict with the police, as he was arrested for robbery prior to going to prison as part of the MOVE 9 in 1978. In addition, prior to joining MOVE, Eddie described drug use that also brought him into violent conflict with the police: "I would be walking down the street smoking some joint and have a cop see me. He'd stop me and I'd get smart and we'd get to fighting, and I'd get locked up." In a fashion similar to the interwar and earlier postwar working-class Philadelphians of the Great Migration generations, Eddie's journey, in his own estimation, from wretch to wonder helped define the miraculous nature of John Africa's philosophy of life to outsiders. As well, his proximity to the underground gave coherence to his narrative of transformation within the discourses of working-class migrant institutions, especially "cults" from the decades before.[23]

Phil Africa's testimony in the 1981 trial suggested the discordant temporality that MOVE's law of life operated through. When asked by defendant Alphonso Robbins how long he had been part of the family, Phil responded, "I've been in the organization a long time. I have not tried to keep count of how long I've been in the organization, such as years, as people would say, because it interferes with my religion" which "teaches that Life has no age." This reimagination of temporality as not measured by the hegemonic clock or calendar and the non-temporal nature of a larger force, "life," reinforced Phil's dedication to the organization: "In practicing my religion I do my activities as they're needed . . . I don't care about the time, the months, the years," he explained.[24]

This theorization of the boundless temporality of life for Phil and other MOVE members also served to inform an alternative understanding of politics and sovereignty. For Phil, this alternative formulation of time as boundless, which allowed him to engage in dedicated service to the work of transformation outlined by the organization, contrasted with that which he ascribed to "this system, this society," which, he argued, was "built around the disguise of deception" wherein "people are respectful of someone if they are wrapped in a five-hundred dollar suit and has alligator shoes"—a reference to then mayor Frank Rizzo. Hegemonic time—the system of clocks and calendars—was connected to political deception, the notion that the wealthy governed in the interest of everyone, allowing the negative social and environmental effects of the system to continue unabated in the present.[25]

While outsiders discredited MOVE, according to Phil, that was because MOVE spoke "the truth, [and] because people have been taught to accept the lie for so long they are afraid." For Phil, this general fear of "truth," as well as the deception of politicians, buttressed an economic and social landscape dependent on the denaturing of the planet. Phil contrasted the simple truth of MOVE's doctrines with this convoluted system that held up destruction as progress: "When MOVE says that the air is polluted, it pollutes everything. And when we tell you that DuPont or General Motors pollutes the air, that's the truth." Those outside of MOVE, those still entangled in the system, had no choice but to help perpetuate it. As Phil argued, "Society depends on people like DuPont and ARCO to pay their mortgages." Here, Phil directly connected the destructive aspects of capitalist production, its so-called collateral effects like pollution, directly to the primary infrastructures of racial capitalist social reproduction and to housing made available through federally insured mortgages.[26]

MOVE members worked to disentangle themselves from these systems because of the false premise of American society, which for them held that everyone was entitled to things. Phil mobilized the analogy of gold to map the sought-after trinkets produced by American capitalism to the social- and earth-defiling systems of abstraction and uneven trade on which they depended. Phil asked those listening to his testimony in court to "look at the gold that people wear . . . That gold is made in Africa, and when it comes over everybody can't have a gold chain." For Phil, the metaphor of gold chains exemplified the global theft of riches from Africa and the exclusion of poor Black communities inside the United States. He argued that only the "people who went and took those gold chains" could have them in the United States. Eventually, this led to social conflict, since "the boys on the corner that don't have a job" would then act to "take it [the gold chain] from you." In contrast, he argued, "MOVE does not believe in the so-called riches that this country has to offer." This, according to Phil, explained the wider society's antagonism for the group and its truth, since others operated under the obscuring ideology that linked commodity consumption and well-being. As he lamented, "This country is based on an illusion that everybody can have what the man in the White House has."[27]

Phil, like Eddie, Jeannette, and the others, situated his transformation under the teachings of John Africa as a turn away from consumerism with all its corroding social and environmental effects. "Before I came to the teachings of John Africa, I used to wear $100 alligator shoes," he reflected. Although Phil did detail his life prior to joining MOVE as fully as the other members of the family testifying during the 1981 trial, he narrated his transformation as part of a collective one whereby he and others joined MOVE and left lives associated with the city's underground. "You look at people's records in the MOVE organization before coming into MOVE, and you see junkies, and you see gold snatchers, and you see drug addicts, you see teachers, you see pimps, you see prostitutes . . . But look at us now," he commanded. The analogy between teachers and hustlers here reinforces MOVE's prickly and discordant politics, casting aspersion on the normalizing institutions held to be in the public good under Keynesian governance and planning, by linking it with the discredited Black underground, and by viewing them as equally destructive entities.[28]

The proximity between MOVE and the underground was further underscored in Phil's testimony as he contrasted the "honest work" the group did "washing cars or fixing up people's houses or cleaning up yards" with other forms of "hustling work." For members of MOVE like Phil Africa, dark agoras, the spaces of shadowy gathering and existence associated with racialized slums, were no less a cognitive and cartographic touchstone than they were for formal urbanists. Yet the spaces of economic and social isolation and the insurgent activities of the social life of the underground, like hustling, inspired MOVE to express the destruction of the infrastructures of standard living and not to remove or exile the vulnerable. The group did not malign drug users, hustlers, or pimps; rather, they identified these groups as some of the system's most acute sufferers and also acknowledged their own former place among them. MOVE sought to proselytize, or as Phil described, "spread health in the community," among those yet suffering the ill effects, albeit they did so from a radically different epistemic entry point articulated under their rubric of return to a natural state that was central to their ideology.

Like the Peace Mission before them, personal physical transformation also manifested an insurgent spatial politics that while never attaining the international reach of Father Divine's Peace Mission, nevertheless reshaped West Philadelphia's landscape. With money from Donald Glassey, an original white member who later turned state's witness against the group in 1978, as well as funds from William "Whit" Smith, the organization made a down payment on adjoined houses at 307–309 North Thirty-Third Street in 1972. The group's efforts to return to a state of nature centered in their rogue "rehabilitation" of the house serving as the organization's headquarters, whereby they sought to define the space as sovereign territory operating outside the legal apparatus of municipal, state, and federal governance and under the authority of John Africa, thus subject only to his "law of life." From the vantage of the communities circumscribed by the Village, they viewed the infrastructures of standard living proposed, projected, and executed under the auspices of dominant urbanism as debilitating, alienating, and ultimately death generating, citing Black people's place at the bottom and the earth-defiling systems on which these infrastructures depended, like oil.

MOVE's efforts to radically rehabilitate their first headquarters contrasted sharply with the efforts of Drexel University to radically reterritorialize Powelton Village, which also helps explain the dialectic of violence between the organization and the state. Beginning in 1959, Drexel joined the University of Pennsylvania, Presbyterian Hospital, the Philadelphia College of Osteopathy, and the College of Pharmacy and Science to create an economic development corporation that continues to function as the University City District. The corporation's task was to "reclaim blighted residential areas in West Philadelphia" to "help neighboring residential areas keep pace with the development of one of the nation's great educational, medical, research and cultural concentrations." Modeled after similar partnerships, such as those of the University of Chicago and Columbia University, that transformed the areas around their urban campuses, this redevelopment agency set its sights on the largely working-class Black community inhabiting the area bounded by Haverford Avenue to the north, rail tracks to Media, Pennsylvania, to the south, Fifty-Second Street to the west, and the Schuylkill River to the east. The agency envisioned a future for West Philadelphia as a competitive center of research and "a community which holds and attracts institutional and cultural facilities" and was explicit for its desire to displace the current residents in order to attract and retain "large numbers of the population not now attracted to the area." The goal was to transform slums into "standard and marketable residential areas served by adequate schools, parks, churches, and shopping." Concomitant with the goal of transforming Philadelphia's "Black Bottom" and the "Village" was their extension and enhancement of the municipal government's various powers to police. In addition to committing to help the city enforce zoning, fire, and housing codes, the organization also sought to "obtain better police protection" for the area. The agency was terribly successful in its efforts. Between 1962 and 1968, it facilitated the destruction of the historic "Black Bottom," one of Philadelphia's oldest and poorest Black neighborhoods, which was razed to make way for the expansion of the institutions.[29]

By the mid-1970s, the area had been radically transformed through urban renewal, setting the scene for MOVE's efforts at a form of Black queer urbanism through rogue rehabilitation—an effort at reclaiming urban space for an expressly anti-urban future. Denouncing the rubrics of rehabilitation promoted by planners and corporate developers, MOVE worked to disconnect their home from the wider infrastructures of standard living and commanded a novel if also resonant vision of territorial sovereignty. The group removed the furnace from their compound and disconnected themselves from electric power and gas energy in order to remake their home according to their principles. They understood these basic urban infrastructures of energy as dangerous hazards that not only threatened to engulf individual homes in inferno (a palpable danger in 1970s Philadelphia) but that also drew on fossil fuels, nuclear power, and other ecologically destructive processes in their maintenance. Rather than seeking "world class" educations for their children, they denounced the Philadelphia school system as a primary disseminator of misinformation. They withdrew their children from public education and replaced the systems education that they understood as brainwashing with an education in the principles of life as articulated in John Africa's philosophy.

In contrast to the deadly and defiling operations of the system, MOVE forwarded what they interchangeably termed a law and a philosophy of life, the core of which was a respect for all living things. In contrast with what they characterized as the materialistic and unhealthy relationship with food, alcohol, and drugs and the dysfunctional social and familial relationships promoted by the system, MOVE's members engaged in a minimalism that reimagined consumption through an ideal of raw vegetarianism, a strict prohibition of alcohol and drugs, and the peaceful reengineering of social relationships.

During his 1981 testimony, MOVE's minister of defense and coordinator of its "underground activities," Delbert Africa, declared himself before the court as the "law and disciple of John Africa." Delbert decried the group's castigation by the press, which he said "scandalized" the group by projecting its own "mental problems" and "frustrations," born of the system, onto MOVE. He addressed the charges that he and his brothers and sisters, as well as their leader were insane, declaring, "We're not crazy." In contrast to what the media described as the group's "gibberish," Delbert asserted the doctrines outlined in the teachings of John Africa as "the truth." Delbert recast the normalizing efforts of the media to tame MOVE by labeling them as crazy and therefore as discredited by contrasting the healthiness of MOVE's members with the "mess of the news rooms," where the colleagues of the journalists discrediting MOVE members "are dying everyday of heart attacks, strokes, cancer." He pointed out that although the media discredited MOVE "for years for being dirty, filthy, out of our minds, they have yet to show one diseased MOVE member." In contrast to the healthiness of MOVE's members, he noted that the same journalists denouncing MOVE "face[d] a medicine cabinet full of pills, pills to wake up, pills to go to sleep, pills to stop diarrhea and pills to start diarrhea." And "yet they'll call us and castigate us as sick and diseased," he continued. Instead of biomedicine and its obsession with a vision of pharmaceutical treatment and well-being through pills, Delbert argued that "the teachings of John Africa . . . are a medicine to cure of this sickness"—the sickness of a society profiting from unhealthiness rather than total well-being. Delbert couched a trenchant critique of the logics of pharmaceutical capital and a US sense of well-being in the heterodox teachings of John Africa, grounding health in a renewed relationship to and practice of one's own body among the community of those equally committed to transformation and transcendence.

MOVE members shared their stripped-down living quarters with dogs, with whom they often shared exercise in their exacting physical regiment of running, taking members sometimes upward of ten miles a day. Outsiders, including neighbors, accused them of creating fetid conditions that supported the growth of creatures usually designated vermin in need of extermination, particularly rats and roaches. Although MOVE denied these accusations of filthiness, calling attention to the irony that the city, for the first time, was concerned that Black children faced roaches and rats and calling attention to the system's perpetuation of life-draining pollution and social, ecological, and spatial relations that promoted unbalance and death. Moreover, MOVE members also countered the assertion that rats were disease-causing agents, recasting the system as the cause of urban rat populations harboring of disease. In one frame, that the most common urban rat populations had their origins in continental France in the age of the colonization of the Americas, MOVE made a valid if not practical point about the erection of global capitalism and the disruption of the spaces of various species habitats as deadly not only humans but even for such a reviled creature as the rat.

To promote global interspecies peace, adherents of MOVE theorized a vision of spatial sovereignty whereby each living thing was afforded the right to its own habitat. This vision of a natural order mapped lateral rather than hierarchical relationships between spaces as well as species. MOVE refitted their Victorian era house into what they termed their "headquarters." MOVE's growing conflict with the police between 1972 and 1978 resulted in part because MOVE claimed a right to violence against the system. According to adherents of MOVE's philosophy, this system, organized through the principles of radical exploitation, was most egregious for its threat to living in the broadest sense of all forms of vital energy. MOVE theorized the world reform system as entangling and colonizing all life and indicted it for having created products like bombs and conditions like pollution with the capacity to extinguish life.

MOVE's sense of autonomy and spatial sovereignty expressed a vision of violence that was sometimes unclear to outsiders in court and in the media who painted the group as wantonly violent. While rejecting weapons and warfare, they did embrace the right for "self-defense." Phil was committed in this belief, stating before the court that "self-defense is in fact what keeps us alive." Further, he held that "when you violate the law of self-defense, which is a guide to your right to duty, to leave yourself open to anything that happens to you, that's when you become hurt." He attested to the violence of the state, which he said both killed his son and withheld recognition of that death by means of bureaucratic violence: "They [the Philadelphia Police Department] killed my son in '76 . . . [and then] they tried to tell us, because my son did not get a birth certificate that he was never born." Phil said John Africa kept him from totally destructive violence against the "sick society" in the aftermath of his infant son's death. Nevertheless, the violence of "the most racist cops in the United States, the Philadelphia Police Department," inspired the group to take up a new strategy of self-defense, which Phil believed "allowed us to survive." "We kept Mayor Frank Rizzo," he noted, "as much as he hates blacks, as much as he hates revolutionaries, as much as he hates poor folks, us being all three things collected together, we were able to keep that man off our backs, to keep him from doing the things he wanted to do to us." MOVE's embrace of self-defense in the growth of their conflict with the police department was in response to the violence of the state, which pressed them to take their visions of radical discordant sovereignty further, leading to the crescendo of the 1978 conflict and the later 1985 bombing.

MOVE's visions of spatial sovereignty and of decolonized urban space were connected to Vincent Leaphart's biography. If Father Divine's followers held that he survived a lynching and a Georgia chain gang, the leader of MOVE survived the internecine carnage of both the US war in Korea and the ongoing travesties of the Vietnam War.

During Vietnam, the United States waged total geographic war seeking to destroy not only strategic military features but also symbiotic ecosystems like villages and forest, as well as infrastructures built over hundreds of years like the complex hydraulic system of the Red River delta on which the bulk of the North Vietnam population depended for living area and basic sustenance through rice cultivation. Alongside the devastation that Vietnamese villagers experienced, Black soldiers likewise experienced disproportionate death, as they were confined to units directly engaged in hand-to-hand combat with Viet Cong forces. Black men's death rate during some years of the conflict was nearly double their percentage of those serving in Vietnam. Like Divine before him, Africa obscured his past, including his military service. And yet in his novel interpretation of the order of being John Africa extended the terrain of peace proposed in the edicts of the Peace Mission, commanding of his adherents a radical respect for all life forms. Here we bear witness to an invective mirroring and therefore inverting the totalizing violence of deforestation, hydraulic destruction, and industrialized murder to which MOVE bore witness. MOVE's designation of sovereignty and power to every living thing, the group's demands for peace except in self-defense, their radical abolitionist call for releasing all people and animals from cages, and the group's practical transformation of their own living sphere so as to minimize consumption and their negative effects on the wider biosphere evolved in dialogue with the violence of late-twentieth-century containment politics. Here we see the ongoing struggle to delimit and foreclose socialist and communist revolutions around the globe and the systematic surveillance and violent assault against Black radicals and "extremists" among others within the context of the United States itself. John Africa's philosophy was a direct injunction against sickness and death, and yet this was not a simple continuation from the era of Divine's authority and adherent-held divinity. Africa and Divine encountered and narrowly survived different regimes of exposure and death. Their parishioners also faced different circumstances. If the violence of unchecked infectious conditions and jail time in post-plantation landscapes of the US South, US Up South, and Caribbean archipelago drew the many to the likes of Father Divine for healing, sustenance, and abundance, the necropolitical landscapes of tedium and austerity of deindustrialization and care service sector growth drew in the adherents of MOVE and other religio-political affiliations (even those marked as apolitical) to the promises of a natural and peaceful existence set apart from the social violence eddying out from violent capital dislocation. If Divine's adherents relinquished biological family, sex, alcohol, gambling and other modes of insurgent Black social life in the city associated with the underground to cultivate a world of devotion, followers of Africa similarly relinquished non-adherent family, narcotics, alcohol, illicit sex, and affiliations with the underground, like neighborhood gang membership, for a novel mode of congregation defined by peace (if also engaged in conflict to achieve it).

Although Philadelphia was not Vietnam between the 1970s and especially in the 1980s under Wilson Goode, Philadelphia's first Black mayor, the city's Black communities experienced a violent reterritorialization whose fundamental premises MOVE challenged. Constrained by severe fiscal austerity, Wilson Goode took a series of actions to create new public and private partnerships for redevelopment, including partnerships with hotel developers to complete the city's convention center and major subsidization through tax breaks and free land in support of the new sports complexes clustered on South Broad Street.[30] As part of an effort to attract and retain capital to the fiscally desperate city, Goode's administration reinforced statutes against graffiti, redoubled the crackdown on the illicit narcotic trade as well as on its use, and worked to sequester illicit sex, drug use, and the de-housed from public view. The removal of these groups to "clean up" downtown by dislocating "undesirable" populations did not engender their permanent removal from the city but rather precipitated the relocation to residential neighborhoods of the illicit sex, drug use, and other activities associated with the vulnerable-turned-expendable, fueling discord as majoritarian, moblike publics marked those engaged in illicit sex as threats to the social order. Vengeful populism here and in my other work describes the dominant political affect of neoliberalism. Building out from the subjects that Inderpal Grewal describes as emerging in relation to the post–September 11, 2001, security state, Achille Mbembe's formulation of enmity, and Neil Smith's description of revanchism, I locate the crystallization of these phenomena in the context of deindustrialization between the 1970s and 80s in the United States.[31] Specifically, vengeful populism describes efforts to rhetorically and physically reterritorialize communities in the wake of capital flight by violently excommunicating those considered social and economic drains on the collective.[32]

The continuities and discontinuities between the movement for international peace led by Divine and the passage of this spirit through the maelstrom of the 1964 Columbia Street Riot and galvanized by exhorters and the emergence of MOVE after 1972 embodies the complexity of the religio-political Black radical tradition that has been traced through this work up and out from the plot and derives much of its kinetic force from the heated transgression of the boundary between the underground and the spaces of set-apart bodies.

Wherever Black insurgency rears, it is overdetermined as being outside of the legitimate terrain, marked as terroristic and violent, or when seeking to avoid confrontation, wary, supplicant, and otherworldly. And yet any metaphysical reordering on the part of Black theologies rehearses and replays the jubilee—the triumphant reordering of being itself—foremost the abolition of the slave and the spiritual baptism of the new world. These automatic figurations of insurgent Black social worlds as being outside the terrain of politics illustrates the dependency of Western political categories of generative politics in liberal and radical variants on the figuration of the dark agora of unsanctioned congregations and illegitimate publics as the present absence defining the normative political spectrum and legitimate political action.

Delbert, like other adherents of John Africa's philosophy of life, contrasted his mission with that of the system. He understood himself, especially in his role as the minister of defense, as the defender not only of his brothers and sisters in the faith but of life itself. He claimed explicitly that his work was "the defense of life." This for Delbert contrasted with the murderousness of the system: "Killing is something this lifestyle perpetuates." He went on to further emphasize the healthiness of MOVE people who he declared "are the healthiest people on earth . . . healthy not only in what you see as body, but all over, and I'm talking about the mind." MOVE's efforts to defend life itself created a new metaphysical challenge to the body in its biopolitical construction, disarticulating the Cartesian duality of mind-body separation and the notion of health registered on the individual body, rather forwarding a vision where health was social, political, and affected by pollution and other collateral effects of the (re)production of the system. "All along since my beginning in this organization, all I've been taught is respect for life [and] . . . how to get healthy," he argued. For Delbert, like the others, understood his transformation through adherence to John Africa's teachings, which had transformed him from the "sickness" perpetuated by the social order: "Before joining MOVE I was sick, he attested. "Now I'm healthy. Before joining MOVE I was weak. Now I'm strong. Before joining MOVE I was disloyal, untrustworthy, full of all kinds of lies and deception. Now I know the meaning of loyalty. I know the meaning of family."[33]

Even following John Africa's violent death and the deaths of ten members in the wake of the police bombing, Delbert, from behind bars as a political prisoner, continued to proselytize the message of their founder and coordinator. In MOVE's brief publication from the mid-1990s, Delbert continued to advocate the fundamental meaning of John Africa's teachings as action: "What our Beloved Founder **JOHN AFRICA** is teaching, exhorting everyone in the grip of oppression to do, is to stop all the 'rap,' all the theorizing, all the barroom and living room debates, the campus 'think tanks,' etc. and get on down and do the work necessary to rid all of LIFE of this foulness." Delbert continued to diagnose the illness-producing effects of the broader system and called on everyday people to take action, as they might in the treatment of cancer or some other ailment. As he wrote, "When you got a cancer you get rid of it . . . when you got a foul degenerate system like this one that's afflicting all of us, it must be done away with for the sake of you, your family, and the generations to come!" Here, Delbert asserted the defiling and life-draining effects of the system as debilitating across generations. According to him, there was no recourse but to transform the system, and the only viable solution was revolution as outlined in the teachings of John Africa. He continued the radical abolitionist demands of MOVE paralleling "hospitals . . . full to the roof with hordes of other sick people waiting for a bed" and "stocked" prisons "overflowing with the financially poor . . . [while] insane politicians make pitches every election bragging about their willingness to throw even more folks in these hellholes." According to Delbert, the system continued to produce social misery for the majority and decadence for the few. He added that there could be no amelioration of the system, only its end. He defined revolution in contrast to the current system: "Revolution ain't war, but peace, revolution won't sicken the world, it'll strengthen all who engage in it. Revolution won't cause separation, but instead, will generate togetherness! Revolution won't bring decay, but will instill generation! Ya'll know why this system work so hard to turn folk away from anything positive? Because it's the positive that means the demise, the death of "their" system of oppression!"[34]

To outsiders, MOVE remained, even to their supporters, brash and prickly. Father Paul Washington of the Church of the Advocate described his interactions with MOVE as complicated given the organization's demanding and discordant exterior facing dynamics as well as its nonconformist political program. Washington described the organization in the early 1970s as "recognizable on the streets of Philadelphia in the 1970s by their dreadlocks, . . . their profane outbursts against 'the system,' and their disruption of public events including Board of Education meetings and meetings of peace groups and other organizations." Washington met the organization directly in 1975 after he began an outreach to them to "try to understand who they were." Washington understood part of the impulse drawing adherents to John Africa's heterodox teachings, including an early 1970s demonstration at the Philadelphia Zoo, where they protested the caging of animals, to be disaffection of Black Power organizing.[35] For Washington, Louise Africa, who was both John Africa's sister and the mother of one of the children who perished in the 1985 PPD bombing of the organization, exemplified the deep dissatisfaction with other forms of social movement work that helped spawn MOVE. He quoted Louise at length, who at various points aligned herself with the Black Panther Party and the writing and political activity of Angela Davis and George Jackson. Washington was drawn directly into contact with MOVE after Christine Washington saw them on television during broadcasts of public board of education meetings. In the 1970s and 1980s, despite the pressure from three decades of social movement work in the city, most entities other than the school board remained closed. MOVE capitalized on the open nature of board of education meetings to stage what others considered disruptive and hostile takeovers of the meeting to promote the teachings of John Africa, to renounce those involved in ordinary processes as reinforcing the system, and to advocate for the release of arrested members of the organization itself. Father Washington crystalized the teachings of John Africa along six primary principles outlined earlier in this chapter.

MOVE's outspokenness and their politics of disruption, which had drawn Janine and other in, repelled many others who viewed them as obnoxious and unproductive. It also attracted the police, who did not receive well MOVE's face-to-face diatribes against them, beginning with their first protests, including at the Philadelphia Zoo. The police department used the discord between MOVE members and neighbors to harass the group and to invade and raid their headquarters on more than one occasion. In response, as noted, MOVE increasingly fortified their headquarters and armed themselves with what they considered the instruments of the system, which they rejected generally but embraced for self-defense and protection of their headquarters.

MOVE's initial actions in 1972 and 1973 included protests against conditions at a long-term-care facility they condemned for mistreating Black elders and protests at the city's zoo against the caging of animals.

The group's use of profanity and its radical abolitionist message drew the ire of police officers. In the context of recent passage of punitive 1972 Pennsylvania legislation, police classified the group's use of profanity as riotous and designated them violent threats to public order. Nearby homeowners complained about MOVE, accusing the group of health hazards and confrontations. During successive raids on the group's original Powelton Village headquarters in the mid-1970s, police beat and arrested members with impunity. The group also accused them of killing Janine Africa's baby, Life Africa, in March 1976, though police disputed this claim.[36]

MOVE members refused to be passive victims of the city's antagonism. On April 2, 1976, a few days after the death of Life Africa, the organization invited city council members Lucien Blackwell and Joseph Coleman, as well as future council member Janie Blackwell, to the headquarters. After a shared meal, Janine led the three to the basement of the headquarters to view Life's body to call attention to violent police attacks sustained by the organization. Louise Africa also used her biweekly column at the Philadelphia Tribune, "On the MOVE," to call out police aggression. "We have time and time again run smack into these politically controlled cops," who, as Louise went on to describe, exhibited sadism in relation to the organization. The police department denied having a role in the death of Life Africa, going so far as to insist that the infant had not existed and, thus, could not have been killed.

When in response, the group began to arm itself in self-defense, seeking weapons through a member who had begun working with ATF agents, neighbors again demanded that the city do something about the group, and officials treated MOVE members as enemy combatants. This posture culminated in 1978 with an extended siege in which officials blockaded MOVE's headquarters, shut off its water supply, and attempted to drown the group in their basement, before eventually raiding and destroying the home. The 1978 violence resulted in the death of a police officer and the incarceration nine members of the group (including Janine), whom the group galvanized around as political prisoners; two of the nine died in state custody, and the other seven served forty-year sentences scattered across Pennsylvania's prisons.

Tensions between the group and police began to escalate in 1977 as the group prepared for a standoff with police and began to stand guard above their fortified front entrance with arms. In 1977, Delbert handed ATF agent George Fincl an incendiary letter addressed to the "Philadelphia Authorities," including the mayor of Philadelphia, "and to the person or persons . . . in charge of the confrontation in front of MOVE headquarters."[37] The letter warned, "Don't attempt to enter MOVE headquarters, or harm MOVE people unless you want an international incident." "We are prepared to get reservoirs, empty out towns and apartment houses, close factories and tie up traffic in the major cities of Europe," the letter continued. Outlining a broader conspiracy, the letter invoked "the Black Guard of Western Europe" with cells in France, Germany, England, and Poland armed and ready to deliver on the threat. The letter suggested that these entities had already placed "two occupants in major hotels and apartment houses in each city" from Chicago to Paris. To prevent the threat of a debilitating strike across North American and Western European cities, MOVE demanded the immediate release of Robert Africa, Gerald Africa, and Conrad Africa, held during that time at Pennsylvania's notorious Graterford Prison in Montgomery County, just outside the city.

MOVE did not seek recourse through the ordinary means of the Western judicial process; it did not try to reverse the judge's or the jury's decisions in these cases through appeal in either the formal sense of legal appeal or in the broader sense of an appeal to the wider public for recognition and empathy. Instead, the organization demanded an end to the incarceration of its members and threatened the infrastructures of standard living—those ensuring the day-to-day reproduction and operation of American and Western European society, including markets, transportation, housing, and water distribution systems. MOVE conjured a large-scale subversive organization capable of terrorism to gain leverage against the powerful forces they viewed as aligned to destroy them along with all the planet's life, human and nonhuman.

Even as MOVE sought to create leverage through the invocation of terrorism, the group continued to see potential in the plot as a future beyond the destruction of the deindustrializing city, articulating a horizon familiar to earlier groups such as the Moorish Science Temple. As part of their negotiations during the siege, the group sought to buy a large farm in Virginia; although these plans were thwarted, according to the group, by the City of Philadelphia's disparagement of them to officials in Virginia, the lasting legacy of plotting as a multidimensional vision of autonomy and sovereignty associated with the set-apart remained active and vibrant. Despite the unprecedented conditions that MOVE faced in the deindustrializing context, they built on a familiar pattern of social-geographic experience and Black working-class worldmaking. The group most pointedly drew together the rubrics associated with dark agoras—both the underground and the set-apart—to generate an abolition politics at the end of the twentieth century.

Coda

Even before I knew I would be composing a segment of the present project about the International Peace Mission movement and its larger-than-life founder, Reverend M. J. "Father" Divine, I was attracted to the power of the Divine Lorraine Hotel, situated between Temple University and Center City (the business district) to mark my relative distance on Broad Street, the main corridor running north-south in Philadelphia. Although the towers of Center City are visible from several miles up Broad Street, this actually makes them useless for accurately assessing relative distance. The Divine Lorraine shell welcomes you to North Philly or beckons you back from the rearview mirror.

At the start of my archival work, the hotel had been engaged for a photographic project that opened in a show in South Philadelphia at what was at the time the Bends and Bones Studio, headed by Diarra and Raea Davis. I went in the waning daylight, when the sun is refracted through Philadelphia's harsh air in the most stunning orange hue, to photograph the building. It was at the time the subject of many a lens because of the ornate grandeur overlaid by the art of some daring taggers. I shot several of what I now recognize as unoriginal photos that I subsequently had to render through digital manipulation to make interesting. These all present a familiar framing of the building, highlighting its former grandeur and its contemporary ruins and thus unintentionally flirting with the genre of ruins porn. Sometime after the Bends and Bones debut of my images, I rediscovered some photographs that I had never printed of a placard secured on the stone bottom wall of the hotel. Titled "Fifteen Theses on How the Divine Lorraine Would Be Better Served as a Divine Sanctuary," the placard was placed by artist and designer Jason Lempieri, who competed in and won a design competition for the resuscitation of the then derelict building. His plan would have made it a citywide crematorium and memorial site. In the placard, Lempieri made his case to the would-be redeveloper. In its first afterlife, the hotel went from being an exclusive preserve of Philadelphia's rich white society to an accessible space that Divine and the members of the Peace Mission understood as an epicenter out of which would spread divine peace and bubbling joy to all, irrespective of "color or creed." In its second afterlife, which has never been brought to fruition, this artist imagined it as a place of public mourning that could "enhance the revitalization of North Broad," already well on its way to being transformed from one of the nation's most important centers of Black urban culture to what Davarian Baldwin terms the "univer-city" by Temple's massive reterritorialization of the neighborhood.[1]

On a trip to Philadelphia in the summer of 2020 for research in the municipal archives and court records for work about the later twentieth century, my partner and I made an intentional trip to the site to see what had become of it. The Divine Lorraine Hotel, unlike the mortuary site envisioned by Limpieri or the eternal site of joy and shared communions practiced by the followers of Divine in the mid-twentieth century, redevelopers have re-created the building as an exclusive luxury housing project with a high-end restaurant on the bottom floor. This transitory nature of the Divine Lorraine, an otherwise unmovable edifice, attests to the complexities of the contemporary landscape shaped by various temporalities lived at different scales and in that, constantly rewritten, even over and against the grooves of their brick-and-mortar materiality and its shifting valuation in global markets.

Whatever we are to make of the building's transit, we must account for the ways that the heterogenous forms of assembly associated with Black living and their formulations for alternative urban futures have been radically displaced by contemporary investments in Center City. For the last decades of the twentieth century, investors, policy makers, police, and ordinary citizens have treated Philadelphia's core neighborhoods as ecologies of risk—sectors of concentrated death, increased morbidity rates, violent crime, and innumerable instances of debilitation requiring policing and containment. Contrasting sharply with this earlier urbanism through dislocation and isolation, discourses in the opening two decades of the twenty-first century about the future of Philadelphia have shifted in favor of heavy economic, civic, and social investment in these same segments prior to COVID-19's unprecedented reshaping of social and economic life. Policy makers, redevelopers, and other organizations driving the "renaissance" are galvanizing the radical transformation of the social and geographic character of the core in the name of "livability." The inverse of the Black-living-in-death that was so acutely associated with the era of deindustrialization but whose genealogy dates back to Progressive thought about the incommensurate nature of Black social forms and generative urban futurity, livability describes an ideological and material schema for the reproduction of the city particular to the unprecedented corporatization and concentration of real estate of the early twenty-first century. Under the rubrics of livability, contemporary city-crafters seek to enhance the capacity for core neighborhoods to (theoretically) attract and sustain urban citizens as consumers—"normal" (white) people and families with sufficient incomes to maintain rising rents and prices for homes as well as services and commodities.[2]

The progenitors and financers of this new vision for Center City and the surrounding residential communities are an elite managerial class governing the city through the concentrated power characteristic of the forms of diffuse ownership associated with corporatization. In the name of stockholder returns, this group envisions a sanitized city in which urbane living and the new urban subjects, defined by consumerism and the securitization it hails, displace "undesirables"—groups marked under financialized urbanism as risky and therefore in need of permanent removal.[3] Philadelphia-based Brandywine Realty Trust exemplifies the ways that major inlays of capital have reterritorialized the core—or violently transformed its material and affective infrastructures. Granted tax subsidies through Pennsylvania's effort to reverse "urban decay" through the Keystone Opportunity Zone initiative, Brandywine built the FMC building at Cira Centre in University City, an area in West Philadelphia that previously had only one skyscraper. These exclusionary properties are prohibitively expensive for the city's ordinary residents and small business owners. Gerard Sweeney, who served as vice president for the real estate development firm LROC, founded Brandywine Trust in 1994. At the time of Brandywine's founding, the company owned three properties at a total capitalization of five million dollars. Currently, with properties spanning from Texas to Pennsylvania, Brandywine holds a portfolio topping out at more than five billion dollars in total investment.[4] In Philadelphia alone in 2019, the company managed a real estate holding of fourteen properties totaling 7,466,095 square feet of commercial and mixed-use space.

Real Estate Investment Trusts (REITs) like Brandywine were codified legally through a rider bill on the Cigar Excise Tax Extension signed by Dwight Eisenhower in September 1960. Although not utilized at a large scale until the 1980s, since 2008, they have been a major site of investment, growing in returns and capitalization disproportionate to other markets in the aftermath of the Great Recession.[5] According to the 1960 legislation, a REIT is defined as an

> unincorporated trust or an unincorporated association . . . (1) which is managed by one or more trustees; (2) the beneficial ownership of which is evidenced by transferrable shares, or by transferable certificates of beneficial interest; (3) which (but for the provisions of this part) would be taxable as a domestic corporation; (4) which does not hold any property primarily for sale to customers in the ordinary course of its trade or business; (5) the beneficial ownership of which is held by 100 or more persons.[6]

Constituted in a similar fashion to mutual funds, REITs open real estate to a dispersed ownership. These corporations manage portfolios encompassing retail and residential properties as well as mortgages. The funds of traditional lenders, while still quite regulated, were transformed in 1999 following the repeal of the 1933 Glass-Steagall Act, which no longer required financial firewalls between lending and investment practices, binding mutual funds, insurance companies, and privatized retirement funds to tenuous urban real estate markets across the United States through REITS like Brandywine. Although collectively, Americans exert little democratic oversight regarding the siting, construction, and development of shopping centers, regional malls, apartments, manufactured homes, and single-family houses or the dispensation of commercial and private mortgages, these things are our collective assets generated from a range of sources that make us inadvertent, passive owners. Indeed, REITs represent a form of concentrated economic power, divorced from ownership, in which ordinary people are unconsciously fueling the violent reterritorialization of the urban and exurban landscapes.[7]

The financialization of real estate and the fracturing of ownership through securities and markets buttress unilateral and undemocratic visions for the city's future, visions that privilege absentee sharehold-ers over residents. To ensure the continued return on investment for these unprecedented outlays of real estate investment, these organiza-tions have begun to exert serious power in shaping the landscape. For example, Brandywine's Sweeney has also positioned himself to serve as a kind of shadow mayor for the neighborhoods surrounding his com-pany's investments near Center City. As of the late 2010s he served as the chairman of both the Schuylkill River Development Corporation (SRDC) and the Center City District Foundation (CCD), two entities of privatized authority that seek to "enhance" municipal governance through private control of collective resources.[8]

This consolidation of power in the hands of redevelopers belies the democratization often associated with "greening" and other less directly punitive modes of transforming the city through livability, revealing their dependency on racial and class exclusion as well as the extension of the carceral apparatus. In summer 2018, CCD opened the first phase of Rail Park, its highly anticipated answer to New York City's High Line. Along with this converted railway in the Callowhill section near historic Chinatown, CCD has also remade and currently manages a number of other small downtown parks, including Dilworth, Sister Cities, John F. Collins, and Cret. If projections for the future of Rail Park are realized, the city will have two major green corridors effectively managed and controlled by a real estate investor with major holdings in the neighbor-hood who faces little oversight with regard to democratic process. While green spaces are potentially beneficial to all residents of cities, CCD, SRDC, and similar organizations around the country employ these ef-forts as part of an effort at attracting wealthy residents, new businesses, and tourists—all groups whose activities are deemed normal because their activities contribute to the city as a site of consumption.

Livability depends on a cartography mapped over and against the forms of Black insurgent social life associated with dark agoras in Center City and the core neighborhoods before 2000, revealing the imbrication of "greening" and other liberal projects of rehabilitation with carceral-ization. Alongside trash cleanup, tree planting, and park management, CCD, for example, hires its own private security force, in effect extending an overall matrix of surveillance and policing. In the name of the collective urban good, redevelopment corporations controlled by real estate interests with little oversight exacerbate inequality, geographic marginality, and criminalization for the damned, those marked as redundant and expendable within the political economy of real estate mogul urbanism ascendant recently to the highest halls of power in the United States.

In addition to the enhancement of the carceral apparatus through the institution of private security, the logics of securitization are also often built into the very fabrics of the infrastructures of livability, giving rise to and supporting the powerful ideology of securitized urban citizenship.[9] "Normal" within the context of securitized urbanism and REIT redevelopment is defined through an individual's or group's predictable, sustained engagement, proximity, and entanglement with stable markets, a respect for authority, and an acceptance of the sanctity of private property. Those disrupting livability and the various social-spatial assemblages erected under its rubrics are marked as outside of citizenship, as the groups that *must be policed* to ensure "progress" through growth and redevelopment. Securitized urban citizenship articulates novel majoritarian blocs centered in the sanctioned uses of semiprivate public space deputized to insure "proper uses" of parks and other infrastructures of livability.

In 2015, a temporary coalition of runners, bicyclists, and agents of real estate development was galvanized by Jon Lyons, who also founded the Facebook group RUN215. Following reports of "five or six teens on mountain bikes" who allegedly harassed and groped an unidentified woman, Lyons created a patrol to informally police the trail. Next, the group organized representatives of the Bicycle Coalition of Philadelphia, the Department of Parks and Recreation, the police, and the SRDC to meet with members of the city council to address the kinds of criminalized gathering associated with if not named explicitly as a problem of unwieldy Black youth. In effect, the temporary coalition formed around advocacy for the normal uses of the park at the expense of those who were deemed as in need of permanent removal. Architects designed the long narrow park for individual walking, running, and cycling rather than for motley groups of teenagers on bicycles—who were coded as not belonging by the inclusion of the description of their "mountain bikes."

The news reports of the incident code and overwrite social-spatial antagonism as sexualized and violent (Black) aggression.

These kinds of contemporary discussions that render social-spatial antagonism and violence though the common trope of Black sexual aggression masks the violence at the heart of the "green" corridor's creation and bolsters new threads of social-political identification expressed in the compulsion to "protect" the collective "green" asset from the disintegration associated with antisocial social life in the city. This newly created green space was assembled directly on top of displaced spaces of often illicit social life, racialized as Black even as it had always included non-Black people. SRDC built its green corridor on Reading Railroad right-of-way land along the Schuylkill River, which had previously been land where the city's Black youth, its queer communities, and the homeless cultivated forms of gathering considered antisocial and that were more often than not marked as criminal and dangerous. In contrast with earlier insurgent uses, the current organization of the space encourages pedestrian and bicycle traffic and employs spatial design for most of its length to prevent the formation of collectives. SRDC did not recover unused land and create a space for living; rather, it expended millions of dollars for the reterritorialization of land to remake it from a space that could only be described by outsiders as dangerous into a zone of enhanced livability. It distilled the knowledge of Black communities about how to activate the postindustrial city while also helping to "clean up" these areas in order to ensure the geographies of normal leisure—quintessentially, the running/ bicycle path under neoliberal regimes of urban governance. In contemporary urban reformism organized through the quest for livability, spaces and spatial practices associated with Blackness are collapsed into sinister darkness, serving in an ongoing sense as the contrastive relief against which the idioms of orderly and generative urban social-geographic life are expressed. Blackness therefore continues to serve as a key to the cartographic syntax and grammar of redevelopment and modernization.

This book historicizes these contemporary formations by placing them within a longer dialectic between insurgent Black social-geographic life and dominant urbanism centered on growth. Specifically, I have examined the distinctive congregations born of the plot in its migration with

Black communities to the city and the ways these congregations shaped Black politics and the city's geography. In the face of urban reform initiatives that routinely flattened Black communities and subjected them to blight and degradation, Black communities crafted this diverse network of insurgent spaces through modes of assembly. I delineate through the work a history of insurgent forms of assembly—dark agoras—the ways they underwrote a distinctive practice of urban placemaking, and the ways that this in turn materialized Black queer urbanism, a set of discordant visions of the urban future emerging from the transposition of the plot from its original context of articulation. The spatial formation of dark agoras and the movement between these forms of congregation that are centered in the ecstatic and other affective modalities and that are usually tamed out of accounts of meaningful political action and social formation served as critical incubators of Black Power's long development and the contours of its expression. The power and possibility of thinking the city from the vantage of dark agoras—those formulations shadowing and terrorizing order but also grounding everyday Black social existence despite debilitating austerity, exclusion, and violence—is relevant if we are to reclaim urban space outside the dictates of cancerous growth, extractionism, ecocide, urbicide, and disposability. These sites and the expressions of Black queer urbanism emerging from them suggest the possibilities of reformulating our collectivity to include the visions for urban futures demoted as heterodox within our current order and suggest paths to communal integration through abolition not only of police and prisons but also of the economic and social interests for which they work, the regime of gendered racial capitalism that currently presents an existential crisis for planetary life, human and nonhuman. There is no livable city without the extirpation of the logics of growth that continue to hold Black life as antithetical to the urban form and its future.

The cultivators of dark agoras, through their emphasis on the realms outside of labor, and the set-apart, through their attendance to fellowship, collectivity, and transformation, provide an unexamined blueprint for an as yet unrealized world.

ACKNOWLEDGMENTS

Foremost, I would like to acknowledge the role that my partner, Hue-wayne, has played in making the publication of this work possible. From low times to times of celebration, beginning with the dissertation iteration of this work up through its final publication, he has been a constant source of inspiration, and our intellectual and artistic orbit together has made this not only possible but fun.

I would like to acknowledge the critical support my family has provided. My mom, Lynnette's, persistent questions about how the work was coming along and her encouragment to finish have been no small contributions to completion. My stepfather, Eddie's, support has also been indispensable. I am grateful to my partner's family, especially his generous parents, Hughlords and Marcia, whose care, support, and prayer have helped me get through this process over many years; I am grateful, too, to his brothers Hughie and Marcello.

Thank you to my siblings, Chris, Jonathan, Amanda, Aaliyah, and Bryanne, for encouraging me and sometimes providing comic and other forms of relief. My sister-cousins Shameka and Chardé, my cousin-niece Trezhure, my aunts Susie, Leverne, and Yvonne, my uncle Billy, my great-aunt Ella Mae, my cousins Erica, Gwen, Donnetta, Dora, Al, Fred, Patrice, James, Quamé, Nikkyeea, Collease, as well as many of my other aunts, uncles, cousins, and extended family have cheered my work in big and small ways all along the journey, sometimes calling and texting me through anxiety they didn't even necessarily know I had.

I am especially indebted to Nijah Cunningham, Jarvis McInnis, and Matthew Morrison. We met in the uncertain years of graduate school, and these brothers have held me down reading my work, directing me to things I should read, and talking me through when things seemed slow or even dismal. Our weekly and sometimes daily text thread has provided a primary sense of comradery and really has been key in sustaining this work.

This work would have been impossible (present limitations acknowledged) without the generous support of my PhD committee. My chair, Samuel K. Roberts Jr., challenged and supported me throughout the process of drafting my dissertation. Elizabeth Blackmar's encouragement and her abiding interest in questions of landscapes and space have been a great boon for this research. Tina Campt opened non-traditional historical methodologies for me. Premilla Nadasen's close engagement with my dissertation and encouragement of this work have continued to nourish this project. There is no way to fully account for the role that Alondra Nelson has played in encouraging and helping to ensure the publication of this work. Her support through genuine mentorship has meant the world to me. She has shared some of the most impactful advice, provided some of my first writing and publication opportunities, and she held me accountable when I needed to do more. I am forever indebted.

Imani Owens, Courtney Bryan, Dialika Sall, Megan French-Marcelin, Romeo Guzman, Carribean Fragoza, Maria John, Daniel Morales, Yesenia Barragan, the late and great Devon Wade, George Aumoithe, Brittney Taylor, Wes Alcenat, Brittaney Graham, Tania Balan-Gaubert, Navid Farnia, Erica Richardson, Shanita Ealey, Dana Cypress, Darnell Moore, Christine Pinnock, Rich Blint, Amaka Okechukwu, Matt Birkhold, Yannick Marshall, Kevin Holt, and Elleza Kelley, along with many others, have also been critical interlocutors and friends throughout the extended work of this project beginning in graduate school.

Carla Shedd's affirmation of work, process, and method was critical early in writing this project. Ruthie Wilson Gilmore's support and critical engagement over the years has challenged me to think more deeply about an abolitionist approach to place.

I am grateful to Sherita Flournoy, Stacy Grover, Ariel Shaw, and Leonel Lombe for their work as undergraduate and graduate research assistants along the way for this project.

I appreciate Mary C. Curtis and Deborah Douglas for their efforts during an Op. Ed. Project writing retreat hosted by Alondra Nelson at Columbia in 2016. Participation in this workshop and Deborah's sustained support for one of my very first public venue publications in the weeks that followed ignited my pen and gave me the confidence to publish.

I am grateful to Maaza Megiste, who challenged me to write lives in their fullness and introduced me to a practice of radical editing during the 2015 Callaloo Fiction Writing Workshop at Oxford, in which she served as my writing mentor. I am thankful for much creative inspiration provided by Wandeka Gayle, Jayson Smith, Klieon John, Arielle John, Nkosi Nkululeko, Monique Hayes, and other participants during that workshop.

The community associated with Columbia's Institute for Research in African American Studies provided a vital lifeline for this work. Sharon Harris has facilitated innumerable impromptu discussions and connections that were essential to my finishing at Columbia. As well, Shawn Mendoza, Josef Sorett, Natasha Lightfoot, Farah Jasmine Griffin, and the now ancestors Steven Gregory and Marcellus Blount all supported and encouraged my work for many years during my dissertation process and beyond. Much of this community's support came in the form of small kindnesses but also in the robust intellectual world IRAAS created for Black students pursuing PhDs across Columbia.

My undergraduate advisor Claudrena Harold's encouragement and support since we met when she organized a Katrina relief event at UVA in 2006 has been essential to the long haul of my work. Her scholarship, pedagogy, and artistry continue to serve as a primary inspiration. Prof. Harold, as I still affectionately call her, has provided wise council to me so many times, written so many letters, and encouraged me so much that I cannot really fully encompass my gratitude in words. She is a brilliant, quiet intellectual force for whom I'm eternally grateful.

Wende Marshall has been an important force in shaping this work. I met Wende during a critical moment in my politicization, and her generous critiques of my thinking and writing have aided in clarifying the stakes of this project. I have also counted on her political comradeship along the way.

I am also grateful to Claire Yoo for her support and generosity and her engagement over the many years.

I continue to draw positive inspiration from dear friends Boston Woolfolk, Krystilyn Washington, Lauren Dobbs, Jessica Foster, and Ryan Wynn, who have always encouraged and supported me over many years. I am thankful for Tory Hairston and Andi Cullins for their intellectual engagement, especially early in my intellectual journey.

Kevin Quashie, whom I met during my postdoctoral fellowship year at Smith College, quickly developed into one of my key friend-mentors in life. I carry in my heart our time, along with dear Daphne Lamoithe, in the little hall where our offices were at Smith's old Nielson Library. That time just after graduate school taught me so much about how to do this work and to attempt to do so with grace and honesty. Kevin embraced me, helped me to heal, and provided a fresh and important model of study.

My original intellectual home at the Carter G. Woodson Institute at University of Virginia has been a godsend for my research, shaping some of my original questions and continuing to support my work over the years. As the Woodson's director, Deborah McDowell was the first person to invite me to discuss my research; she brought me back there more than once to present my scholarship and always kept me in the network of the Woodson, for which I am grateful.

I will never forget the foundation the Black studies faculty at UVA provided for my intellectual development before graduate school as well. The first person to ever mention concepts of race and place was Ian Grandison. That conversation in his office planted an important seed. I am thankful to Marlon Ross, who has encouraged my work over the years. Corey Walker has also supported my work since undergraduate days. Robert Fatton's critical lessons in Marxist political theory continue to shape my approach. Cindy Hoehler-Fatton's support was vital to my successful matriculation into graduate school and connected me with the vital resources provided by the Institute for the Recruitment of Teachers Program.

Sonya Donaldson, Deidre Cooper Owens, LuAnn Williams, Todne Thomas, Brandi Hughes, Z'étoile Imma, Tim Lovelace, and Alwin Jones provided important models of Black studies scholarship in my formative years. I will always carry in my heart the feeling of engaging intellectual community that I shared with Adom Getachew, Solomé Rose, Octavia Philips, and Claudrena Harold when I first started hanging out at the Woodson.

This work was supported by the Taft Research Center at the University of Cincinnati. Littisha Bates, James Mack, and other members of University of Cincinnati's Black Faculty Association also provided vital support for my well-being and the incubation of this project during my time in

Cincinnati. Derrick Broomes has been a good brother, always checking in and sending positive energy. I am thankful for him. I am grateful to Aimee Meredith Cox for integrating me into her family during my years in Cincinnati. Her wonderful sister, Jennifer Cox, and her generous parents Larry and Mary Cox were my rocks there. A special thank you to Michelle Watts, who since meeting me has demonstrated such radical generosity and kindness. Carolette Norwood is an inspiration and has been a good friend over the course of the years, sharing generously in ideas and support. My WGSS colleagues at Cincinnati—Amy Lind, Deb Meem, Ashley Currier, Valerie Weinstein, Olga Sanmiguel-Valderrama, and Giao Tran—invested energy in me and my work.

The last rounds of working through this manuscript really benefited from the Schomburg Fellowship. My co-fellows Melissa Cooper, Anasa Hicks, Grace L. Sanders Johnson, T. Urayoán Noel, Russell Rickford, Ebony Jones, Kali Tambree, Andrew Anastasi, Stephanie Crease, Rebecca Hall, Eve Meltzer, and Phyllis Ross provided great critical feedback on penultimate drafts of many of the chapters in this work. I am especially thankful for my overlapping time with Malachi Crawford at the Schomburg. Our conversations about Black religious life and politics nourished this book greatly. I must also single out the brilliant and generous Brent Hayes Edwards, the fellowship program's leader. Brent asked some of the most provocative and thoughtful questions of this work, for which I am indebted and grateful.

I would like to thank Karen and Larry "Papa" Falcon in Philadelphia for their keen interest and support of this research. I happened on Papa's ministry one day while walking and engaging the landscape of West Philadelphia. I have loved and appreciated his wisdom since. Ms. Karen, founder of the Jubilee School in Philadelphia, is an important model of meaningful history and pedagogy, and her students' work to memorialize victims of the police bombing of MOVE inspired me greatly in the final chapter.

Two of my closest friends in this work are Justin Hosbey and Randi Gill-Sadler. I met them during an unsuccessful attempt on the job market, and their questions, engagement, and insight have been key to my work. Justin and I have collaborated extensively on conceptualizing and curating work centering Black ecologies. Our collaboration has left an indelible mark on my thinking. Randi is one of the most critical scholars

I know, and her deep engagement with the archives of Black feminist writing and thought has inspired me tremendously, inviting me to ask important questions of the subjects and worlds covered in this work.

I am thankful for the friendship and support of Emerald Rutledge, La Marr Bruce, Julius Fleming, Adam McNeil, and Antoine Johnson. The Mastermind's working group, organized by Charisse Burden-Stelly and including Shamara Wyllie Alhassan, Randi Gill-Sadler, Sandy Placido, Jesús Smith, Jarvis Givens, Brian Kwoba, Ashley Farmer, Takiyah Harper Shipman, and Adom Getachew, provided important space for this work as well as for feedback.

Thank you to Keisha Blain, Ashley Farmer, and Melissa Shaw for their support. Keisha put me on to editing *Black Perspectives,* which helped to expand my knowledge of Black studies tremendously. She also supported early research that became central to this work in her role as editor. Ashley's and Melissa's thoughtfulness, especially when I edited the blog, stands out, and I am forever grateful.

I am grateful for my eighth grade English teacher Ruth E. Tobey, whose early and consistent support of my writing has encouraged me over the years.

I am thankful to Cheryl Hicks, Sarah Haley, and LaShawn Harris for modeling important Black feminist urban history on the page but also for their kind support in real-life interactions, engaging my work as community.

This work has benefitted from critical engagements with scholarly communities at the University of Tennessee-Knoxville, Princeton University, University of Virginia, University of Massachusetts-Boston, University of Edinburgh, the Museum of Modern Art's Mellon-Marron Research Consortium, New Jersey City University, University of Wisconsin, University of Sussex, Harvard University, Columbia University, University of Cincinnati, and Smith College, as well as during panels at the Association for the Study of African American Life and History, the African American Intellectual History Society, American Studies Association, National Women's Study's Association, American Society for Environmental History, American Association of Geographers, US Intellectual History Society, Organization of American Historians, American Historical Association, and the Association of Humanist Sociology.

NOTES

INTRODUCTION

1 For the centrality of Du Bois to the emergence of US sociology, see Aldon Morris, *The Scholar Denied: W. E. B. Du Bois and the Birth of Modern Sociology* (Oakland: University of California Press, 2017); and Earl Wright II, *The First American School of Sociology: W. E. B. Du Bois and the Atlanta Sociological Laboratory* (New York: Routledge, 2017). On the intellectual centrality of the *Philadelphia Negro,* see Marcus Anthony Hunter, *Black Citymakers: How The Philadelphia Negro Changed Urban America* (Oxford University Press, 2013).

2 See *Wandering: Philosophical Performances of Racial and Sexual Freedom* (Durham, NC: Duke University Press, 2014), Sarah Jane Cervenak's instructive work that uses wandering as a critical counterpoint and a point of the possibilities of freedom as opposed to Enlightenment theories of rationality seeking to contain Blackness.

3 W. E. B. Du Bois, *The Philadelphia Negro: A Social Study* (1899; repr., Philadelphia: University of Pennsylvania Press, 1996), 221.

4 Ibid. The significance I assign to this formation of the circle at the altar benefits from my engagement with Nina Angela Mercer's dissertation proposal "Transnational Ritual Poetics of Blackness in Performance."

5 Du Bois, *The Philadelphia Negro,* 67.

6 See Saidiya Hartman, *Wayward Lives, Beautiful Experiments: Intimate Histories of Social Upheaval* (New York: W. W. Norton, 2019).

7 See Terrion L. Williamson, *Scandalize My Name: Black Feminist Practice and the Making of Black Social Life* (New York: Fordham University Press, 2016), 9.

8 Aimee Meredith Cox, *Shapeshifters: Black Girls and the Choreography of Citizenship* (Durham, NC: Duke University Press, 2015), 28.

9 Pekka Hämäläinen, *Lakota America: A New History of Indigenous Power* (New Haven, CT: Yale University Press, 2019), 9.

10 Tiffany Lethabo King, *The Black Shoals: Offshore Formations of Black and Native Studies* (Durham, NC: Duke University Press, 2019.

11 For an astute account of the historical relationship between kinship and commercialization through the Atlantic slave trade, see Jennifer Morgan, *Reckoning with Slavery: Gender, Kinship, and Capitalism in the Early Black Atlantic* (Durham, NC: Duke University Press, 2022).

12 Kathryn Benjamin Golden, "'Armed in the Great Swamp': Fear, Maroon Insurrection, and the Insurgent Ecology of the Great Dismal Swamp," *Journal of African American History* 106, no. 1 (2021): 1–26; Alex A. Moulton, "Towards the Arboreal Side-Effects of Marronage: Black Geographies and Ecologies of the Jamaican Forest," *Environment and Planning E: Nature and Space*, May 2022, https://doi.org/10.1177/25148486221103757.

13 Marshall contrasts Western conceptions of domination through dominion with indigenous Hawaiian conceptualizations of reciprocity between human communities, spiritual and ancestral realms, and the land and waterscapes of inhabitance. See Wende Marshall, *Potent Mana: Lessons in Power and Healing* (Albany: State University of New York Press, 2013).

14 Sarah Haley, *No Mercy Here: Gender, Punishment, and the Making of Jim Crow Modernity* (Chapel Hill: University of North Carolina Press, 2016). On the character of Jim Crow as a regime of real estate profiteering, see N. D. B. Connolly, *A World More Concrete: Real Estate and the Remaking of Jim Crow South Florida* (Chicago: University of Chicago Press, 2014).

15 Adom Getachew, *Worldmaking after Empire: The Rise and Fall of Self-Determination* (Princeton, NJ: Princeton University Press, 2019).

16 Nijah Cunningham, "The Nonarrival of Black Freedom (c. 12.6.84)," *Women & Performance* 27, no. 1 (2017): 112–20.

17 I am indebted to Elizabeth Blackmar for introducing me to a generative conceptualization of landscape studies and directly to the work of J. B. Jackson while I was a teaching assistant in her magisterial course The Making of the Modern American Landscape at Columbia. See J. B. Jackson, *Discovering the Vernacular Landscape* (New Haven, CT: Yale University Press, 1986), 86. For a generative analysis of temporality through the "spatializing logics of black patience" in the context of the civil rights struggle, see Julius B. Fleming, "Transforming Geographies of Black Time: How the Free Southern Theater Used the Plantation for Civil Rights Activism," *American Literature* 91, no. 3 (September 2019): 587–617. My emphasis on fleeting architectures of relation is not to undermine the realities of the ways that diasporas have created architectural features shaping broader US vernacular architectures. The porch is the primary example of this more permanent incorporation of Black architectural traditions in the US context. Marcus Hunter, *Black Citymakers: How the Philadelphia Negro Changed Urban America* (New York: Oxford University Press, 2013); Zandria F. Robinson, *This Ain't Chicago: Race, Class, and Regional Identity in the Post-Soul South* (Chapel Hill: University of North Carolina Press, 2014).

18 Katherine McKittrick, *Demonic Grounds: Black Women and the Cartographies of Struggle*, (Minneapolis: University of Minnesota Press, 2006); Clyde Woods, *Development Arrested: The Blues and Plantation Power in the Mississippi Delta* (London: Verso 2017); Clyde Woods, *Development Drowned and Reborn: The Blues and Bourbon Restorations in Post-Katrina New Orleans*, ed. Jordan Campt and Laura Pulido (London: Verso, 2017); Rashad Shabazz, *"Spatializing Black-*

ness: Architectures of Confinement and Black Masculinity in Chicago (Urbana: University of Illinois Press, 2015); Jarvis McInnis, "Black Women's Geographies and the Afterlives of the Sugar Plantation," *American Literary History* 31, no. 4 (Winter 2019): 741–74; Justin Hosbey, "Refusing Unliveable Destinies: Toward a Future for Black Life in New Orleans," *Fire!!!* 5, no. 1 (2018): 35–47; K. Ian Grandison, "The Other Side of the 'Free' Way," in *Race and Real Estate*, ed. Adrienne Brown and Valerie Smith (Oxford: Oxford University Press, 2015), 195–230; Hilda Lloréns, *Making Livable Worlds: Afro-Puerto Rican Women Building Environmental Justice* (Seattle: University of Washington Press, 2021); Ashanté M. Reese, *Black Food Geographies: Race, Self-Reliance, and Food Access in Washington, D.C.* (Chapel Hill: University of North Carolina Press, 2019); Tiffany Lethabo King, *The Black Shoals: Offshore Formations of Black and Native Studies* (Durham, NC: Duke University Press, 2019.

19 Nathan Hare, "Black Ecology," *Black Scholar* 1, no. 6 (April 1970): 2–8; J. T. Roane and Justin Hosbey, "Mapping Black Ecologies," *Current Research in Digital History* 2 (August 23, 2019), https://doi.org/10.31835/crdh.2019.05; Monica White, *Freedom Farmers: Agricultural Resistance and the Black Freedom Movement* (Chapel Hill: University of North Carolina Press, 2018); Danielle Purifoy and Louise Seamster, "What Is Environmental Racism For? Place-Based Harm and Relational Development," *Environmental Sociology* 7, no. 2 (2021), doi:10.1080/23251042.2020.179033 1; Carlyn Ferrari, "Anne Spencer's 'Natural' Poetics," *CLA Journal* 61, no. 4 (2018): 185–200.

20 Kevin Quashie. *Black Aliveness, or a Poetics of Being* (Durham, NC: Duke University Press, 2021). In this work, Quashie expands on his work on Black interiority to analyze being as a mode of becoming in and through relation. Also see his *The Sovereignty of Quiet beyond Resistance in Black Culture* (New Brunswick, NJ: Rutgers University Press, 2012).

21 Kevin Quashie, *Black Aliveness, or a Poetics of Being* (Durham, NC: Duke University Press, 2021), 12.

22 On erotic sovereignty, see Mireille Miller Young, *A Taste of Brown Sugar: Black Women in Pornography* (Durham, NC: Duke University Press, 2014); J. T. Roane, "Werking the Black Underground: On the Insurgent Politics of the 'Ho,'" *Martyr's Shuffle*, https://www.themartyrsshuffle.com/single-post/werking-the-black-underground-on-the-insurgent-politics-of-the-ho.

23 Cathy J. Cohen, "Punks, Bulldaggers, and Welfare Queens: The Radical Potential of Queer Politics?" *GLQ* 3, no. 4 (1997): 437–65.

24 Hortense Spillers "Mama's Baby, Papa's Maybe: An American Grammar Book," *Culture and Countermemory: The "American" Connection* 17, no. 2 (Summer 1987): 64–81; Evelyn Hammonds, "Black (H)holes and the Geometry of Black Female Sexuality," in *The Black Studies Reader*, ed. Jacqueline Bobo, Cynthia Hudley, and Claudine Michel, (New York: Routledge, 2004), 301–14; Sarah Haley, "'Like I Was a Man': Chain Gangs, Gender, and the Domestic Carceral Sphere in Jim Crow Georgia," *Signs* 39, no. 1 (2013): 53–77; C. Riley Snorton, *Black on Both Sides: A*

Racial History of Trans Identity, (Minneapolis: University of Minnesota Press, 2017); L. H. Horton-Stallings, *Funk the Erotic: Transaesthetics and Black Sexual Cultures* (Urbana: University of Illinois Press, 2015).

25 Louis Wirth, "Urbanism as a Way of Life," *American Journal of Sociology* 44, no. 1 (1938): 1–24.

26 Jaquelyn Dowd Hall, "The Long Civil Rights Movement and the Political Uses of the Past," *Journal of American History* 91 (March 2005): 1233–63.

27 Brian Purnell and Jeanne Theoharris, eds., *The Strange Careers of the Jim Crow North: Segregation and Struggle outside of the South* (New York: New York University Press, 2019); Matthew Countryman, *Up South: Civil Rights and Black Power in Philadelphia* (Philadelphia: University of Pennsylvania Press, 2005).

28 Sundiata Keita Cha-Jua and Clarence Lang, "The 'Long Movement' as Vampire: Temporal and Spatial Fallacies in Recent Black Freedom Studies," *Journal of African American History* 92, no. 2 (2007): 265–88.

29 Treva B. Lindsey, *Colored No More: Reinventing Black Womanhood in Washington, D.C.* (Urbana: University of Illinois Press, 2017).

30 Brittney C. Cooper, *Beyond Respectability: The Intellectual Thought of Race Women* (Urbana: University of Illinois Press, 2017); Martha S. Jones, *Vanguard: How Black Women Broke Barriers, Won the Vote, and Insisted on Equality for All*, 1st ed. (New York: Basic Books, 2020).

31 *Dreams Are Colder than Death*, directed by Arthur Jaffa (2014, Onye Anyanwu et al., BFI Distribution).

32 Rinaldo Walcott, "Outside in Black Studies: Reading from a Queer Place in the Diaspora," in *Black Queer Studies: A Critical Anthology*, ed. E. Patrick Johnson and Mae Henderson (Durham, NC: Duke University Press, 2005), 93; Candice Jenkins, *Private Lives, Proper Relations: Regulating Black Intimacy* (Minneapolis: University of Minnesota Press, 2007).

33 Charles Ashley Hardy, "Race and Opportunity: Black Philadelphia during the Era of the Great Migration, 1916–1930" (PhD diss., Temple University, 1989).

34 Ibid.

35 I borrow this formulation from Rahma Haji, who made this distinction in my 2017 Black Queer Urbanism seminar at Smith College. I am also indebted to ongoing discussions and unpublished collective writing done with Kwame Holmes that centered werk. I am also inspired by a phenomenal talk by Tiffany Lethabo King thinking outside the rubric of work through Black and indigenous intimacies: "Losing Faith in Works: Black and Indigenous Relations," Institute for Humanities Research, Arizona State University, February 18, 2021. Also see J. T. Roane, "Werking the Black Underground: On the Insurgent Politics of the 'Ho,'" *Martyr's Shuffle*, https://www.themartyrsshuffle.com/single-post/werking-the-black-underground-on-the-insurgent-politics-of-the-ho.

36 Cheryl Hicks, *Talk with You Like a Woman: African American Women, Justice, and Reform in New York, 1890–1935* (Chapel Hill: University of North Carolina Press, 2010); LaShawn Harris, *Sex Workers, Psychics, and Numbers Runners: Black*

Women in New York City's Underground Economy (Urbana: University of Illinois Press, 2016); Sarah Haley, *No Mercy Here: Gender, Punishment, and the Making of Jim Crow Modernity* (Chapel Hill: University of North Carolina Press, 2016); Sharon Harley, "'Working for Nothing but a Living': Black Women in the Underground Economy," in *Underground Sister Circle: Black Women and Work*, ed. Sharon Harley and the Black Women and Work Collective (New Brunswick, NJ: Rutgers University Press, 2002), 48–66; Kali N. Gross, *Colored Amazons: Crime, Violence, and Black Women in the City of Brotherly Love, 1880–1910* (Durham, NC: Duke University Press, 2006).

37   Dianne M. Stewart Diakité and Tracey E. Hucks, "Africana Religious Studies: Toward a Transdisciplinary Agenda in an Emerging Field," *Journal of Africana Religions* 1, no. 1 (2013): 28–77, doi:10.5325/jafrireli.1.1.0028; James Padillioni Jr., "Cosmic Literacies and Black Fugitivity," *Black Perspectives* (December 20, 2017), https://www.aaihs.org/cosmic-literacies-and-black-fugitivity/; Shamara W. Alhassan, "We Stand for Black Livity!": Trodding the Path of Rastafari in Ghana," *Religions* 11, no. 7 (2020): 374, https://doi.org/10.3390/rel11070374; Jason Young, *African Atlantic Religion in Kongo and the Lowcountry South in the Era of Slavery* (Baton Rouge: Louisiana State University Press, 2011); Omise'eke Natasha Tinsley, *Ezili's Mirrors: Imagining Black Queer Genders* (Durham, NC: Duke University Press, 2018); Josef Sorett, *Spirit in the Dark: A Religious History of Racial Aesthetics* (New York: Oxford University Press, 2019).

38   Deidre Helen Crumbley, *Saved and Sanctified: The Rise of a Storefront Church in Great Migration Philadelphia* (Gainesville: University of Florida Press, 2012).

39   Ashon T. Crawley, *Blackpentecostal Breath: The Aesthetics of Possibility* (New York: Fordham University Press, 2017), 24.

40   Anthea D. Butler, *Women in the Church of God in Christ Making a Sanctified World* (Chapel Hill: University of North Carolina Press, 2007)

41   J. T. Roane, "On the Spiritual Geography of Black Working-Class Washington," *Black Perspectives* (June 20, 2017), https://www.aaihs.org/on-the-spiritual-geography-of-black-working-class-washington/.

42   Imani Uzuri, "The Sacred Migration of Sister Gertrude Morgan," in *Women and Migration: Responses in Art and History*, ed. Deborah Willis, Ellyn Toscano, and Brooks Nelson (Cambridge, UK: Open Book Publishers, 2019), 581–604, https://books.openbookpublishers.com/10.11647/obp.0153.pdf.

43   For the language of wayward Black religious worlds, see Ahmad Greene Hayes's insightful engagement with Saidiya Hartman's *Wayward Lives* in "Wayward Negro Religions in the Twentieth-Century Slum," *Journal of African American History* 106, no. 1; *Kincraft: The Making of Black Evangelical Sociality* (Durham, NC: Duke University Press, 2021).

44   Malachi D. Crawford, *Black Muslims and the Law: Civil Liberties from Elijah Muhammad to Muhammad Ali* (Lanham, MD: Lexington Books, 2016); Edward E. Curtis, *Black Muslim Religion in the Nation of Islam, 1960–1975* (Chapel Hill: University of North Carolina Press, 2009); Ula Y. Taylor, *The Promise of Patriarchy:*

Women and the Nation of Islam (Chapel Hill: University of North Carolina, 2018); Yvonne Patricia Chireau and Nathaniel Deutsch, *Black Zion: African American Religious Encounters with Judaism* (New York: Oxford University Press, 2000).

45 Elsa Barkley Brown, "Negotiating and Transforming the Public Sphere: African American Political Life in the Transition from Slavery to Freedom," *Public Culture* 7 (1994): 107–46.

46 Erica Edwards, *Charisma and the Fictions of Black Leadership* (Minneapolis: University of Minnesota Press, 2012), i–xvi.

47 Fabian, Johannes. "An African Gnosis—For a Reconsideration of an Authoritative Definition," *History of Religions* 9, no. 1 (1969): 42–58.

48 Albert Camus, *The Rebel: An Essay on Man in Revolt* (New York: Knopf, 1956).

49 Eric Voegelin, *The Collected Works of Eric Voegelin*, vol. 5, *Modernity without Constraint: The Political Religions, the New Science of Politics, and Science, Politics, and Gnosticism*, ed. Manfred Henningsen (Columbia: University of Missouri Press, 2000).

50 Erica Edwards, *Charisma and the Fictions of Black Leadership*; Cedric Robinson, "Malcolm Little as a Charismatic Leader," in *Cedric J. Robinson: On Racial Capitalism, Black Internationalism, and Cultures of Resistance*, ed. H. L. T. Quan (London: Pluto Press, 2019), 267–94; Tiffany N. Florvil, *Mobilizing Black Germany: Afro-German Women and the Making of a Transnational Movement* (Urbana: University of Illinois Press, 2020); Shana Redmond, *Everything Man: The Form and Function of Paul Robeson* (Durham, NC: Duke University Press, 2020).

51 Here I draw on Robin D.G. Kelley's influential description of Black "freedom dreams." See Robin D. G. Kelley, *Freedom Dreams: The Black Radical Imagination* (Boston: Beacon Press, 2002).

52 Aliyyah I. Abdur-Rahman, "The Black Ecstatic," *GLQ* 24, no. 2–3 (2018): 343–65.

53 The complex terrain of this interstitial space is informed by the sharp theorizing of L. H. Stallings through the paradigm of funk; see *Funk the Erotic: Transaesthetics and Black Sexual Cultures* (Urbana: University of Illinois Press, 2015). This theorization of the ecstatic as both grounding and disorienting, as a disarticulation between the mind and the body, also benefits from La Marr Jurrelle Bruce, *How to Go Mad without Losing Your Mind: Madness and Black Radical Creativity* (Durham, NC: Duke University Press, 2021).

54 Paolo Boccagni, "What's in a (Migrant) House? Changing Domestic Spaces, the Negotiation of Belonging and Home-Making in Ecuadorian Migration Housing," *Theory and Society*, 31, no. 3 (2014): 277–93.

55 I am indebted to critical feedback from Brent Hayes Edwards, who suggested the relation of transposition as a way of describing geographic transfers through visions of the past and the left-behind continuing to inhabit a present imaginary. I am also indebted to the work that Reese does around nostalgia in thinking Washington's Black food geographies and modes of self-reliance.

56 Here, within the demarcation of urban planning discourse, Black people embodied something akin to nothingness. See Calvin L. Warren, *Ontological Terror: Blackness, Nihilism, and Emancipation* (Durham, NC: Duke University Press, 2018.

1. PLOTTING THE HISTORICAL ORIGINS OF DARK AGORAS

1 Kevin Quashie, *Black Aliveness, or a Poetics of Being* (Durham, NC: Duke University Press, 2021), 9.

2 Sylvia Wynter, "Novel and History, Plot and Plantation," *Savacou* 5 (1971): 95–102. I am indebted to Nijah Cunningham, who first introduced me to this essay by Wynter.

3 Sonya Pomentier, *Cultivation and Catastrophe: The Lyrical Ecology of Modern Black Literature* (Baltimore, MD: Johns Hopkins University Press, 2017), 41.

4 Lynn Rainville, *Hidden History: African American Cemeteries in Central Virginia* (Charlottesville: University of Virginia Press, 2014).

5 Dianne D. Glave, *Rooted in the Earth: Reclaiming the African American Environmental Heritage* (Chicago: Lawrence Hill Books, 2010).

6 Angela Davis, "Reflections on the Black Woman's Role in the Community of Slaves," *Black Scholar* 12, no. 6 (1981): 2–15.

7 See Whitney Battle-Baptiste, "Sweepin' Spirits: Power and Transformation on the Plantation Landscape, in *Archaeology and Preservation of Gendered Landscapes*, ed. Sherene Baugher and Suzanne Spencer-Wood (New York: Springer, 2010), 81–94.

8 Sarah Haley, *No Mercy Here: Gender, Punishment, and the Making of Jim Crow Modernity* (Chapel Hill: University of North Carolina Press, 2016), 198.

9 The terminology of a radical spatial ecological tradition draws on Cedric Robinson's conception of the Black radical tradition. See Cedric J. Robinson, *Black Marxism: The Making of the Black Radical Tradition*, 2nd ed. (Chapel Hill: University of North Carolina Press, 2000). On the nature of migratory Black ecological imaginaries, I draw on public remarks made by Hilda Lloréns during POLLEN20, "Contested Natures: Power, Possibility, Prefiguration," Black keynote, 3rd Biennial Conference of the Political Ecology Network (POLLEN), September 22–25, 2020, Brighton, UK.

10 Karla F. C. Holloway, *Passed On: African American Mourning Stories, A Memorial* (Durham, NC: Duke University Press, 2003), 2.

11 Sharon Patricia Holland, *Raising the Dead: Readings of Death and (Black) Subjectivity* (Durham, NC: Duke University Press, 2000), 15.

12 Vincent Brown, *The Reapers Garden: Death and Power in the World of Atlantic Slavery* (Cambridge, MA: Harvard University Press, 2008), 152–57.

13 Nyle Forte, "Refusing to Give Death the Last Word," *Boston Globe*, June 4, 2020, https://www.bostonglobe.com/2020/06/04/opinion/refusing-give-death-last-word/.

14 Dagmawi Woubshet, *The Calendar of Loss: Race, Sexuality, and Mourning in the Early Era of AIDS* (Baltimore, MD: Johns Hopkins University Press, 2015), 3. For further reflection on the way that proximity to death reorients Black life, also see Darius Bost's *Evidence of Being: The Black Gay Cultural Renaissance and the Politics of Violence* (Chicago: University of Chicago Press, 2018).

15 Amaka Okechukwu, "Urban Social Hauntings: Disappearing Gravestone Murals in Gentrifying Brooklyn," *Environment and Planning D: Society and Space* (December 2021), https://doi.org/10.1177/02637758211059539.

16 H. R. McIlwaine and Wilmer L. Hall, eds., *Executive Journals of the Council of Colonial Virginia* (Richmond, VA, 1925–1945), 1:86–87. Also in Warren M. Billings, *The Old Dominion in the Seventeenth Century: A Documentary History of Virginia, 1609–1689* (Chapel Hill: University of North Carolina Press, 1975), 160.

17 Nicholas May, "Holy Rebellion: Religious Assembly Laws in Antebellum South Carolina and Virginia," *American Journal of Legal History* 49, no. 3 (2009): 237–56.

18 Eugene D. Genovese, *Roll, Jordan, Roll: The World the Slaves Made* (New York: Vintage, 1976); Albert Raboteau, *Slave Religion: The "Invisible Institution" in the Antebellum South* (Oxford: Oxford University Press, 1978). As Browne notes, to cut down on possible conspiracy, the Common Council of New York City in 1722 regulated burials to no more than twelve attendees plus pallbearers and gravediggers. Simone Browne, *Dark Matters: On the Surveillance of Blackness* (Durham, NC: Duke University Press, 2015), 78.

19 Lynn Rainville, *Hidden History: African American Cemeteries in Central Virginia* (Charlottesville: University of Virginia Press, 2014).

20 Barbara Heath, "Space and Place within Plantation Quarters in Virginia, 1700–1825," in *Cabin, Quarter, Plantation: Architecture and Landscapes of North American Slavery*, ed. Clifton Ellis and Rebecca Ginsburg (New Haven, CT: Yale University Press, 2010), 156–76.

21 Katherine McKittrick, *Demonic Grounds: Black Women and the Cartographies of Struggle* (Minneapolis: University of Minnesota Press, 2006), 37–64.

22 Rebecca Ginsberg, "Escaping through a Black Landscape," in *Cabin, Quarter, Plantation: Architecture and Landscapes of North American Slavery* (New Haven, CT: Yale University Press, 2010), 54; Stephanie M. H. Camp, *Closer to Freedom: Enslaved Women and Everyday Resistance in the Plantation South* (Chapel Hill: University of North Carolina Press, 2004); Dell Upton, "White and Black Landscapes in Eighteenth-Century Virginia," *Places* 2, no. 2 (1982): 95–119.

23 *Slave Narratives: A Folk History of Slavery in the United States from Interviews with Former Slaves*, vol. 8 (Washington, DC: Federal Writer's Project of the Works Progress Administration, 1936), Manuscript/Mixed Material. Retrieved from the Library of Congress, https://www.loc.gov/item/mesn080/.

24 Saidiya Hartman also references this scene. As she explains, "These day-to-day and routine forms of contestation operated within the confines of relations of power and simultaneously challenged those very relations as these covert and chameleonic practices both complied with and disrupted the demands of the system through the expression of a counter-discourse of freedom." Hartman, *Scenes of Subjection: Terror, Slavery, and Self-Making in Nineteenth-Century America* (New York: Oxford University Press, 1997), 68. On the alternative waterscapes of the enslaved, see Kevin Dawson, *Undercurrents of Power: Aquatic Culture in the African Diaspora* (Philadelphia: University of Pennsylvania Press, 2018).

25 Sharla Fett, *Working Cures: Healing, Health, and Power on Southern Slave Planta-tions* (Chapel Hill: University of North Carolina Press, 2002); Yvonne Chireau, *Black Magic: Religion and the African American Conjuring Condition* (Berkeley: University of California Press, 2003).

26 *Slave Narratives.*

27 Harriet A. Washington, *Medical Apartheid: The Dark History of Experimenta-tion on Black Americans from Colonial Times to the Present* (New York: Broadway Books), 36.

28 Marguerite T. Williams, "A History of Erosion in the Anacostia River Basin" (PhD diss., Catholic University Press, 1942).

29 Frederick Law Olmstead, *The Cotton Kingdom: A Traveller's Observations on Cot-ton and Slavery in the American Slave States: Based Upon Three Former Volumes of Journeys and Investigations by the Same Author,* vol. 1 (New York: Mason Brothers, 1862), 35–37.

30 Katherine McKittrick, *Demonic Grounds: Black Women and the Cartographies of Struggle* (Minneapolis: University of Minnesota Press, 2006).

31 Olmsted, *The Cotton Kingdom,* 29.

32 Ibid., 27.

33 Browne, *Dark Matters.*

34 I borrow the language of the otherwise from Ashon T. Crawley, *Blackpentecosta Breath: The Aesthetics of Possibility* (New York: Fordham University Press, 2017).

35 Olmsted, *The Cotton Kingdom,* 35.

36 Ibid.

37 Ibid.

38 Ibid., 36.

39 Frederick Douglass, *Narrative of the Life of Frederick Douglass: An American Slave* (Minneapolis: Lerner Publishing Group, 1976), 26.

40 Clyde Woods, *Development Arrested: The Blues and Plantation Power in the Mis-sissippi Delta* (London: Verso Books, 2017).

41 James Lindsay Smith, *The Autobiography of James L. Smith Including, Also, Remi-niscences of Slave Life, Recollections of the War, Education of Freedmen, Causes of Exodus, Etc.* (1881; repr., Chapel Hill: University of North Carolina Press, 2000), electronic edition.

42 La Marr Jurelle Bruce, "Interludes in Madtime: Black Music, Madness, and Meta-physical Syncopation," *Social Text* 34, no. 4 (December 2017): 4; See also Bruce's significant work on madness, *How to Go Mad without Losing Your Mind: Madness and Black Radical Creativity* (Durham, NC: Duke University Press, 2020).

43 Wendel Marshall, "Tasting Earth: Healing, Resistance Knowledge, and the Chal-lenge to Dominion," *Anthropology and Humanism* 37, no. 1 (2012): 84–99.

44 Terrion L. Williamson, *Scandalize My Name: Black Feminist Practice and the Mak-ing of Black Social Life* (New York: Fordham University Press, 2017), 9.

45 Tera Hunter, *Bound in Wedlock: Slave and Free Black Marriage in the Nineteenth Century* (Cambridge, MA: Harvard University Press, 2017).

46 Joy James, "The Womb of Western Theory: Trauma, Time Theft and the Captive Maternal," *Carceral Notebooks* 12 (2016): 253.

47 Angels Davis, "Reflections on the Black Woman's Role in the Community of Slaves," *Black Scholar* 12, no. 6 (1971): 2–15. For an engagement with Davis's insights about reproduction and resistance in the context of the emergence of "biocapitalism" in the 1970s, see Alys Eve Weinbaum, "Gendering the General Strike: W. E. B. Du Bois's *Black Reconstruction* and Black Feminism's 'Propaganda of History,'" *South Atlantic Quarterly* 112, no. 3 (Summer 2013): 437–64.

48 Jennifer Morgan, *Reckoning with Slavery: Gender, Kinship, and Capitalism in the Early Black Atlantic* (Durham, NC: Duke University Press, 2021): 60.

49 Jessica Marie Johnson, *Wicked Flesh: Black Women, Intimacy, and Freedom in the Atlantic World* (Philadelphia: University of Pennsylvania Press, 2020).

50 Alan Taylor, *The Internal Enemy: Slavery and War in Virginia* (New York: W. W. Norton, 2013), 70–71.

51 Minnie Fulkes, interviewed by Susie Byrd, in *Slave Narratives: A Folk History of Slavery in the United States from Interviews with Former Slaves*, vol. 17 (Washington, DC: Federal Writer's Project of the Works Progress Administration, 1940).

52 Marriah Hines, interviewed by David Hoggard, *Federal Writers' Project: Slave Narrative Project*, vol. 17, *Virginia, Berry-Wilson*, 1936, manuscript/mixed material, https://www.loc.gov/item/mesn170/.

53 Aliyyah I. Abdur-Rahman, "The Black Ecstatic," *GLQ* 24, no. 2–3 (2018): 343–65.

54 Smith, *The Autobiography of James L. Smith*, 27.

55 Abdur-Rahman, "The Black Ecstatic," 350.

56 Fulkes, "Interview of Minne Fulkes."

57 Saidiya Hartman, *Scenes of Subjection*.

58 Richard Slaughter, interview by Claude W. Anderson, December 27, 1936, in *Slave Narratives: A Folk History of Slavery in the United States from Interviews with Former Slaves*, vol. 17 (Washington, DC: Federal Writer's Project of the Works Progress Administration, 1940), manuscript/mixed material, https://www.loc.gov/item/mesn170/.

59 Interview with Page Harris, in *Slave Narratives: A Folk History of Slavery in the United States from Interviews with Former Slaves*, vol. 8 (Washington, DC: Federal Writer's Project of the Works Progress Administration, 1940): 22–25.

60 Ibid.

61 For an important reading of Albert's work and its importance, see Anne C. Bailey, *African Voices of the Atlantic Slave Trade: Beyond the Silence and the Shame* (Boston: Beacon Press, 2006): 95–114.

62 Tony C. Perry, "In Bondage when Cold Was King: The Frigid Terrain of Slavery in Antebellum Maryland," *Slavery & Abolition* 38, no. 1 (2017): 23–36, doi:10.1080/01 44039X.2017.1284923.

63 Octavia V. Rogers Albert, *The House of Bondage, or, Charlotte Brooks and Other Slaves, Original and Life Like, As They Appeared in Their Old Plantation and City Slave Life; Together with Pen-Pictures of the Peculiar Institution, with Sights and*

Insights into Their New Relations as Freedmen, Freemen, and Citizens (New York: Hunt and Eaton, 1890), 4–5.

64 Ibid., 12.

65 Du Bois, *Black Reconstruction*, 86.

66 Charlie Davenport, interview by Edith Wyatt Moore, *Federal Writers' Project: Slave Narrative Project*, vol. 9, *Mississippi*, 1936, manuscript/mixed material, https://www.loc.gov/item/mesn090/.

67 David Scott, *Conscripts of Modernity: The Tragedy of Colonial Enlightenment* (Durham, NC: Duke University Press, 2004).

68 Thavolia Glymph, "Du Bois's *Black Reconstruction* and Slave Women's War for Freedom," *South Atlantic Quarterly* 112, no. 3 (July 2013): 489–505.

69 Saidiya Hartman "The Belly of the World: A Note on Black Women's Labors," *Souls* 18, no. 1 (July 2016): 166–73.

70 Alys Eve Weinbaum "Gendering the General Strike: W. E. B. Du Bois's *Black Reconstruction* and Black Feminism's 'Propaganda of History,'" *South Atlantic Quarterly* 112, no. 3 (July 2013): 437–63.

71 Tera W. Hunter, *Bound in Wedlock: Slave and Free Black Marriage in the Nineteenth Century* (Cambridge, MA: Belknap Press of Harvard University Press, 2017).

72 Farah Jasmine Griffin, *Read until You Understand: The Profound Wisdom of Black Life and Literature* (New York: W. W. Norton, 2021), 15–32.

2. CROSSING THE THRESHOLDS BETWEEN WORLDS

1 In this schedule, Fauntleroy's name is marked as "Larence"; however, the other details match information from the census for Lawrence Fauntleroy. Agriculture Schedule, Selected Federal Census Non-Population Schedules, 1850–1880, OS page 13, line 2, enumeration date June 1, 1880.

2 Oyster Platt Records microfilm, Library of Virginia.

3 *Virginia, Marriages, 1785–1940*. Salt Lake City, Utah: FamilySearch, 2013 (found on Ancestry.com); year: 1880; census place: Essex, Virginia; roll: 1364; page: 221c; enumeration district: 022; census year: 1880; census place: Center Cross Precinct, Essex, Virginia; archive collection number: T1132; roll: 22; page: 13; line: 8; schedule type: agriculture.

4 Oyster Platt Records for Essex County 1892–1902, Library of Virginia.

5 Sarah Haley, *No Mercy Here: Gender, Punishment, and the Making of Jim Crow Modernity* (Chapel Hill: University of North Carolina Press, 2016).

6 Ashanté M. Reese, *Black Food Geographies: Race, Self-Reliance, and Food Access in Washington, D.C.* (Chapel Hill: University of North Carolina Press, 2019), 91; Lorena Muñoz, "Selling Nostalgia: The Emotional Labor of Immigrant Latina Food Vendors in Los Angeles," *Food and Foodways* 25, no. 4 (2017): 289.

7 Here I also draw on discussions with artist Huewayne Watson regarding the nature of Black lines of mobility.

8 Carter G. Woodson, *The Rural Negro* (Washington, DC: Association for the Study of Negro Life and History, 1930), 139.

9 Mrs. W's recollections to Black anthropologist Arthur Huff Fausest formed part of the ethnographic base of Fauset's *Black Gods of the Metropolis*, his classic 1942 treatment of unorthodox Black religious communities in Philadelphia and New York. Miscellaneous pages and notes, box 5, Arthur Huff Fauset papers, Kislak Center for Special Collections, Rare Books and Manuscripts, University of Pennsylvania.

10 Ahmad Greene-Hayes, "Wayward Negro Religions in the Twentieth-Century Slum," *Journal of African American History* 106, no. 1 (2021): 117–21.

11 **W. E. B.** Du Bois, *The Philadelphia Negro: A Social Study* (1899; repr., Philadelphia: University of Pennsylvania Press, 1996), 67.

12 See Saidiya Hartman, *Wayward Lives, Beautiful Experiments: Intimate Histories of Social Upheaval* (New York: W. W. Norton, 2019).

13 Woodson, *The Rural Negro.*

14 Allison Davis, "The Negro Church and Associations in the Lower South June 1940, Myrdal Carnegie Study," microfilm reel 2, Carnegie-Myrdal Study of the Negro in America Research Memoranda Collection, Sc Micro F-13242, Schomburg Center for Research in Black Culture, Manuscripts, Archives and Rare Books Division, New York Public Library.

15 Ibid.

16 Woodson, *The Rural Negro*, 139.

17 Davis, "The Negro Church."

18 St. Clair Drake, "The Negro Church and Associations in Chicago," Myrdal Carnegie Study, microfilm reel 2, Carnegie-Myrdal Study of the Negro in America Research Memoranda collection, Sc Micro F-13242, 308, Schomburg Center for Research in Black Culture, Manuscripts, Archives and Rare Books Division, New York Public Library.

19 Ibid., Sc Micro F-13242, 309.

20 Ibid.

21 Ibid.

22 Ersula Ore, *Lynching: Violence, Rhetoric, and American Identity* (Jackson: University Press of Mississippi, 2019).

23 St. Clair Drake, "The Negro Church."

24 Ibid.

25 Sherrod Johnson File, the Dupree African-American Pentecostal and Holiness Collection, Schomburg Center for Research in Black Culture, New York Public Library, New York; Art Peters, "From Back Room Pastor to Leader of Thousands: Bishop Johnson Forbade Members to Smoke, Drink Or use make-Up," *Philadelphia Tribune*, February 25, 1961.

26 Charles Ashley Hardy, "Race and Opportunity: Black Philadelphia during the Era of the Great Migration, 1916–1930" (PhD diss., Temple University, 1989), 421.

27 Ibid.

28 Ibis., 425.

29 Hortense Spillers, "Moving on Down the Line," *American Quarterly* 40, no. 1 (1989): 89

30 Charles Tindley, "The World's Conqueror," in *A Book of Sermons* (Philadelphia: C. F. Tindley, 1932), 96.

31 Charles Tindley, "The Frailty and Limitations of Mankind," in *A Book of Sermons*, 52–53.

32 Hardy, "Race and Opportunity," 419.

33 Ibid., 422–23.

34 For the analysis of the parameters of Black feminism in Blues women performances, see Angela Y. Davis, *Blues Legacies and Black Feminism: Gertrude "Ma" Rainey, Bessie Smith, and Billie Holiday* (New York: Pantheon, 1998).

35 Hardy, "Race and Opportunity," 336.

36 Pamphlets and printed material, Schomburg Center, New York Public Library, pdf, 2.

37 Reynold N. El, Letter from the president, January 1967, pamphlets and printed material, Schomburg Center, New York Public Library, pdf, 2.

38 Ibid.

39 Moorish Voice, pamphlets and printed material, Schomburg Center, New York Public Library, pdf, 2.

40 Ibid.

41 For example, see Priscilla McCutcheon, "'Returning Home to Our Rightful Place': The Nation of Islam and Muhammad Farms," *Geoforum* 49 (2013): 61–70; and Priscilla McCutcheon, "Growing Black Food on Sacred Land: Using Black Liberation Theology to Imagine an Alternative Black Agrarian Future," *Environment and Planning D, Society & Space* 39, no. 5 (2021): 887–905, https://doi.org/10.1177/02637758211032975.

42 Martin Gelman, "Adat Beyt Moshe—The Colored House of Moses, A Study of the Contemporary Negro Religious Community and Its Leader" (Philadelphia: Graduate School of Arts and Sciences, 1965), 180–255, https://repository.upenn.edu/edissertations/354.

43 Ibid., 192–93.

44 Ibid., 155.

45 For the complex interfaces between Black and Jewish communities, see Yvonne Patricia Chireau and Nathaniel. Deutsch, *Black Zion African American Religious Encounters with Judaism* (New York: Oxford University Press, 2000).

46 "He Lives," Holy Temple Church, Philadelphia, African-American Pentecostal and Holiness collection, Schomburg Center for Research in Black Culture, Manuscripts, Archives and Rare Books Division, New York Public Library.

47 Ibid.

48 Ibid.

49 Ibid.

50 Ibid.

51 Reverend Eugene Rivers (The HistoryMakers A2007.063), interviewed by Larry Crowe, February 12, 2007, The HistoryMakers Digital Archive, session 1, tape 4, story 1, "Reverend Eugene Rivers Describes His Religious Background."

52 Ibid.

3. DARKNESS AS BLACKNESS AND DEATH

1 "'What Makes Johnny Bad?': A Statement on Juvenile Delinquency among Negroes in Philadelphia,'" Cooperating Council of Agencies Serving Negro Youth (February1 1942), unpaginated, pamphlets, Temple Urban Archive. For contextualizing this pamphlet in the wider production of the juvenile delinquent, see Paula Austin, *Coming of Age in Jim Crow D.C.: Navigating the Politics of Everyday Life* (New York: New York University Press, 2019); and Carl Suddler, *Presumed Criminal: Black Youth and the Justice System in Postwar New York* (New York: New York University Press, 2020).

2 See John F. Bauman, *Public Housing, Race, and Renewal: Urban Planning in Philadelphia 1920–1974* (Philadelphia: Temple University Press, 1987); and Matthew Countryman, *Up South: Civil Rights and Black Power in Philadelphia* (Philadelphia: University of Pennsylvania Press, 2007).

3 See Marcus Hunter, *Black Citymakers: How the Philadelphia Negro Changed Urban America* (New York: Oxford University Press, 2013).

4 See Bauman, *Public Housing.*

5 There is a critical genealogy of the family dislodging it from the domain of nature and given and revealing its constructedness. Donald Bender, "A Refinement of the Concept of Household: Families Co-residence and Domestic Functions," *American Anthropologist* 69, no. 5 (October 1967): 493–504; David M. Schneider, *American Kinship: A Cultural Account* (Chicago: University of Chicago Press, 1968). Also see David Schneider, "What Is Kinship All About?," in *Kinship Studies in the Morgan Centennial Year* (Washington, DC: Anthropological Association of Washington, 1972), 257–74. In this piece, Schneider casts doubt as to whether non-Western cultures recognized kinship as a unified domain of inquiry, understanding, or interpretation. Rayna Rapp, "Family and Class in Contemporary America: Notes toward an Understanding of Ideology," in *Rethinking the Family: Some Feminist Questions*, ed. Barrie Thorne and Marilyn Yalom (New York: Longman, 1982), 168–87. For the formulation of the family as a terrain of struggle, see Rayna Rapp, Ellen Ross, and Renate Bridenthal, "Examining Family History," *Feminist Studies* 5, no. 1 (Spring 1979): 174–200; Barbara Ehrenreich and Deidre English, "The Manufacture of Housework," *Socialist Revolution* 5, no. 26 (1975): 5–40; Carole Lopate, "The Irony of the Home Economics Movement," *Edcentric* no. 31–32 (November 1974): 40–42; Michael Anderson, "Family and Class in 19th-Century Cities," *Journal of Family History* 2 (1977): 144. For historical treatment of the family in different periods and contexts, see Louise Tilly, "Individual Lives and Family Strategies in the French Proletariat," *Journal of Family History* 4, no. 2 (June 1979): 137–52; Carol B. Stack, *All Our Kin: Survival Strategies in a Black Community*

(New York: Harper and Row, 1974); Joyce A. Ladner, *Tomorrow's Tomorrow: The Black Woman* (New York: Doubleday, 1971). Also see Molly Dougherty, *Becoming a Woman in Rural Black Culture* (New York: Holt, Rinehart and Winston, 1978); Kath Weston, *Families We Choose: Lesbians, Gays, Kinship* (New York: Columbia University Press, 1991), 127; Stephanie Coontz, *The Social Origins of Private Life: A History of American Families 1600–1900* (New York: Verso, 1988).

6 Lawrence Friedman, *Government and Slum Housing: A Century of Frustration* (Chicago: Rand McNally, 1968)

7 Ibid. Emphasis mine.

8 Ibid.

9 Ibid.

10 Bernard J. Newman, *Housing in Philadelphia Today*, Philadelphia Housing Association, 1928, Temple Urban Archive Pamphlet Collection.

11 Newman, *Housing in Philadelphia Today*, Philadelphia Housing Association, 1929–30. On the politics of defecation as an imperial formation, see Warwick Anderson, *Colonial Pathologies: American Tropical Medicine, Race, and Hygiene in the Philippines* (Durham, NC: Duke University Press, 2006)

12 The film, directed by Irving Lerner, was nominated for an Academy Award for best documentary.

13 Eric J. Sandeen, "The Design of Public Housing in the New Deal: Oscar Stonorov and the Carl Mackley Houses," *American Quarterly* 37, no. 15: 647.

14 Bernard J. Newman, *Housing in Philadelphia Today*, Philadelphia Housing Association, 1936, Temple Urban Archive Pamphlet Collection.

15 Jean Coman, Associate Management Supervisor Housing Division, Observed and Recorded July 31 to August 6, 1936, Federal Emergency Administration of Public Works Housing Division, "Report of Recreation and Welfare Activities of the Carl Mackley Houses, Project No. H-1," Philadelphia, PA, September 1936, 14.

16 Ibid.

17 Bauman delineates two visions for public housing and urban renewal in Philadelphia. He shows how they shaped the transition from public housing as a temporary "waystation" for workers in the 1930s to segregated and isolated "welfare centers" in the 1970s. See *Public Housing, Race, and Renewal.*

18 See Gail Radford, "The Federal Government and Housing During the Great Depression," in *From Tenements to the Taylor Homes: In Search of an Urban Housing Policy in Twentieth Century America*, ed. John F. Bauman et al. (University Park: Pennsylvania State University Press, 2000), 102–20

19 Brent Hayes Edwards, *Epistrophies: Jazz and the Literary Imagination* (Cambridge, MA: Harvard University press, 2017), 242.

20 Ibid.

21 Bernard J. Newman, *Housing in Philadelphia Today*, Philadelphia Housing Association, 1940, Temple Urban Archive Pamphlet Collection

22 Arnold Hirsh, "Choosing Segregation: Federal Housing Policy between Shelley and Brown," in *From Tenements to the Taylor Homes: In Search of an Urban Hous-*

ing Policy in Twentieth Century America, ed. John F. Bauman et al. (University Park: Pennsylvania State University Press, 2000): 210.

23 Roy Lubove, *The Progressives and the Slums: Tenement House Reform in New York City, 1890–1917* (Pittsburgh: University of Pittsburgh Press, 1962); Eugenie Ladner Birch, "Edith Elmer Wood and the Genesis of Liberal Housing Thought, 1910–1942" (PhD diss., Columbia University, Architecture and Planning, 1976); Carol Ann Christensen, "The American Garden City: Concepts and Assumptions" (PhD diss., University of Minnesota, 1977).

24 Valerie Sue Halverson Pace, "Society Hill, Philadelphia: Historic Preservation and Urban Renewal in Washington Square East" (PhD diss., University of Minnesota, 1976), 95–97.

25 Mel Scott, *American City Planning since 1890* (Berkeley: University of California Press, 1969); Isaac Adams Jr., "Values as a Dimension of the Professional Culture of American City Planners" (PhD diss., University of California Los Angeles, 1976).

26 The Antiquities Act of 1906, which gave the president the power to protect historic sites from demolition, was vital in rendering preservation a national phenomenon. The law was backed by John D. Rockefeller.

27 See *Berman v. Parker* (1954), the Supreme Court case that upheld condemnation for a slum clearance project and was later successfully used in Wisconsin and Massachusetts to uphold architectural design controls against due process objections. Cities concerned about aesthetics could act over the private interests of individuals.

28 For example see, Arthur H. Estabrook, *The Jukes in 1915* (Washington, DC: Carnegie Institution of Washington, 1916).

29 Theodore M. Porter, *The Rise of Statistical Thinking, 1820–1900* (Princeton, NJ: Princeton University Press, 1986); Libby Schweber, *Disciplining Statistics: Demography and Vital Statistics in France and England, 1830–1885* (Durham, NC: Duke University Press, 2006); Michel Foucault, *The Government of the Living: Lectures at the College of France*, trans. Graham Burchell (New York: Palgrave Macmillian, 2014).

30 Edith Elmer, *Recent Trends in American Housing* (New York: Macmillan, 1931); Birch, "Edith Elmer Wood."

31 For a kind of urtext for pessimism around the social and biological futures of Black communities dating from the 1890s, see Frederick L. Hoffman, "Race Traits and Tendencies of the American Negro," *Publications of the American Economics Association*, vol. 11, Issues 1–4, 1896. W. E. B. Du Bois challenged this fatalistic notion of Black life that dominated the fields of criminology, actuarial science, sociology, and demography from the 1890s. W .E. B. Du Bois, *The Philadelphia Negro: A Social Study* (1899; repr., New York: Benjamin Blom, 1967): Aldon D. Morris, *The Scholar Denied: W. E. B. Du Bois and the Birth of Modern Sociology* (Oakland, CA: University of California Press, 2015); Earl Wright II, *W. E. B. Du Bois and the Atlanta Sociological Laboratory: The First American School of*

Sociology (New York: Ashgate Books, 2016). For an astute analysis of the impact of Progressive thought on notions of Black psychological pathology and damage, see Daryl Scott, *Contempt and Pity: Social Policy and the Image of the Damaged Black Psyche, 1880–1996* (Chapel Hill: University of North Carolina Press, 1997).

32 Edmund Bacon, "Lower City Taxes?" ENB Writings 1939–1949, Penn Architecture and Design Library 278.I.22.

33 Ibid.

34 Ibid.

35 Ibid.

36 Ibid.

37 Edmund Bacon, "Urban Redevelopment: An Opportunity for City Rebuilding," speech delivered October 11, 1949, at the National Planning Conference of the American Society of Planning Officials, ENB Writings 1939–1949, 278.I.22.

38 Bacon, "Lower City Taxes?"

39 Bacon, "Urban Redevelopment."

40 Ibid.

41 Ibid.

42 Ibid.

43 Ibid.

44 Oscar Stonorov and Louis I. Kahn, *You and Your neighborhood: A Primer for Neighborhood Planning* (New York: Revere Copper and Brass, 1944).

45 Bacon, "Urban Redevelopment."

46 "Better Philadelphia Exhibition," Edmund N. Bacon Collection 292, Architectural Archives, University of Pennsylvania. For the wider context see, Timothy Mennel, "'Miracle House Hoop-La': Corporate Rhetoric and the Construction of the Postwar American House," *Journal of the Society of Architectural Historians* 64, no. 3: 340–61.

47 Better Philadelphia Exhibition," Edmund N. Bacon Collection 292, Architectural Archives, University of Pennsylvania.

48 Ibid.

49 Carol Ann Christensen, "The American Garden City: Concepts and Assumptions" (PhD diss., University of Minnesota Press, 1977).

50 Ibid., 81.

51 Ibid., 79, 81.

52 Ibid., 72, 74.

53 Ibid., 84.

54 Oral History, Edmund N. Bacon Research Collection, 1973–2004.

55 "Negro Delinquency—Whose Responsibility?," in *Crime Prevention—A Report of the Crime Prevention Association of Philadelphia for the Year 1944,* Crime Prevention Association of Philadelphia.

56 "Thirteen Years of Investing in Good Citizenship, A report of the Philadelphia Public Housing Authority," Philadelphia Public Housing Authority, 1950.

57 Ibid.

58 Ibid.

59 John Gahbauer, "Natural Law Theory through the Eyes of Hobbes, Grotius and Pufendorf" *Eudaimonia: The Georgetown Philosophical Review* (Spring 2005): 38–40.

60 Bernard J. Newman, *Slum Clearance and Constitutional Law*, Temple Urban Archive Pamphlet Collection, 1935.

61 Ibid.

62 Oral History, Edmund N. Bacon Research Collection, 1973–2004.

63 Bacon, "Society Hill."

64 Neil Smith, *American Empire: Roosevelt's Geographer and the Prelude to Globalization*, 1st ed. (University of California Press, 2004), 66.

65 For a revelatory history of the spatial dynamics of American globalism, see the late geographer Neil Smith's historical and geographic treatment of contemporary globalism in which he locates it within the decades long career of "Roosevelt's geographer," Isaiah Bowman; Smith, *American Empire*.

66 For generative work on the sonic dynamics of minstrelsy and for a deep understanding of this signification's importance, see the work of Matthew Morrison "Blacksound," in *Oxford Handbook on Western Music and Philosophy*, ed. Nanette Nielsen, Jerrold Levinson, and Tomas McCauley (New York: Oxford University Press, 2020), 556–77; "Towards and Inclusive Musicology: Race, Blacksound, and the (Re)Making of Musicological Discourse," *Journal of the American Musicological Society* 72, no. 3. (2019): 781–823; "The Sound(s) of Subjection: Constructing American Popular Music and Racial Identity through Blacksound," *Women & Performance: A Journal of Feminist Theory* 27, no. 1 (February 2017): 13–24; "Race and the Boundaries of Musicology," *Journal of the American Musicological Society* 65, no. 3 (Fall 2012): 851–61.

67 For an account of the ways that WFIL-TV and Dick Clark respected segregation in order to build a regional following for the show *American Bandstand* and the conflicts in the neighborhood where the show was actually produced, see Matthew F. Delmont, *The Nicest Kids in Town: American Bandstand, Rock "n" Roll, and the Struggle for Civil Rights in 1950s Philadelphia* (Berkeley: University of California Press, 2012).

68 Katherine McKittrick, *Black Geographies and the Politics of Place* (Boston: South End Press, 2007).

4. THE PEACE MISSION MOVEMENT AND BLACK QUEER URBANISM IN PHILADELPHIA

1 On the role of Black anthropologists in shaping conceptions of Black modernity, see Daphne Lamothe, *Inventing the New Negro: Narrative, Culture, and Ethnography* (University of Pennsylvania Press, 2008).

2 In utilizing the language of "Up South," I am drawing on Matthew Countryman's assessment of Philadelphia's social and political organization in the mid- and late twentieth century. See Matthew Countryman, *Up South: Civil Rights and Black*

Power in Philadelphia (Philadelphia: University of Pennsylvania Press, 2005). I am also drawing in this designation on Zandria Robinson and Marcus A. Hunter's analysis of "Black maps" of the United States; see Marcus Anthony Hunter and Zandria F. Robinson, *Chocolate Cities: The Black Map of American Life* (Berkeley: University of California Press, 2018).

3 Jasbir K. Puar, *The Right to Maim: Debility, Capacity, Disability*, (Durham, NC: Duke University Press, 2017), 9. Puar's conceptualization builds on Julie Livingston, *Debility and Moral Imagination in Botswana* (Bloomington: University of Indiana Press 2005).

4 Miscellaneous pages and notes, box 5, Arthur Huff Fauset papers, Kislak Center for Special Collections, Rare Books and Manuscripts, University of Pennsylvania.

5 I am indebted to Erica Edwards theorization of the "charismatic scenario" and Cedric Robinson's engagement with Malcolm X's charisma. See the introduction.

6 Miscellaneous pages and notes, box 5, Arthur Huff Fauset papers, Kislak Center for Special Collections, Rare Books and Manuscripts, University of Pennsylvania.

7 Anthea Butler, "Observing the Lives of the Saints: Sanctification and Practice in Everyday Life," in *Practicing Protestants: Histories of Christian Lives in America*, ed. Laurie Maffly-Kipp, Leigh Schmidt, and Mark Valeri (Baltimore, MD: Johns Hopkins University Press, 2006).

8 Imani Perry, *May We Forever Stand: A History of the Black National Anthem* (Chapel Hill: University of North Carolina Press, 2018).

9 See Robert Weisbrot's *Father Divine: The Utopian Evangelist of the Depression Era Who Became an American Legend* (Boston: Beacon Press, 1983).

10 For a more elaborated list of properties purchased and repurposed by the PMM on the East Coast,. This is information I culled primarily from the Baltimore *Afro-American*, which covered Divine and the PMM's purchase practices extensively between 1932 and 1965.

11 See Marcus Hunter, *Black Citymakers: How the Philadelphia Negro Changed Urban America*, (New York: Oxford University Press, 2013).

12 Letter from Celestine Fulchon, Father Divine papers, folder 4, Manuscript, Archives, and Rare Book Library, Emory University, Atlanta, GA.

13 Hunter, *Black Citymakers*.

14 Peaceful Nimrod to Father Divine about opening of Mission in Oakland dated August 8, 1944, Father Divine papers, folder 4, Manuscript, Archives, and Rare Book Library, Emory University, Atlanta, GA.

15 Anonymous adherent in Richmond, California, to Father Divine dated August 23, 1944, Father Divine papers, folder 4, Manuscript, Archives, and Rare Book Library, Emory University.

16 Wonderful Sincere Grace to Father Divine about her work in the kitchen at the Oakland Mission, August 9, 1944, Father Divine papers, folder 4, Manuscript, Archives, and Rare Book Library, Emory University, Atlanta, GA.

17 Robert O. Self, *American Babylon: Race and the Struggle for Postwar Oakland* (Princeton, NJ: Princeton University Press, 2005); and Chris Rhomberg, *No There*

There: Race, Class, and Political Community in Oakland (Berkeley: University of California Press, 2005).

18 Banquet and Dedication Invitation, February 1947, Emory Rare Books and Manuscripts, Emory University.

19 "'Broke' Father Divine Outlives 'Rich' Daddy Grace: Father Divine, nearly Ninety, in 'Excellent Health', Followers Say," *Philadelphia Tribune*, January 30, 1960, 1.

20 "Whites Say They'll Tear This Boardwalk Down; Father Divine Says, 'Go Ahead. If I Need a Boardwalk, I'll Build Another,'" *Baltimore Afro-American*, March 28, 1942, 3.

21 "Father Divine's Taxes Raised 1,000 Per Cent," *Baltimore Afro-American*, October 16, 1943, 1.

22 "Whites Object to Heaven; Divine Loses Calif. Estate," *Baltimore Afro-American*, March 29, 1947, 15.

23 "Kingdom Funds Come from 'Father's' Factories and Farms: Confessions Not Source of Father Divine's Income," *Baltimore Afro-American*, June 15, 1935, 7.

24 See the Righteous Government Platform, Father Divine papers, Manuscript, Archives, and Rare Book Library, Emory University, Atlanta GA.

25 Mrs. M. J. Divine (Mother Divine), *The Peace Mission Movement* (Philadelphia: Imperial Press, 1982), 23.

26 Ibid., 24.

27 Ruth Boas, "My Thirty Years with Father Divine," *Ebony Magazine* (May 1965).

28 Wilson Jeremiah Moses, *Black Messiahs and Uncle Toms* (University Park: Pennsylvania State University Press, 1982), 12. On critical fabulation see Saidiya Hartman, "Venus in Two Acts," *Small Axe* 12, no. 2 (2008): 1–14.

29 See John Hoshor, *God in a Rolls Royce: The Rise of Father Divine, Madman, Menace, or Messiah?* (New York: Hillman-Curl, 1936); Robert A. Parker, *The Incredible Messiah: The Deification of Father Divine* (Boston: Little, Brown, 1937); Sara Harris, *Father Divine: Holy Husband* (Garden City, NY: Permabooks, Doubleday & Co, 1953).

30 Leonard Norman Primiano "'Bringing Perfection in These Different Places': Father Divine's Vernacular Architecture of Intention," *Folklore* 115, no. 1 (2004): 3–26.

31 Dedication and Consecration of the Unity Mission Church Home and Training School, Inc., Father Divine papers, box 1, Manuscript, Archives, and Rare Book Library, Emory University, Atlanta, GA.

32 Constitution of the Unity Mission Church, Father Divine papers, Manuscript, Archives, and Rare Book Library, Emory University.

33 Peace Mission Constitution, 21–22, Father Divine papers, Manuscript, Archives, and Rare Book Library, Emory University.

34 This specific information is drawn from Menu, Circle Mission Church (Philadelphia, Pennsylvania), 27th Anniversary Banquet, April 28, 1974, box 4, folder 11. Other representative examples include the following: Menu, International Peach Banquet, 1953 box 4, folder 12; Menu, United Mission Church (Philadelphia, Pennsylvania), 28th Anniversary Banquet, April 29, 1974, box 4, folder 14; menu,

United Mission Church (Philadelphia, Pennsylvania), 31st Anniversary Banquet, April 29, 1977, box 4 folder 15; All in Peace Mission Menus, Divine papers, Manuscript, Archives, and Rare Book Library, Emory University.

35 Father Divine, "Kingdom of God Is Not Meat and Drink but Righteousness," Sermon, Father Divine AMI Collection, Schomburg MIRS.

36 Harvey Young, *Embodying Black Experience: Stillness, Critical Memory, and the Black Body* (Ann Arbor: University of Michigan Press, 2012).

37 See Marshall, "Tasting Earth." Marshall revisits indigenous Hawaiian claims around eating and earth in relation to sovereignty struggles in the 1990s. In a very different register of the symbolic significance of eating, see Allen Feldman's treatment of the *braai* or Afrikaaner barbecue in relation to the economy of violence in South Africa under formal apartheid, in "Strange Fruit: The South African Truth Commission and the Demonic Economies of Violence," *Social Analysis: The International Journal of Social and Cultural Practice* 46, no. 3 (2002): 234–65.

38 M. J. Divine to Dorothy Moore, September 21, 1948, Dorothy L. Moore papers, Manuscript, Archives, and Rare Book Library, Emory University.

39 Jill Watts, *God, Harlem USA: The Father Divine Story* (Berkeley: University of California Press, 1992), 36, 47.

40 "Says Divine Broke Home," *Baltimore Afro-American*, January 9, 1937, 19.

41 "Ofay Hubby Quits His Wife's Kisses for Father Divine," *Baltimore Afro-American*, September 22, 1934.

42 Ibid.

43 "Ma Leaves Pa and Seven Children; Divine Blamed," *Baltimore Afro-American*, July 27, 1935, 12.

44 "Wife Charges Husband Deserted Her for Father Divine: Mate Granted Her Freedom," *Baltimore Afro-American*, November 26, 1949, A19.

45 "Wife Cools after Following Divine," *Baltimore Afro-American*, February 10, 1934, 1.

46 Ula Y. Taylor, *The Promise of Patriarchy: Women and the Nation of Islam* (Chapel Hill: University of North Carolina Press, 2017).

47 Miss Mary Justice, three page undated letter, Father Divine papers, box 1, folder 1.

48 Marshall, "Tasting Earth"; Wende Marshall, *Potent Mana: Lessons in Power and Healing* (Albany: State University of New York Press, 2013).

49 Correspondence, Father Divine papers, box 1, Peace Mission Menus, Manuscript, Archives, and Rare Book Library, Emory University.

50 Correspondence, Dorothy L. Moore papers, Manuscript, Archives, and Rare Book Library, Emory University.

51 Ibid.

52 Ibid.

53 M. J. Divine to Dorothy Moore, September 21, 1948, Dorothy L. Moore papers, Manuscript, Archives, and Rare Book Library, Emory University.

54 Wonie to Dorothy Moore, September 24, 1948, Dorothy L. Moore papers, Manuscript, Archives, and Rare Book Library, Emory University.

55 Father Divine Emory Archive, undated, unsigned correspondence, box 1, folder 1.
56 Unsigned, Correspondence to Father Divine, June 20, 1946, box 1.
57 Correspondence, Mrs. E. M. Terry to Father Divine, undated, box 1.

5. INSURGENT BLACK SOCIAL-SPATIAL LIFE AND THE GEOGRAPHY OF THE 1964 "RIOT"

1 Lenora E. Berson, *Case Study of a Riot: The Philadelphia Story* (New York: Institute of Human Relations Press, 1966), 15.
2 On the earlier disturbance, see "52nd & Arch Riot Hearing Thursday: 3 Cops Hurt; Youths Charge Police Brutality," *Philadelphia Tribune*, January 22, 1963, 8. "Suspect's Arrest Triggers Near-Riot at 13th and South: Angry Crowd Seethes as Cops Subdue Victim Witnesses Claim Patrol Wagon Was Driven Over Man," *Philadelphia Tribune*, March 5, 1963, 8.
3 Here I borrow June Jordan's terminology for the youth and others who constituted the 1964 rebellion in Harlem. She used "teenage multitude" in a letter subsequently published in *Civil Wars* to reinscribe Black youth in their tenderness and possibility resisting the narrative of them as disillusioned delinquents. June Jordan, "Letter to Michael," in *Civil Wars* (Boston: Beacon Press, 1981), 16–22.
4 Stephen Best, *None like Us: Blackness, Belonging, Aesthetic Life* (Durham, NC: Duke University Press, 2018), 115.
5 Chris Perry, "False Killing Rumor Triggered Riot: Tiff between Husband and Wife Resulted in Car Blocking Street," *Philadelphia Tribune*, September 1, 1964, 1
6 Patricia Turner, *I Heard It through the Grapevine: Rumor in African American Culture* (Berkeley: University of California Press, 1993).
7 Kwame A. Holmes, "What's the Tea: Gossip and the Production of Black Gay Social History," *Radical History Review* 122 (2015): 55–69.
8 James C. Scott, *Domination and the Arts of Resistance* (New Haven, CT: Yale University Press, 1990), 203.
9 Berson, *Case Study of a Riot*, 16.
10 I am referring to Jordan's letter. She scripts powerfully the metaphor of the annihilative capacity of the police through the metaphor of nuclear warfare. Jordan, "Letter to Michael."
11 For example, see June Jordan, *His Own Where* (New York: Thomas and Crowell, 1971); June Jordan, *New Room, New Life* (New York: Crowell, 1975), in *Ms. Magazine*, box 49, folder 8, June Jordan Papers, Schlesinger Library, Radcliffe Institute.
12 Navid Farnia, "On 'Looting' in an Apartheid State," *Black Perspectives*, July 6, 2020, https://www.aaihs.org/on-looting-in-an-apartheid-state/.
13 Ranajit Guha, "The Prose of Counter-Insurgency," in *Selected Subaltern Studies*, ed. Ranajit Guha and Gayatri Chakravorty (Oxford: Oxford University Press, 2013), 46.
14 Huewayne Watson, "Self-Emancipating Slaves: Rethinking the 1831 Rebellion in Jamaica as Revolution" (master's thesis, Institute for Research in African American Studies, Columbia University, 2011).

15 See *Online Etymology Dictionary*, s.v. "riot," https://www.etymonline.com/search?q=riot.

16 For the critical history of this era through an elegant historicization and analysis of "self-determination's" transformation from the interwar to the postwar period, see Adom Getachew, *Worldmaking after Empire: The Rise and Fall of Self-Determination* (Princeton, NJ: Princeton University Press, 2019).

17 I draw here upon the insightful work of Therí Pickens to parse the different temporal and spatial dynamics of Blackness's construction and the articulation of madness. Pickens theorizes mad Black and mad Blackness as disrupting "the ocular and linear legacies of the West's conception of space and time, respectively." See Pickens, *Black Madness: Mad Blackness* (Durham, NC: Duke University Press, 2019)

18 Alexis Pauline Gumbs, "The Problem with the Past Tense," *Black Perspectives*, July 10, 2018, https://www.aaihs.org/the-problem-with-the-passive-past-tense/.

19 Brent Hayes Edwards, *Epistrophies: Jazz and the Literary Imagination* (Cambridge, MA: Harvard University Press, 2017): 231–32.

20 "300 Negroes Riot in Philadelphia: 7 Policemen and 22 Others Injured in 12-Block Area—Stores Are Looted," *New York Times*, August 29, 1964.

21 "Typist Charged in Inciting Negro Riots in Philadelphia," *New York Times,* September 18, 1964, 24; "Philadelphia Riot Trial Starts," *New York Times*, November 10, 1964, 35.

22 Berson, *Case Study of a Riot*.

23 Chris Perry, "False Killing Rumor Triggered Riot: Tiff between Husband and Wife Resulted in Car Blocking Street," *Philadelphia Tribune*, September 1, 1964. In attending to Odessa Bradford's testimony in this way, I draw on the work of Marisa Fuentes in a different context to recover the voices of accused and condemned Black women from archives of repression. See Marisa J. Fuentes, *Dispossessed Lives: Enslaved Women, Violence, and the Archive* (Philadelphia: University of Pennsylvania Press, 2016).

24 Matthew Countryman, *Up South: Civil Rights and Black Power in Philadelphia* (Philadelphia: University of Pennsylvania Press, 2005), 166.

25 Cited in Berson, *Case Study of a Riot*, 18–19.

26 Sadie Tanner Mossell Alexander, "Education and Social Change: The Citizen's Role in Achieving Civil Rights," draft 1966. Sadie Tanner Mossell Alexander Papers, box 72, folder 2, University of Pennsylvania, University Archives.

27 On the historical significance of white shopkeepers and credit in Black food geographies in a different context, see Ashanté Reese's engagement with the Deanwood neighborhood in Washington's historical development prior to the construction of large supermarkets after the 1960s. Ashanté M. Reese *Black Food Geographies: Race, Self-Reliance, and Food Access in Washington, D.C.* (Chapel Hill: University of North Carolina Press, 2020).

28 Christina Sharpe, *In the Wake: On Blackness and Being* (Durham, NC: Duke University Press, 2016): 113–20.

29 Philadelphia Police Department Investigation Report 520587, August 30, 1964, Philadelphia Department of City Records.
30 Philadelphia Police Department Investigation Report 528925, September 2, 1964, Philadelphia Department of City Records.
31 Philadelphia Police Department Investigation Report 531694, August 31, 1964, Philadelphia Department of City Records.
32 Philadelphia Police Department Investigation Report 532209, September 1, 1964, Philadelphia Department of City Records.
33 My thinking here around the importance of these spaces of Black self-making in what might otherwise register as the confines of the neighborhood is indebted to a series of informal conversations and texts about Black placemaking with Elleza Kelley.
34 Philadelphia Police Department Investigation Report 541693, September 4, 1964, Philadelphia Department of City Records.
35 Philadelphia Police Department Investigation Report 541696, September 4, 1964, Philadelphia Department of City Records.
36 Philadelphia Police Department Investigation Report 540726, September 5, 1964, Philadelphia Department of City Records.
37 Philadelphia Police Department Investigation Report 540726, September 5, 1964, Philadelphia Department of City Records.
38 Philadelphia Police Department Investigation Report 535663, September 2, 1964, Philadelphia Department of City Records.
39 Here I'm influenced by Rashid Khalidi's engagement with Palestinian resistance to occupation by the Israeli Defense Forces. See Rashid Khalidi, *The Hundred Years' War on Palestine: A History of Settler Colonialism and Resistance, 1917–2017* (New York: Henry Holt, 2020).
40 Rinaldo Walcott, *On Property* (Windsor: Biblioasis, 2021), 61.
41 Vicky Osterweil, *In Defense of Looting: A Riotous History of Uncivil Action* (Bold Type Books, 2020).
42 Philadelphia Police Department Investigation Report 527404, August 29, 1964, Philadelphia Department of City Records. See C. Riley Snorton, *Black on Both Sides: A Racial History of Trans Identity* (Minneapolis: University of Minnesota Press, 2017)
43 Philadelphia Police Department Investigation Report 526494, August 29, 1964, Philadelphia Department of City Records.
44 This recalls Sarah Haley's work on Black fugitivity and refusal in the context of Georgia's emergent carceral institutions and their work in the era of Jim Crow's emergence and consolidation to engender Black women violently.
45 Philadelphia Police Department Investigation Report 527375, August 29, 1964, Philadelphia Department of City Records.
46 Berson, *Case Study of a Riot*, 14.
47 Berson, *Case Study of a Riot*, 15.
48 Philadelphia Police Department Investigation Report 537788, September 3, 1964, Philadelphia Department of City Records.

49 Philadelphia Police Department Investigation Report 535604, September 2, 1964, Philadelphia Department of City Records.

50 Philadelphia Police Department Investigation Report 535609, August 29, 1964, Philadelphia Department of City Records.

51 Philadelphia Police Department Investigation Report 536798, September 3, 1964, Philadelphia Department of City Records.

52 Philadelphia Police Department Investigation Report #531651, August 31, 1964, Philadelphia Department of City Records.

6. ON THE MOVE

1 Philadelphia Special Investigation Commission (MOVE) Records, box 65, folder 3, Urban Archive, Temple University. Also see a more recent narrative of this at the organization's website, https://onamove.com/move-9/janine-africa/.

2 Celeste Henery, "Why Black Women Can't Breathe," *Black Perspectives*, February 21, 2019, https://www.aaihs.org/why-black-women-cant-breathe/.

3 Julie Livingston, *Debility and the Moral Imagination in Botswana* (Bloomington: Indiana University Press, 2005), muse.jhu.edu/book/9079.

4 Ian G. R. Shaw, "Worlding Austerity: The Spatial Violence of Poverty," *Environment and Planning D: Society and Space* 37, no. 6 (2019): 971–89, https://doi.org/10.1177/0263775819857102.

5 Philadelphia Special Investigation Commission (MOVE) Records, box 65, folder 3, Temple Urban Archive.

6 Philadelphia Special Investigation Commission (MOVE) Records, box 65, folder 3, Temple Urban Archive.

7 Micol Seigel, *Violence Work: State Power and the Limits of the Police* (Durham, NC: Duke University Press, 2018).

8 Ula Taylor, *The Promise of Patriarchy: Women and the Nation of Islam*, (Chapel Hill: University of North Carolina Press, 2017)

9 Shamara Wyllie Alhassan, "Rastafari Women's Early-Twentieth Century World-making," Immanent Frame, https://tif.ssrc.org/2022/04/01/rastafari-womens-early-twentieth-century-world-making/.

10 Ashley Farmer, *Remaking Black Power: How Black Women Transformed an Era* (Chapel Hill: University of North Carolina Press, 2017).

11 Matthew Countryman, *Up South: Civil Rights and Black Power in Philadelphia* (Philadelphia: University of Pennsylvania Press, 2005), 325; Heather Anne Thompson, "Saying Her Name," *New Yorker*, May 16, 2021.

12 Richard Kent Evans, *MOVE: An American Religion* (Oxford: Oxford University Press, 2020).

13 Philadelphia Special Investigation Commission (MOVE) Records, box 65, folder 3, Temple Urban Archive.

14 Aliyyah I. Abdur-Rahman, "The Black Ecstatic," *GLQ* 24, no. 2–3 (2018): 350.

15 *25 Years Ona MOVE*, self-published pamphlet by organization. Accessed through Schomburg Center.

16 Alondra Nelson, *The Social Life of DNA: Race, Reparations, and Reconciliation after the Genome* (Boston: Beacon Press, 2016); Also see Alondra Nelson, "Bio Science: Genetic Genealogy Testing and the Pursuit of African Ancestry," *Social Studies of Science* 38, no. 5 (October 1, 2008): 759–83, doi:10.2307/25474607.

17 Yannick Marshall, "An Appeal–Bring the Maroon to the Foreground in Black Intellectual History," *Black Perspectives*, June 19, 2020, https://www.aaihs.org/an-appeal-bring-the-maroon-to-the-foreground-in-black-intellectual-history/.

18 MOVE adds to and diverges from a significant tradition of Black health politics in its expression of health as a production of the social and economic conditions of society. Alondra Nelson, *Body and Soul: The Black Panther Party and the Fight against Medical Discrimination* (Minneapolis: University of Minnesota Press, 2011). See also Samuel K. Roberts Jr., *Infectious Fear: Politics, Disease, and the Health Effects of Segregation*, 1st ed. (Chapel Hill: University of North Carolina Press, 2009); David McBride, *Integrating the City of Medicine: Blacks in Philadelphia Health Care, 1910–1965* (Philadelphia: Temple University Press, 1988); Keith Wailoo, *Dying in the City of the Blues: Sickle Cell Anemia and the Politics of Race and Health*, 1st ed. (Chapel Hill: University of North Carolina Press, 2001); Vanessa Northington Gamble, *Making a Place for Ourselves: The Black Hospital Movement, 1920–1945* (Oxford: Oxford University Press, 1995); Susan Reverby, *Examining Tuskegee: The Infamous Syphilis Study and Its Legacy*, 1st ed. (Oxford: University of North Carolina Press, 2009); James H. Jones, *Bad Blood: The Tuskegee Syphilis Experiment*, rev. ed. (New York: Free Press, 1993); Allen M. Hornblum, *Acres of Skin: Human Experiments at Holmesburg Prison*, 1st ed. (New York: Routledge, 1999); Harriet A. Washington, *Medical Apartheid: The Dark History of Medical Experimentation on Black Americans from Colonial Times to the Present* (New York: Doubleday, 2006); Patricia A. Turner, *I Heard It through the Grapevine: Rumor in African-American Culture* (Berkeley: University of California Press, 1994).

19 "Neighbors Claim They're Terrorized by MOVE Folk," *Philadelphia Tribune*, August 12, 1975, 24.

20 Ibid.

21 Louise Africa, "ON THE MOVE by Louise Africa Disciple of JOHN AFRICA," *Philadelphia Tribune*, August 30, 1975, 5.

22 Ibid.

23 Eddie Africa Testimony from 1981 Trial, box 65, folder 3, Philadelphia Special Investigation (MOVE) Commission Records, SCRC 605, Special Collections Research Center, Temple University Libraries, Philadelphia, Pennsylvania.

24 Phil Africa's Testimony from 1981 Trial, box 65, folder 1, Philadelphia Special Investigation (MOVE) Commission Records, SCRC 605, Special Collections Research Center, Temple University Libraries, Philadelphia, Pennsylvania.

25 Ibid.

26 Ibid.

27 Ibid.

28 Ibid.

29 West Philadelphia Corporation. n.d. *West Philadelphia Corporation: A Word to Our Friends*, Temple Urban Archive, Pamphlet Collection.

30 Thomas Turcol and Idris M. Diaz, "Marriot Approved by Council 12–5 Vote Allows Center to Proceed." *Philadelphia Inquirer*, December 15, 1989, A1; Vanessa Williams, "Goode Says Teams May Stay Now New PA Offer Raises His Hopes," *Philadelphia Inquirer*, December 6, 1989, A1; Wayne Browne, "Philadelphia Sports: Are We Being Robbed?" *Philadelphia Tribune*, 1992, A1.

31 Achille Mbembe, "The Society of Enmity," *Radical Philosophy* 200 (November/December 2016): 23–35; Inderpal Grewal, *Saving the Security State: Exceptional Citizens in Twenty-First-Century America* (Durham, NC: Duke University Press, 2017); Neil Smith, *The New Urban Frontier: Gentrification and the Revanchist City* (New York: Routledge, 2016).

32 Smith, *The New Urban Frontier*; Katharyne Mitchell, "Pre-Black Futures," *Antipode* 41, no. S1 (2010): 239–61.

33 Delbert Africa Testimony from 1981 Trial, box 65, folder 1, Philadelphia Special Investigation (MOVE) Commission Records, SCRC 605, Special.

34 Delbert Africa, "Application Don't Need No Conversation," *First Day*, no. 3, Father Paul Washington Papers, Temple Blochson Collection, box 26, folder 1.

35 Linn Washington, "MOVE: A Double Standard of Justice?" *Yale Journal of Law and Liberation* (1989): 67–82, https://openyls.law.yale.edu/bitstream/handle/20.50 0.13051/7718/09_1YaleJL_Lib67_1989_.pdf?sequence=2&isAllowed=y.

36 *25 Years Ona MOVE.*

37 Philadelphia Special Investigation Commission (MOVE), box 64, folder 3, Temple Urban Archive.

CODA

1 For a generative and striking look at the effects of universities on these transformations, see Davarian Baldwin, *In the Shadow of the Ivory Tower: How Universities Are Plundering Our Cities* (New York: Bold Type Books, 2021).

2 Given the nature of these speculative outlays of finance in the urban landscape, I use the qualifier *theoretically* because these investment properties could remain empty given the nature of recent market fluctuations and also because I hold hope that the various insurgent forms of urban life might soon overtake the luxury condos and apartments for ordinary people. For a compelling analysis of the relationship between aesthetic Blackness and gentrification see Brandi Summers, *Black in Place: The Spatial Aesthetics of Race in a Post-Chocolate City* (Chapel Hill: University of North Carolina Press, 2019).

3 For a useful development of the articulation of the damned or wretched of the earth, see Katherine McKittrick and Clyde Woods's introduction to their edited volume, *Black Geographies and the Politics of Place* (Cambridge, MA: South End Press, 2007), 1–13.

4 This history is featured on Brandwine Realty Trust's website, http://www.brandy-winerealty.com (accessed May 1, 2018).

5 For an account of the rise of real estate investment trusts in the context of exurban development, see Elizabeth Blackmar, "Of REITS and Rights: Absentee Ownership at the Periphery," in *City, Country, Empire: Landscapes in Environmental History*, ed. Jeffry M. Diefendorf and Kurk Dorsey (Pittsburgh: University of Pittsburgh Press, 2005), 81–98.

6 Public Law 86–779, September 14, 1960.

7 For an influential and important interpretation of the emergence of modern corporations defined by dispersed ownership and concentrated power, see Adolf Berle and Gardiner Means, *The Modern Corporation and Private Property* (New York: Harcourt, Brace & World, 1932). For Berle's extension of this into an important critique of mutual funds (and by extension contemporary REITS), see Adolph Berle, *Power without Property: A New Development in American Political Economy* (London: Sidgwick and Jackson, 1959).

8 My invocation of a shadow mayor invokes the analysis forwarded by Franz Neuman in which he analyzes the rise of the Nazis in Germany as a function of monopolistic capitalism and the attendant forms of autocracy that proliferated in all aspects of German society; see his *Behemoth: The Structure and Practice of National Socialism, 1933–1944* (Oxford: Oxford University Press, 1942).

9 Inderpral Grewal, *Saving the Security State: Exceptional Citizens in Twenty-First-Century America* (Durham, NC: Duke University Press, 2017); Achille Mbembe, "The Society of Enmity," *Radical Philosophy* 200 (November-December 2016): 23–35; Jasbir K. Puar, *The Right to Maim: Debility Capacity, Disability* (Durham, NC: Duke University Press, 2017).

INDEX

Page numbers in *italics* indicate figures

Bey, R. Yancey, 102
Bey, Yvonne, 102
biocapitalism, 266n47
Black architectural traditions, 258n18
Black austerity, 193–94
"Black Bottom," 231
Black children: in Black community,
170–71; in Black migrant cultures, 126;
Black queer urbanism and, 151–52;
education of, 137–38; religion and,
171–72; in US, 117–19, 145–46. *See also*
"Black delinquency"
Black commons: Black people in, 48;
Black queer urbanism and, 68–69;
in Civil War, 58; ecologies of, 23, 52;
fugitives in, 37–38; Jim Crow laws for,
33–34, 66; plotting in, 13–14, 42, 62–66,
74; in politics, 41, 48–49; public spaces
and, 47; racism and, 26; rebellion in,
184; Slaughter on, 53–54; slavery and,
24; social spaces in, 34; society in,
39; in underground spaces, 204–5;
violence in, 46–47, 71, 221
Black community: Adat Beyt Moshe
community, 102–7; Black children in,
170–71; Black migrant cultures and, 11,
77; for Black people, 6–7, 22, 29–30, 39,
41–42; Black women in, 15; celebration in, 49–50; charisma in, 25–26;
Christianity in, 9; churches in, 1–2, 82;
death in, 263n14; drugs in, 210–11, 229;
exclusion of, 228; food in, 45–47, 164,
277n37, 279n27; housing for, 137–38;
marriage in, 170–71; in MTSA, 99–102;
nostalgia in, 68–69; pessimism in,
272n31; in Philadelphia, 161, 235–36;
police in, 181–82, 185–86, 189–92; in
politics, 65, 250; religion in, 78–81, 79,
85–86, 149–50, 268n9; in rural spaces,
77–78; sex in, 97; in slavery, 32; spiri-
tuality in, 84; stereotypes of, 188–89,
215–16, 220–21; transformation in,
71–72; in US, 214; working class, 210

"Black delinquency": Blackness and,
133–34; Black youth and, 278n3; Crime
Prevention Association of Philadel-
phia on, 138–39; in politics, 139–40;
stereotypes of, 120–26, 225–26; in
urban spaces, 117–19; in US, 144–45;
violence and, 141–42. *See also* slums
Black feminism, 10, 20, 269n34
Black formalism, 153
Black Gods of the Metropolis (Fauset), 147,
268n9
Black health politics, 282n18
Black interiority, 259n20
Black Jacobins (James, C. L. R.), 59
Black Lives Matter, 156
Black Matrix theory, 48
Black metaphysical rebellion, 50–51
Black migrant cultures: in antebellum
period, 40–41; Black children in, 126;
Black community in, 77; Black queer
urbanism and, 70–71; Black women
in, 94–95, 98–99, 166; in Chicago, 7–8;
citymaking by, 25; community and, 11;
Du Bois on, 62; ecologies of, 263n9;
in Great Migration, 2–3; housing
for, 83, 120–21; integration with, 138;
landscapes of, 22–23; plotting in, 98,
175–76; to police, 184–85; religion and,
99–101, 155; from rural spaces, 167;
after slavery, 5; in society, 34; society in, 76; from the South (US), 133;
stereotypes of, 118–19, 141; transformation of, 89–90; underground spaces
for, 16–17; in urban spaces, 1, 18, 23,
74, 87, 94; from Virginia, 56–57; in
working class, 148; worldmaking by, 6,
24, 72–73
Black nationalism, 192–93
Blackness: anti-Blackness, 27, 31, 37;
"Black delinquency" and, 133–34; gender and, 22; in politics, 119, 177; racism
and, 12, 24–25; stereotypes and, 279n17
Black Panther Party, 239

ABOUT THE AUTHOR

J. T. ROANE, a native of Tappahannock, Virginia, is Assistant Professor of Africana Studies and Geography and Andrew W. Mellon chair in the Institute for the Study of Global Racial Justice at Rutgers University. He received his PhD in history from Columbia University, where he also received a graduate certificate in Women's, Gender, and Sexuality Studies, and he is a 2008 graduate of the Carter G. Woodson Institute at the University of Virginia.